Decoding the TOEFL® iBT

Advanced

READING

INTRODUCTION

For many learners of English, the TOEFL® iBT will be the most important standardized test they ever take. Unfortunately for a large number of these individuals, the material covered on the TOEFL® iBT remains a mystery to them, so they are unable to do well on the test. We hope that by using the *Decoding the TOEFL® iBT series*, individuals who take the TOEFL® iBT will be able to excel on the test and, in the process of using the book, may unravel the mysteries of the test and therefore make the material covered on the TOEFL® iBT more familiar to themselves.

The TOEFL® iBT covers the four main skills that a person must learn when studying any foreign language: reading, listening, speaking, and writing. The *Decoding the TOEFL® iBT* series contains books that cover all four of these skills. The *Decoding the TOEFL® iBT* series contains books with three separate levels for all four of the topics as well as the *Decoding the TOEFL® iBT Actual Test* books. These books are all designed to enable learners to utilize them to become better prepared to take the TOEFL® iBT. This book, *Decoding the TOEFL® iBT Reading Advanced*, covers the reading aspect of the test. It is designed to help learners prepare for the Reading section of the TOEFL® iBT. Finally, the TOEFL® iBT underwent a number of changes in August 2019. This book—and the others in the series—takes those changes into account and incorporates them in the texts and questions, so readers of this second edition can be assured that they have up-to-date knowledge of the test.

Decoding the TOEFL® iBT Reading Advanced can be used by learners who are taking classes and also by individuals who are studying by themselves. It contains ten chapters, each of which focuses on a different reading question, and one actual test at the end of the book. Each chapter contains explanations of the questions and how to answer them correctly. It also contains passages of varying lengths, and it focuses on the types of questions that are covered in the chapter. The passages and question types in *Decoding the TOEFL® iBT Reading Advanced* are the same difficulty levels as those found on the TOEFL® iBT. Individuals who use *Decoding the TOEFL® iBT Reading Advanced* will therefore be able to prepare themselves not only to take the TOEFL® iBT but also to perform well on the test.

We hope that everyone who uses *Decoding the TOEFL® iBT Reading Advanced* will be able to become more familiar with the TOEFL® iBT and will additionally improve his or her score on the test. As the title of the book implies, we hope that learners can use it to crack the code on the TOEFL® iBT, to make the test itself less mysterious and confusing, and to get the highest grade possible. Finally, we hope that both learners and instructors can use this book to its full potential. We wish all of you the best of luck as you study English and prepare for the TOEFL® iBT, and we hope that *Decoding the TOEFL® iBT Reading Advanced* can provide you with assistance during the course of your studies.

Michael A. Putlack
Stephen Poirier
Allen C. Jacobs

TABLE
OF
CONTENTS

ABOUT THE TOEFL® iBT READING SECTION

Changes in the Reading Section

TOEFL® underwent many changes in August of 2019. The following is an explanation of the changes that have been made to the Reading section.

Format

The number of passages that appear in the Reading section is either 3 or 4. The time given for the Reading section is either 54 (3 passages) or 72 (4 passages) minutes.

Passages

The length of each passage has been slightly shortened. A typical Reading passage is between 690 and 710 words. However, there are some passages with as few as 670 words.

In addition, there is a heavier emphasis on science topics. This includes topics such as biology, zoology, and astronomy.

There are sometimes pictures accompanying the text. They are used to provide visual evidence of various objects discussed in the passage. On occasion, there are also pictures used for glossary words.

The glossary typically defines 0-2 words or phrases.

Questions

There are only 10 questions per Reading passage now. This is a decrease from the 12-14 questions that were asked on previous tests.

Question Types

TYPE 1 Vocabulary Questions

Vocabulary questions require the test taker to understand specific words and phrases that are used in the passage. Each of these questions asks the test taker to select another word or phrase that is the most similar in meaning to a word or phrase that is highlighted. The vocabulary words that are highlighted are often important words, so knowing what these words mean can be critical for understanding the entire passage. The highlighted words typically have several different meanings, so test takers need to be careful to avoid selecting an answer choice simply because it is the most common meaning of the word or phrase.

- There are 1-3 Vocabulary questions per passage.
- Passages typically have 2 Vocabulary questions.

TYPE 2   Reference Questions

Reference questions require the test taker to understand the relationships between words and their referents in the passage. These questions most frequently ask the test taker to identify the antecedent of a pronoun. In many instances, the pronouns are words such as *he, she,* or *they* or *its, his, hers,* or *theirs.* However, in other instances, relative pronouns such as *which* or demonstrative pronouns such as *this* or *that* may be asked about instead.

- There are 0-1 Reference questions per passage. However, these questions rarely appear anymore.

TYPE 3   Factual Information Questions

Factual Information questions require the test taker to understand and be able to recognize facts that are mentioned in the passage. These questions may be about any facts or information that is explicitly covered in the passage. They may appear in the form of details, definitions, explanations, or other kinds of data. The facts which the questions ask about are typically found only in one part of the passage—often just in a sentence or two in one paragraph—and do not require a comprehensive understanding of the passage as a whole.

- There are 1-3 Factual Information questions per passage. There is an average of 2 of these questions per passage.
- Some Factual Information questions require test takers to understand the entire paragraph, not just one part of it, to find the correct answer.

TYPE 4   Negative Factual Information Questions

Negative Factual Information questions require the test taker to understand and be able to recognize facts that are mentioned in the passage. These questions may be about any facts or information that is explicitly covered in the passage. However, these questions ask the test taker to identify the incorrect information in the answer choices. Three of the four answer choices therefore contain correct information that is found in the passage. The answer the test taker must choose therefore either has incorrect information or information that is not mentioned in the passage.

- There are 0-2 Negative Factual Information questions per passage.

TYPE 5 **Sentence Simplification Questions**

Sentence Simplification questions require the test taker to select a sentence that best restates one that has been highlighted in the passage. These questions ask the test taker to recognize the main points in the sentence and to make sure that they are mentioned in the rewritten sentence. These rewritten sentences use words, phrases, and grammar that are different from the highlighted sentence. Sentence Simplification questions do not always appear in a passage. When they are asked, there is only one Sentence Simplification question per passage.

- There are 0-1 Sentence Simplification questions per passage.
- The answer choices for these questions are approximately half the length of the sentences being asked about.

TYPE 6 **Inference Questions**

Inference questions require the test taker to understand the argument that the passage is attempting to make. These questions ask the test taker to consider the information that is presented and then to come to a logical conclusion about it. The answers to these questions are never explicitly stated in the passage. Instead, the test taker must infer what the author means. These questions often deal with cause and effect or comparisons between two different things, ideas, events, or people.

- There are 0-2 Inference questions per passage. Most passages have at least 1 Inference question though.
- The difficulty level of these questions has increased. In some cases, test takers must be able to understand an entire paragraph rather than only a part of it.

TYPE 7 **Rhetorical Purpose Questions**

Rhetorical Purpose questions require the test taker to understand why the author mentioned or wrote about something in the passage. These questions ask the test taker to consider the reasoning behind the information being presented in the passage. For these questions, the function—not the meaning—of the material is the most important aspect for the test taker to be aware of. The questions often focus on the relationship between the information mentioned or covered either in paragraphs or individual sentences in the passage and the purpose or intention of the information that is given.

- There are 1-2 Rhetorical Purpose questions per passage.
- There is a special emphasis on these questions. Some questions ask about entire sentences, not just words or phrases.

TYPE 8 Insert Text Questions

Insert Text questions require the test taker to determine where in the passage another sentence should be placed. These questions ask the test taker to consider various aspects, including grammar, logic, connecting words, and flow, when deciding where the new sentence best belongs. Insert Text questions do not always appear in a passage. When they are asked, there is only one Insert Text question per passage. This question always appears right before the last question.

- There are 0-1 Insert Text questions per passage.
- There is a special emphasis on these questions. Almost every passage now has 1 Insert Text question.

TYPE 9 Prose Summary Questions

Prose Summary questions require the test taker to understand the main point of the passage and then to select sentences which emphasize the main point. These questions present a sentence which is essentially a thesis statement for the entire passage. The sentence synthesizes the main points of the passage. The test taker must then choose three out of six sentences that most closely describe points mentioned in the introductory sentence. As for the other three choices, they describe minor points, have incorrect information, or contain information that does not appear in the passage, so they are all therefore incorrect. This is always the last question asked about a Reading passage, but it does not always appear. Instead, a Fill in a Table question may appear in its place.

- There are 0-1 Prose Summary questions per passage.
- There is a special emphasis on these questions. Almost every passage now has 1 Prose Summary question.

TYPE 10 Fill in a Table Questions

Fill in a Table questions require the test taker to have a comprehensive understanding of the entire passage. These questions typically break the passage down into two—or sometimes three—main points or themes. The test taker must then read a number of sentences or phrases and determine which of the points or themes the sentences or phrases refer to. These questions may ask the test taker to consider cause and effect, to compare and contrast, or to understand various theories or ideas covered. This is always the last question asked about a Reading passage, but it does not always appear. Instead, a Prose Summary question may appear in its place.

- There are 0-1 Fill in a Table questions per passage.
- These questions rarely appear anymore. Prose Summary questions are much more common than Fill in a Table questions.

HOW TO USE THIS BOOK

Decoding the TOEFL® iBT Reading Advanced is designed to be used either as a textbook in a classroom environment or as a study guide for individual learners. There are 10 chapters in this book. Each chapter provides comprehensive information about one type of reading question. There are 5 sections in each chapter, which enable you to build up your skills on a particular reading question. At the end of the book, there is one actual test of the Reading section of the TOEFL® iBT.

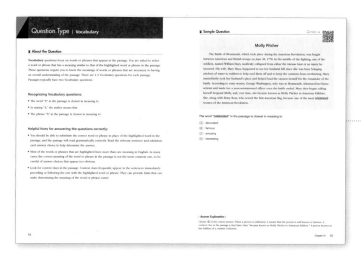

▌ Question Type

This section provides a short explanation of the question type. It contains examples of typical questions so that you can identify them more easily and hints on how to answer the questions. There is also a short reading passage with one sample question and explanation.

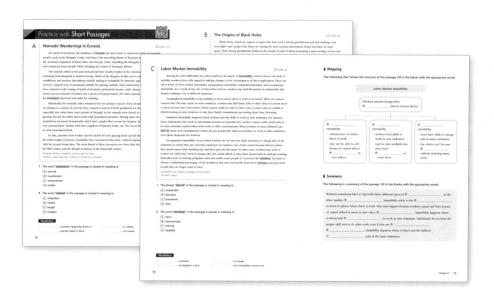

▌ Practice with Short Passages

This part contains three reading passages that are between 300 and 400 words long. Each reading passage contains one or two questions of the type covered in the chapter and has a short vocabulary section.

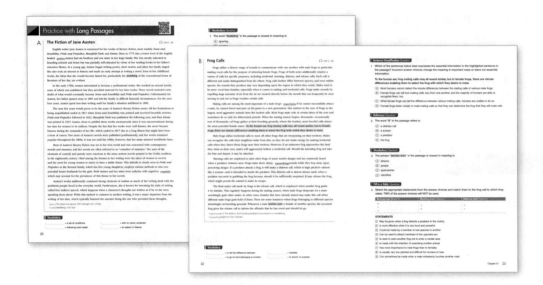

Practice with Long Passages

This section has two reading passages that are between 500 and 600 words long. Each reading passage contains four questions. There is one question about the type of question covered in the chapter. The other three questions are of various types. There is also a short vocabulary section after each passage to test your knowledge.

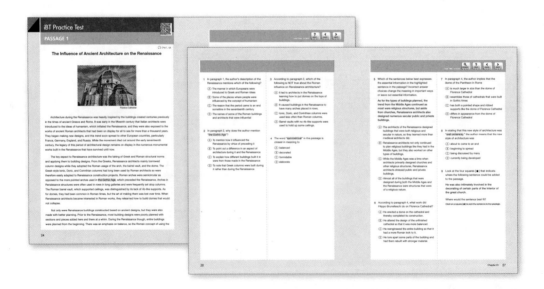

iBT Practice Test

This part has two full-length reading passages with 10 questions each.

▌ Vocabulary Review

This section has two vocabulary exercises using words that appear in the passages in the chapter.

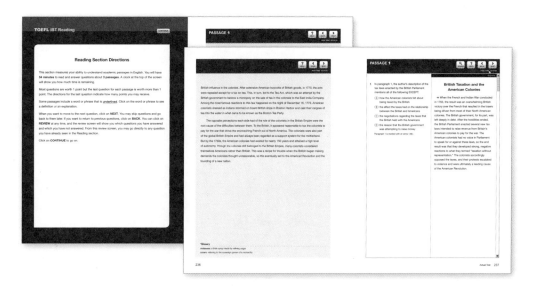

▌ Actual Test (at the end of the book)

This section has 1 Reading test, which contains 3 full-length reading passages with 10 questions each.

Chapter **01**

Vocabulary

Question Type | Vocabulary

◪ About the Question

Vocabulary questions focus on words or phrases that appear in the passage. You are asked to select a word or phrase that has a meaning similar to that of the highlighted word or phrase in the passage. These questions require you to know the meanings of words or phrases that are necessary to having an overall understanding of the passage. There are 1-3 Vocabulary questions for each passage. Passages typically have two Vocabulary questions.

Recognizing Vocabulary questions:

• The word "X" in the passage is closest in meaning to

• In stating "X," the author means that

• The phrase "X" in the passage is closest in meaning to

Helpful hints for answering the questions correctly:

• You should be able to substitute the correct word or phrase in place of the highlighted word in the passage, and the passage will read grammatically correctly. Read the relevant sentence and substitute each answer choice to help determine the answer.

• Most of the words or phrases that are highlighted have more than one meaning in English. In many cases, the correct meaning of the word or phrase in the passage is not the most common one, so be careful of answer choices that appear too obvious.

• Look for context clues in the passage. Context clues frequently appear in the sentences immediately preceding or following the one with the highlighted word or phrase. They can provide hints that can make determining the meaning of the word or phrase easier.

Molly Pitcher

The Battle of Monmouth, which took place during the American Revolution, was fought between American and British troops on June 28, 1778. In the middle of the fighting, one of the soldiers, named William Hays, suddenly collapsed from either the intense heat or an injury he incurred. His wife, Mary Hays, happened to see her husband fall since she was busy bringing pitchers of water to soldiers to help cool them off and to keep the cannons from overheating. Mary immediately took her husband's place and helped load the cannon herself for the remainder of the battle. According to some stories, George Washington, who was at Monmouth, witnessed her brave actions and made her a noncommissioned officer once the battle ended. Mary then began calling herself Sergeant Molly, and, over time, she became known as Molly Pitcher in American folklore. She, along with Betsy Ross, who sewed the first American flag, became one of the most celebrated women of the American Revolution.

The word "celebrated" in the passage is closest in meaning to

Ⓐ decorated

Ⓑ famous

Ⓒ amusing

Ⓓ interesting

| Answer Explanation |

Choice Ⓑ is the correct answer. When a person is celebrated, it means that the person is well known or famous. A context clue in the passage is that Mary Hays "became known as Molly Pitcher in American folklore." A person known in the folklore of a country is famous.

A | Nomadic Wanderings in Eurasia

🎧 CH01_2A

For much of its history, the landmass of **Eurasia** has been home to numerous tribes of nomadic people, such as the Mongols, Goths, and Huns. One prevailing theme of Eurasian nomadic history has been the westward expansion of these tribes into Europe. Some, including the Mongols, moved vast distances and conquered many people while changing the course of European history.

The nomadic tribes in the past and present have mostly resided in the enormous **steppe** region stretching from Mongolia to Eastern Europe. Much of the Steppes, as this area is called, is flat and windblown and receives intermittent rainfall, making it unsuitable for intensive agriculture. It does, however, support seas of grasslands suitable for grazing animals. Thus, historically, the majority of nomads' lives centered on the raising of herds of livestock, particularly horses, cattle, sheep, and goats. While their horses served as beasts of burden and a means of transportation, the other animals provided meat and milk for sustenance and wool and hides for clothing.

Historically, the nomadic tribes wandered for two primary reasons. First, because of their dependence on animals as a means of survival, they roamed in search of fresh grasslands for their herds. This was especially true when there were periods of drought, so the nomads were forced to move to seek better grazing. Second, the tribes had to deal with population pressures. During times of abundance, tribal populations increased dramatically, which had a ripple effect across the Steppes. As larger tribes sought new grazing lands, warfare with their neighbors frequently broke out. The losers then migrated westward to seek unoccupied lands.

In time, pressure from warfare and the desire for new grazing lands spread the nomads across nearly the entire length of Eurasia. Eventually, they encountered the more civilized regions of Europe and clashed with the people living there. The most famed of these incursions are those that led to the fall of Rome in the fifth century and the Mongol invasions of the thirteenth century.

*Eurasia: the land covered by both Europe and Asia
*steppe: a very large plain covered with grass and few trees

1 The word "sustenance" in the passage is closest in meaning to

  Ⓐ survival

  Ⓑ nourishment

  Ⓒ enhancement

  Ⓓ protein

2 The word "clashed" in the passage is closest in meaning to

  Ⓐ integrated

  Ⓑ traded

  Ⓒ fought

  Ⓓ mingled

Vocabulary

- _____ = sporadic; happening off and on
- _____ = animals raised on farms
- _____ = to wander
- _____ = an invasion

The Origins of Black Holes

Black holes, which are regions of space that have such a strong gravitational pull that nothing—not even light—can escape from them, are among the most unusual phenomena found anywhere in outer space. Their strong gravitational fields are the results of each of them possessing a mass as large as ten suns compressed into a space no larger than that of a large metropolis such as New York City. Astronomers have difficulty detecting black holes since they **emit** no electronic radiation; therefore, their presence is inferred by the absence of such radiation or by the drawing of material from a nearby cloud of **interstellar** matter toward the black hole.

Every black hole begins as a star that dies and promptly collapses on itself, but not all stars that perish become black holes. Stars three times as large as the sun or smaller become white dwarf stars when they die while those between four and eight times the size of the sun usually transform into neutron stars. To become a black hole, a star must be even greater in size. When one of these giant stars exhausts its hydrogen and helium fuel through the course of nuclear reactions, its outer shell weakens and collapses, resulting in a massive explosion called a supernova.

The core of the star remains at the center of the explosion. As the star falls inward, a gargantuan amount of material gets squeezed into a tiny area through the force of gravity. This is the beginning of a black hole. Next, something unusual happens: The collapsing star's material reaches what is known as the event horizon. This is the region on the boundary of the black hole where time seems to slow to a standstill to observers located far away. As the material reaches the event horizon, it can no longer escape from the black hole since both matter and light are drawn inward. But because of how time slows so much, distant observers will never actually witness the material cross the event horizon and enter the black hole. As a result, astronomers do not know what happens to the material drawn into a black hole.

*emit: to send out; to release
*interstellar: related to or located in the region in space between stars

1 The word "exhausts" in the passage is closest in meaning to

(A) renews

(B) tires

(C) finishes

(D) reduces

2 In stating that time seems to "slow to a standstill," the author means that time seems to

(A) halt

(B) compress

(C) advance

(D) pass

Vocabulary

• _____ = something impressive or unusual   • _____ = a star that has exploded

• _____ = condensed; pressed together   • _____ = very large; huge

C Labor Market Immobility

Among the chief difficulties in a labor market is its degree of **immobility**, which refers to the lack of mobility workers have with regard to making changes to the circumstances of their employment. There are three kinds of labor market immobility: geographical immobility, industrial immobility, and occupational immobility. As a result of any one of these three factors, workers may find themselves in undesirable jobs despite wishing to be in different situations.

Geographical immobility is the inability to move where there is work to be found. There are various reasons why this may occur. In some instances, workers may find better jobs in other cities yet cannot move to them because they own homes which cannot easily be sold. In other cases, workers may be unable to afford housing in new locations or may have family commitments preventing them from relocating.

Industrial immobility happens when workers lack the skills to work in new industries. For instance, those individuals who work in automobile factories as assembly line workers cannot easily switch jobs to become insurance underwriters who work in office environments. When workers in some industries get laid off, those now-unemployed workers do not possess the skill set necessary to work in other industries, even those desperate for workers.

Occupational immobility occurs when workers do not have the skills necessary to change jobs in the industries in which they are currently employed. For instance, law clerks cannot become lawyers unless they spend many years studying law and then pass the bar exam. In other cases, workers may want to acquire the skills they need to change jobs but cannot afford to leave their present jobs to undergo training. Remedies such as training programs exist and enable some people to overcome this handicap. Yet there is always a substantial percentage of the workforce that does not benefit from these **schemes** and gets stuck in jobs they no longer want to have.

*immobility: the inability to change one's position
*scheme: a plan

---

1 The phrase "laid off" in the passage is closest in meaning to

Ⓐ suspended

Ⓑ demoted

Ⓒ transferred

Ⓓ fired

2 The word "handicap" in the passage is closest in meaning to

Ⓐ injury

Ⓑ disadvantage

Ⓒ infirmity

Ⓓ disability

Vocabulary

- _____ = unwanted
- _____ = an obligation; a duty
- _____ = to change
- _____ = all of the abilities a person has

Mapping

The following chart shows the structure of the passage. Fill in the blanks with the appropriate words.

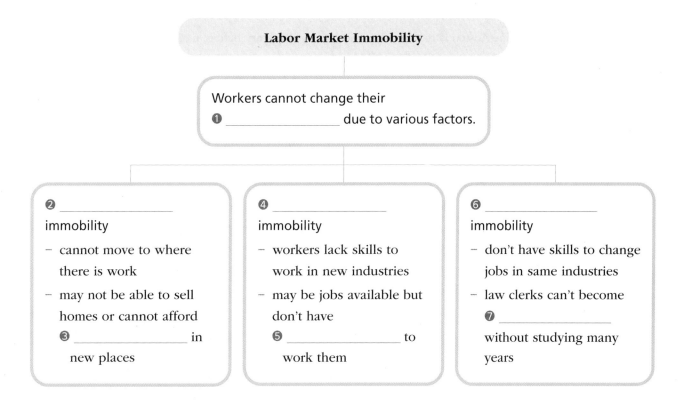

Labor Market Immobility

Workers cannot change their
❶ _____ due to various factors.

❷ _____
immobility
- cannot move to where there is work
- may not be able to sell homes or cannot afford ❸ _____ in new places

❹ _____
immobility
- workers lack skills to work in new industries
- may be jobs available but don't have ❺ _____ to work them

❻ _____
immobility
- don't have skills to change jobs in same industries
- law clerks can't become ❼ _____ without studying many years

Summary

The following is a summary of the passage. Fill in the blanks with the appropriate words.

Workers sometimes have to deal with three different types of ❶ _____ in the

labor market. ❷ _____ immobility refers to the ❸ _____

to move to places where there is work. This may happen because workers cannot sell their homes

or cannot afford to move to new cities. ❹ _____ immobility happens when

workers lack ❺ _____ to work in new industries. Individuals do not have the

proper skill sets to do other work even if jobs are ❻ _____.

❼ _____ immobility happens when workers lack the skills to

❽ _____ jobs in the same industries.

A | The Fiction of Jane Austen

CH01_3A

   English writer Jane Austen is renowned for her works of literary fiction, most notably *Sense and Sensibility*, *Pride and Prejudice*, *Mansfield Park*, and *Emma*. Born in 1775 into a lower level of the English landed **gentry**, Austen had six brothers and one sister in her large family. She was mostly educated at boarding schools and home but was partially self-educated by virtue of her reading books in her father's extensive library. At a young age, Austen began writing poetry, short stories, and plays her family staged. She also took an interest in history and made an early attempt at writing a novel. Even in her childhood works, the ideas that she would become famed for, particularly her snubbing of the conventional forms of literature of her day, are evident.

   In the early 1790s, Austen determined to become a professional writer. She worked on several novels, none of which was published, but they provided material for her later works. These novels included early drafts of what would eventually become *Sense and Sensibility* and *Pride and Prejudice*. Unfortunately for Austen, her father passed away in 1805 and left the family in difficult financial circumstances. For the next four years, Austen spent less time writing until her family's situation stabilized in 1809.

   The next few years would prove to be the acme of Austen's literary fiction career. All her frustrations at being unpublished ended in 1811 when *Sense and Sensibility* was printed and received favorable reviews. *Pride and Prejudice* followed in 1813, *Mansfield Park* was published the following year, and then *Emma* was printed in 1815. Austen chose to publish these works anonymously since it was unconventional during her time for women to be authors. Despite the fact that her works were well known, she never became famous during the remainder of her life, which ended in 1817 due to a long illness that might have been a form of cancer. Two more of Austen's novels were published posthumously, and her works remained popular throughout the 1800s. It was not until the 1900s, however, that her name attained worldwide fame.

   Most of Austen's literary fiction was set in her own world and was concerned with contemporary morals and manners, and her novels are often referred to as "comedies of manners." Her uses of the elements of comedy and parody were reactions to the more serious novels penned in the Gothic tradition in the eighteenth century. Chief among the themes in her writing were the place of women in society and the need for young women to marry to have a stable future. This attitude is clearly seen in *Pride and Prejudice* as the Bennett family, which has five young daughters, employs various methods to win over potential future husbands for the girls. Both Austen and her sister were unlucky with regard to **nuptials**, which may account for the prevalence of this theme in her novels.

   Austen's works additionally contained strong elements of realism as much of her writing dealt with the problems people faced in the everyday world. Furthermore, she is known for inventing the style of writing called free indirect speech, which happens when a character's thoughts are written as if he or she were speaking them aloud. While this method is common in modern writing, it was a major departure from the writing of her time, which typically featured the narrator being the one who provided these thoughts.

*gentry: the class in England right beneath the nobility
*nuptial: wedding; marriage

Vocabulary

• _____ = a set of conditions	• _____ = with no name; unnamed
• _____ = following one's death	• _____ = an aspect or feature

1 The word "snubbing" in the passage is closest in meaning to

(A) ignoring

(B) creating

(C) admiring

(D) rebuking

2 According to paragraph 3, which of the following is true about Jane Austen?

(A) She published an average of one book a year from 1811 until the year that she died.

(B) Her works achieved a level of fame that she did not receive until after her death.

(C) Her first work went on to become the novel of hers that was printed the most.

(D) She was the most famous of all the authors whose works were published in the 1810s.

3 In paragraphs 4 and 5, the author's description of Jane Austen's writing style mentions all of the following EXCEPT:

(A) the kinds of characters whom she preferred to use as the narrators of her stories

(B) the type of style that she wrote before anyone else had ever done so

(C) the connection between her works and those that were published in the Gothic Era

(D) the two major themes that were featured in most of her works

4 An introductory sentence for a brief summary of the passage is provided below. Complete the summary by selecting the THREE answer choices that express the most important ideas of the passage. Some sentences do not belong because they express ideas that are not presented in the passage or are minor ideas in the passage.

Jane Austen published several novels that were often about the morals and manners of her time and were written in her own unique style.

ANSWER CHOICES

1. Austen was the first author to write down the thoughts of characters to make it seem as though they were speaking out loud.

2. Between 1811 and 1815, Austen published several novels that she is still known for writing today.

3. Austen did not do very much writing in the years that immediately followed the death of her father.

4. One of the major themes in Austen's works, such as *Pride and Prejudice*, was the role of women in society.

5. During her life, Austen published all of her novels anonymously since women in her time were not usually writers.

6. From 1811 to the present day, Austen has sold more works than almost any other female author writing in the English language.

Frog Calls

Frogs utilize a diverse range of sounds to communicate with one another with male frogs in particular making vocal calls for the purpose of attracting female frogs. Frogs of both sexes additionally employ a variety of calls for specific purposes, including territorial, warning, distress, and release calls. Each call is different and easily distinguished from the others. Frog calls further differ between species, and even within species, the sounds they produce may vary depending upon the region in which they reside. Males tend to be more vocal than females, especially when it comes to mating and territorial calls. Frogs make sounds by expelling large amounts of air from the air sac located directly below the mouth that can frequently be seen moving in and out as frogs vocalize certain calls.

Mating calls are among the most important of a male frog's **repertoire**. If he cannot successfully attract a mate, he cannot breed and pass on his genes to a new generation. Size matters in the case of frogs as the largest, most aggressive animals have the loudest calls. Most frogs mate only at certain times of the year and sometimes do so only for abbreviated periods. When the mating season begins, thousands—occasionally tens of thousands—of frogs gather at their breeding grounds, where the loudest, most forceful calls attract the most potential female mates. To the human ear, frog mating calls may all sound similar, but to female frogs, there are minute differences enabling them to select the frog with which they desire to mate.

Male frogs utilize territorial calls to warn off other frogs that are trespassing on their territory. Males can recognize the calls their neighbors make from afar, so they do not waste energy by making territorial calls when they detect those frogs near their territory. However, if an unknown frog approaches the land they claim as their own, males will aggressively bellow a territorial call. Should the intruding frog not take the hint and depart, it may be attacked.

Warning calls are employed to alert other frogs of some nearby danger and are commonly heard when a predator ventures near. Frogs make short, sharp, **squawking** sounds while they hop away upon perceiving danger. If a predator attacks a frog, it will make a distress call, which is high pitched—almost like a scream—and is intended to startle the predator. This distress call is almost always made when a predator succeeds in grabbing the frog because, should it be sufficiently surprised, it may release the frog, which might permit the animal to make its escape.

The final major call made by frogs is the release call, which is employed when another frog grabs it by mistake. This regularly happens during the mating season, when male frogs desperate for a mate unwittingly grab other males. In other cases, females that have already mated may make this call when different male frogs grab hold of them. There are some instances when frogs belonging to different species intermingle on breeding grounds. Whenever a male latches onto a female of another species, the accosted frog gives the release call to inform the offender that he has erred and should let go.

*repertoire: all of the skills or techniques possessed by someone or something
*squawking: loud and high pitched

Vocabulary

• _____ = to tell the difference between	• _____ = hostilely
• _____ = to go on land belonging to another	• _____ = to shock; to surprise

Sentence Simplification Question

1   Which of the sentences below best expresses the essential information in the highlighted sentence in the passage? Incorrect answer choices change the meaning in important ways or leave out essential information.

To the human ear, frog mating calls may all sound similar, but to female frogs, there are minute differences enabling them to select the frog with which they desire to mate.

(A) Most humans cannot detect the minute differences between the mating calls of various male frogs.

(B) Female frogs can tell how mating calls vary from one another, and the majority of humans are able to recognize them, too.

(C) While female frogs can tell the difference between various mating calls, humans are unable to do so.

(D) Female frogs listen closely to male mating calls so that they can determine the frog that they will mate with.

Reference Question

2   The word "it" in the passage refers to

(A) a distress call

(B) a scream

(C) a predator

(D) the frog

Vocabulary Question

3   The phrase "latches onto" in the passage is closest in meaning to

(A) attacks

(B) grasps

(C) approaches

(D) identifies

Fill in a Table Question

4   Select the appropriate statements from the answer choices and match them to the frog call to which they relate. TWO of the answer choices will NOT be used.

Mating Call (Select 3)	Warning Call (Select 2)	Release Call (Select 2)
•		•
•	•	•
•	•	

STATEMENTS

1 May be given when a frog detects a predator in the vicinity

2 Is more effective when it is very loud and powerful

3 Could be made by a member of one species to another

4 Can be used to attract members of the opposite sex

5 Is used to warn another frog not to enter a certain area

6 Is made with the intention of surprising another animal

7 Has more importance to male frogs than to females

8 Is usually very low pitched and difficult for humans to hear

9 Can sometimes be made when a male mistakenly touches another male

CH01_4A

The Influence of Ancient Architecture on the Renaissance

Florence Cathedral

Architecture during the Renaissance was heavily inspired by the buildings created centuries previously in the times of ancient Greece and Rome. It was early in the fifteenth century that Italian architects were introduced to the ideas of humanism, which initiated the Renaissance, and they were also exposed to the works of ancient Roman architects that had been on display for all to see for more than a thousand years. They began making new designs, and this trend soon spread to other European countries, particularly France, Germany, England, and Russia. While the movement died out around the early seventeenth century, the legacy of this period of architectural design remains on display in the numerous monumental works built in the Renaissance that have survived until now.

The key aspect to Renaissance architecture was the taking of Greek and Roman structural norms and applying them to building designs. From the Greeks, Renaissance architects mainly borrowed column designs while they adopted the Roman usage of the arch, the barrel vault, and the dome. The Greek-style Ionic, Doric, and Corinthian columns had long been used by Roman architects so were therefore easily adapted to Renaissance construction projects. Roman arches were semicircular as opposed to the more pointed arches used in the Gothic Age, which preceded the Renaissance. Arches in Renaissance structures were often used in rows in long galleries and were frequently set atop columns. The Roman barrel vault, which supported ceilings, was distinguished by its lack of rib-like supports. As for domes, they had been common in Roman times, but the art of making them was lost over time. When Renaissance architects became interested in Roman works, they relearned how to build domes that would not collapse.

Not only were Renaissance buildings constructed based on ancient designs, but they were also made with better planning. Prior to the Renaissance, most building designs were poorly planned with sections and pieces added here and there at a whim. During the Renaissance though, entire buildings were planned from the beginning. There was an emphasis on balance, so the Roman concept of using the square as a base for buildings was employed. Another adoption was symmetrical façades on buildings. As for the types of buildings planned, the trend from the Middle Ages continued as most were religious structures, but aside from churches, Renaissance architects also designed numerous secular public and private buildings.

Florence, Italy, was the center of the Renaissance when it began. One of its earliest adherents was Filippo Brunelleschi (1377-1446), who believed in building designs with order and symmetry, much like the Roman buildings he admired. One of the major projects in Florence during his day was the still-unfinished Florence Cathedral. Work on it had begun in 1296, but it was still incomplete in the early fifteenth century as the planned dome had not been constructed. Brunelleschi was commissioned to complete the project and, after considerable effort, successfully fulfilled his mission. He based most of the dome's construction on observations he had made of the dome of the Pantheon in Rome. While his dome utilized Roman engineering principles, it was not a true Roman dome as it had a pointed shape and used ribbed supports, much like those found in Gothic architecture.

Nevertheless, Florence Cathedral and its dome are typically considered the first structures done in the Renaissance style. Brunelleschi received more commissions after he completed the cathedral, and both his influence and design notions spread. By the end of the fifteenth century, this new style of architecture was well underway in Italy and was spreading to other lands. During this time, which is called the High Renaissance, great architectural works were undertaken. Among the most famous was St. Peter's Basilica in the Vatican. ◼1 Considered the pinnacle of Renaissance architecture, it was designed by several architects, including Michelangelo. ◼2 It took nearly a century to be designed and constructed and underwent several important revisions during that time. ◼3 Its final shape was that of a Latin cross, and it had vast interior spaces and one of the largest domes in the world on its top. ◼4 The Greek and Roman influences are easy to see in its façade, columns, many arches, and grand dome, which dominates the skyline of Rome to this day.

*Glossary

façade: the front of a building, especially one that is decorated

pinnacle: a peak; an acme

1 In paragraph 1, the author's description of the Renaissance mentions which of the following?

  (A) The manner in which Europeans were introduced to Greek and Roman ideas

  (B) Some of the places where people were influenced by the concept of humanism

  (C) The reason that the period came to an end sometime in the seventeenth century

  (D) The names of some of the Roman buildings and architects that were influential

2 In paragraph 2, why does the author mention "the Gothic Age"?

  (A) To mention how it influenced the Renaissance by virtue of preceding it

  (B) To point out a difference in an aspect of architecture during it and the Renaissance

  (C) To explain how different buildings built it in were from those made in the Renaissance

  (D) To note that Greek columns were built during it rather than during the Renaissance

3 According to paragraph 2, which of the following is NOT true about the Roman influence on Renaissance architecture?

  (A) It led to architects in the Renaissance learning how to put domes on the tops of buildings.

  (B) It caused buildings in the Renaissance to have many arches placed in rows.

  (C) Ionic, Doric, and Corinthian columns were used less often than Roman columns.

  (D) Barrel vaults with no rib-like supports were used to hold up some ceilings.

4 The word "symmetrical" in the passage is closest in meaning to

  (A) balanced

  (B) decorated

  (C) formidable

  (D) elaborate

5   Which of the sentences below best expresses the essential information in the highlighted sentence in the passage? Incorrect answer choices change the meaning in important ways or leave out essential information.

As for the types of buildings planned, the trend from the Middle Ages continued as most were religious structures, but aside from churches, Renaissance architects also designed numerous secular public and private buildings.

(A) The architects of the Renaissance designed buildings that were both religious and secular in nature, so they learned more than medieval architects did.

(B) Renaissance architects not only continued to plan religious buildings like they had in the Middle Ages, but they also worked on other types of buildings.

(C) While the Middle Ages was a time when architects primarily designed churches and other religious structures, Renaissance architects stressed public and private buildings.

(D) Almost all of the buildings that were designed during both the Middle Ages and the Renaissance were structures that were of a religious nature.

6   According to paragraph 4, what work did Filippo Brunelleschi do on Florence Cathedral?

(A) He erected a dome on the cathedral and thereby completed its construction.

(B) He altered the design of the unfinished cathedral so that it was more balanced.

(C) He reengineered the entire building so that it had a more Roman look to it.

(D) He tore apart some parts of the building and had them rebuilt with stronger material.

7   In paragraph 4, the author implies that the dome of the Pantheon in Rome

(A) is much larger in size than the dome of Florence Cathedral

(B) resembles those of cathedrals that were built in Gothic times

(C) has both a pointed shape and ribbed supports like the dome of Florence Cathedral

(D) differs in appearance from the dome of Florence Cathedral

8   In stating that this new style of architecture was "well underway," the author means that the new style of architecture was

(A) about to come to an end

(B) beginning to spread

(C) being discussed by many

(D) currently being developed

9   Look at the four squares [■] that indicate where the following sentence could be added to the passage.

He was also intimately involved in the decorating of certain parts of the interior of the great church.

Where would the sentence best fit?

Click on a square [■] to add the sentence to the passage.

10 Directions: An introductory sentence for a brief summary of the passage is provided below. Complete the summary by selecting the THREE answer choices that express the most important ideas of the passage. Some sentences do not belong because they express ideas that are not presented in the passage or are minor ideas in the passage. **This question is worth 2 points.**

> Drag your answer choices to the spaces where they belong. To remove an answer choice, click on it. To review the passage, click on VIEW TEXT.

Architects during the Renaissance were influenced by both the ancient Greeks and Romans.

-
-
-

ANSWER CHOICES

1. St. Peter's Basilica, which was created during the High Renaissance, is considered one of the greatest buildings made during that time.

2. Architects such as Filippo Brunelleschi, who worked on Florence Cathedral, were inspired by the Pantheon and other works from the past.

3. Variations of the Roman arch, barrel vault, and dome were employed in many buildings made during the Renaissance.

4. Greek columns were a common feature of numerous buildings that were designed in the Renaissance.

5. Work on Florence Cathedral took more than one hundred years, but it was finally completed by Filippo Brunelleschi.

6. Ideas about humanism spread after the Middle Ages and helped the Renaissance get its start in the 1400s.

PASSAGE 2

The Palace at Versailles

One of the world's most opulent palaces is located in Versailles, which is approximately twenty kilometers outside Paris, France. The palace was home to the rulers of France from the late seventeenth century until the onset of the French Revolution in 1789. From its humble beginnings as a hunting lodge, the palace at Versailles was transformed into a gigantic structure containing hundreds of rooms, elaborate gardens and water fountains, and a population of servants equal to that of a small city.

The region surrounding the village of Versailles was an untouched swath of wild, undeveloped land and was full of game and natural beauty in the early seventeenth century. As a young man, King Louis XIII hunted there and fell in love with the splendor of Versailles. In 1623, he purchased some land and constructed a small hunting lodge there. It became a refuge for him, a place where he could escape from his tiresome duties as king and the palace **intrigues** and mobs of Paris. King Louis XIII became king at the age of eight following his father's death, and this resulted in him having a troublesome life. His mother, Marie de' Medici, who belonged to the powerful Medici family of Florence, Italy, became his **regent**. Her role was supposed to end when Louis turned thirteen years old, but his domineering mother held onto power until he was sixteen. During the early years of his reign, Louis was beset by various factions of individuals wishing to topple him from power and by wars both internal and external.

Only with the ascendancy of the powerful, skilled diplomat Cardinal Richelieu to Louis's ruling council in 1624 did some measure of peace come about. Unfortunately, Richelieu and Marie frequently clashed and struggled to gain the king's favor. This came to a head on November 1630, when an event occurred called the Day of the Dupes because those who thought they had succeeded actually lost. Marie obtained the support of numerous nobles due to their growing dislike of France's involvement in the costly Thirty Years' War. Marie secreted the king to her own Luxembourg Palace in Paris in order to influence him to remove Richelieu from power. Richelieu found them, and after a confrontation, Marie believed she had won the struggle. Louis subsequently fled to his hunting lodge in Versailles. After taking some time to reflect upon his rash decision, the next day, Louis summoned Richelieu to Versailles, reconciled with him, and banished his mother and her supporters from court life.

This event set the tone for Louis's future. He began spending more time away from the courtly intrigues of Paris and soon improved his Versailles hunting lodge. Between 1631 and 1633, the hunting lodge was expanded into a palace that was U-shaped with two extending wings. After Louis's death in 1643, his infant son became King Louis XIV. At first, the new king was uninterested in his father's small palace, but after he became older, Louis became smitten with Versailles and transformed it into the seat of power in France. Louis XIV spent very much treasure and time making Versailles the envy of Europe by greatly expanding the main structures and by constructing lavish gardens and water fountains.

In Louis XIV's mind, the palace had become a symbol of France and its power. It was essentially a showpiece designed to cow France's enemies and friends alike. **1** It also suited his ideas of absolutism and showed off his wealth and supreme position as the ruler of France. **2** Louis XIV additionally felt a desire to stay away from Paris. **3** The main royal residences in Paris were hemmed in by the growing city, so there was no room for expansion. **4** Much like his father, he mistrusted the nobility and the mobs of Paris. Eventually, Louis XIV insisted that all government business be conducted in Versailles. Nobles would have to travel to Versailles and spend the night there as his guests if they wanted anything from him. By demanding that nobles visit Versailles, Louis XIV may have also felt that this would stop them from creating their own powerbases in their regional homelands far from Versailles.

*Glossary

intrigue: underhanded or secret dealings between individuals

regent: a person that rules for a monarch who is a minor or disabled in some way

11 According to paragraph 1, which of the following is true about the palace at Versailles?

(A) It was planned as a hunting lodge but later became the world's largest museum.

(B) It suffered a great amount of damage during the French Revolution in 1789.

(C) It served as the home of the leaders of France for a period of around 100 years.

(D) It was located in the heart of Paris, which was the capital of France at that time.

12 The word "domineering" in the passage is closest in meaning to

(A) overbearing

(B) greedy

(C) competent

(D) skilled

13 In paragraph 2, the author implies that the reign of Louis XIII

(A) transformed France into the most powerful country in Europe

(B) lasted longer than that of any other French king

(C) caused most of the problems that resulted in the French Revolution

(D) was not a time when there was peace in the kingdom

14 The author discusses "the Day of the Dupes" in paragraph 3 in order to

(A) mention what happened on the day that Louis XIII became the king of France

(B) explain why Louis XIII decided to spend more time living in Paris than at Versailles

(C) describe the event that led to Cardinal Richelieu gaining power in the king's court

(D) show how palace intrigues resulted in a civil war that killed many people in France

15 Which of the sentences below best expresses the essential information in the highlighted sentence in the passage? Incorrect answer choices change the meaning in important ways or leave out essential information.

After taking some time to reflect upon his rash decision, the next day, Louis summoned Richelieu to Versailles, reconciled with him, and banished his mother and her supporters from court life.

- (A) Louis talked to Richelieu about the rash decision he had made, and then the two men worked together to force Louis's mother and her allies to leave Versailles.
- (B) Louis reconsidered his choice and had Richelieu visit Versailles, where the two men solved their problems, and Louis then made his mother and her supporters leave.
- (C) Because Richelieu managed to convince Louis he had made a rash decision concerning his mother, she and her supporters were permitted to remain at court in Versailles.
- (D) Life at Versailles changed considerably when Louis began making sudden decisions such as the time when he reconciled with Richelieu and banished his mother from court.

16 In stating that Louis "became smitten with Versailles," the author means that Louis

- (A) stayed there very often
- (B) wanted to expand it
- (C) liked it very much
- (D) told people about it

17 Which of the following can be inferred from paragraph 4 about the palace at Versailles?

- (A) Most of the nobles in France desired to avoid going there.
- (B) Nearly every ruler in Europe visited it at some point.
- (C) No other palace cost as much money to build as it did.
- (D) It became one of the most luxurious palaces in Europe.

18 The phrase "hemmed in by" in the passage is closest in meaning to

- (A) approached by
- (B) visible to
- (C) constrained by
- (D) in control of

19 Look at the four squares [■] that indicate where the following sentence could be added to the passage.

For instance, those individuals who visited the palace were often intimidated by its sheer size and beauty.

Where would the sentence best fit?

Click on a square [■] to add the sentence to the passage.

20 **Directions:** An introductory sentence for a brief summary of the passage is provided below. Complete the summary by selecting the THREE answer choices that express the most important ideas of the passage. Some sentences do not belong because they express ideas that are not presented in the passage or are minor ideas in the passage. **This question is worth 2 points.**

> Drag your answer choices to the spaces where they belong. To remove an answer choice, click on it. To review the passage, click on **VIEW TEXT**.

During the reigns of Louis XIII and Louis XIV of France, the palace at Versailles expanded greatly in size and importance.

-
-
-

ANSWER CHOICES

1 Louis XIII was encouraged by his mother, Marie de' Medici, to purchase land in Versailles in order to construct a palace there.

2 Both kings of France spent a lot of time and money making the palace at Versailles much larger than it was originally.

3 Cardinal Richelieu often visited Louis XIII at Versailles, particularly after the Day of the Dupes took place.

4 Louis XIV transferred his court to Versailles and used it to show off the power and the wealth of his country.

5 When it was first built, Versailles was merely a hunting lodge that Louis XIII visited to get away from Paris.

6 Because there were so many courtly intrigues in Paris, the monarchs of France decided to spend all of their time in Versailles.

■ Vocabulary Review

A Complete each sentence with the appropriate word from the box.

circumstances	initiate	phenomenon	humble	compressed

1 The couple welcomed the visitors into their _____ home.

2 The _____ were right for the businessman to run for president.

3 The two blocks were _____ against each other and could not be separated.

4 Earthquakes are a natural _____ that can be devastating at times.

5 The company has plans to _____ a project dedicated to scientific advancement.

B Complete each sentence with the correct answer.

1 Michelle has a strong **commitment** to _____ at all times.

   a. do her duty   b. relax

2 As an **adherent** of mountain climbing, Jeff is a _____ of the art of climbing high places.

   a. practitioner   b. researcher

3 We did not know _____ since the letter was written **anonymously**.

   a. the letter's date   b. the writer's name

4 There was **intermittent** rain all day long, so it _____.

   a. stopped and started a lot   b. did not stop raining for hours

5 You should not _____ and **trespass** on it.

   a. take something that is not yours   b. go onto land that is not yours

6 As the **supreme** ruler of the country, Marcus could _____.

   a. ask Congress for permission to act   b. do anything he wanted

7 There were several _____ competing, and each **faction** had a lot of support.

   a. companies   b. groups

8 The animals _____ as they **roam** across the plain.

   a. walk wherever they want   b. stay near one another

9 The men discarded the **undesirable** items since they were _____.

   a. valuable to everyone   b. unwanted by anyone

10 The soldiers reacted **aggressively** by behaving in a _____ manner to the people.

   a. peaceful   b. hostile

Chapter 02

Reference

Question Type | Reference

▨ About the Question

Reference questions focus on the relationships between words and their referents in the passage. You are asked to identify what the antecedent of a pronoun is. There are often questions with subject pronouns such as *he, she, it,* and *they* and object pronouns such as *him, her,* and *them.* There are also questions with relative pronouns such as *which* and demonstrative pronouns such as *this, that, these,* and *those.* There are 0-1 Reference questions for each passage. However, these questions rarely appear anymore. There may be 1 Reference question in an entire Reading section, or there may be none.

Recognizing Reference questions:

• The word "X" in the passage refers to

Helpful hints for answering the questions correctly:

• The correct answer choice can always fit into the sentence. So try inserting each answer choice into the sentence to see which one reads the best.

• All four of the answer choices always appear in the same order as they are written in the passage. They are also the exact words or phrases that appear in the passage.

• On rare occasions, the correct answer appears in the passage after the highlighted word. Most of the time, however, it can be found before the highlighted word.

Penny Presses

In the United States in the 1830s, there was a high rate of literacy amongst all classes of people, yet large numbers of individuals, particularly those belonging to the working class, did not read newspapers on a daily basis. The main reason was that the cost—six cents—was considered exorbitant. Sensing a business opportunity, Benjamin Day established *The Sun*, a newspaper in New York City, in 1833, and he started selling it for a penny per issue. This is widely considered to be the first of the penny presses that came to be prevalent during that decade. Day not only sold his newspaper for a low price, but he also hired newsboys to sell it on street corners, which increased its popularity. While *The Sun* did not have the most rigorous standards and its reporting was often shoddy, it became financially successful. This caused a number of other penny presses to spring up around New York City as well as in other large metropolitan areas.

The word "it" in the passage refers to

(A) the cost

(B) a business opportunity

(C) *The Sun*

(D) New York City

| Answer Explanation |

Choice ⓒ is the correct answer. The "it" that was being sold for a penny per issue was *The Sun*. Note that of all four answer choices, the only one that could be sold is the newspaper. By using the process of elimination, it is possible to find the correct answer.

A | The Use of Light in Art Galleries

CH02_2A

Art galleries are structures in which artists can display all types of works of art, including paintings, etchings, drawings, photographs, and sculptures. To enhance the appearance of every work of art, the display area needs to be well lit. At the same time, however, each artwork must be protected from **exposure** to too much light since that can cause works such as paintings and drawings to fade and thereby get ruined. Finding a happy medium between not enough light and too much of it requires considerable skill and experience.

The most common form of lighting used to **illuminate** artwork is indoor spotlights on tracks attached to the ceiling near where the work is being displayed. Using tracked lighting is beneficial as it permits the lights to be moved more easily when the light patterns require adjusting. Recessed lights—those which are embedded in walls and ceilings—can be useful so long as they are not fixed in place but can instead be easily moved to create ideal light patterns. Most art gallery curators state that a combination of tracked and recessed light fixtures is ideal because the tracked lights focus directly on the artwork while the recessed lights are used on the nearby walls to provide an ambient light source which can enhance the mood surrounding the work.

Regarding the angle of the lights, it depends upon the height of the ceiling and the size of the artwork. Caution must be taken to avoid creating too many areas with shadows or to have the lights cause a glare on the artwork. Furthermore, the lights should not be bare bulbs burning directly on the artwork but should be filtered in some way to mute the lighting. According to experts, low voltage bulbs are the best to use when lighting artwork. Above all, natural light should be avoided since the ultraviolet rays in direct sunlight will damage artwork, particularly paintings, over time. Thus artwork should be placed in a room where sunlight cannot directly hit it.

*exposure: the condition of being opened to something
*illuminate: to brighten; to light up

1 The word "they" in the passage refers to

Ⓐ the lights

Ⓑ the light patterns

Ⓒ recessed lights

Ⓓ walls and ceilings

2 The word "it" in the passage refers to

Ⓐ time

Ⓑ artwork

Ⓒ a room

Ⓓ sunlight

Vocabulary

• _____ = enclosed; sunken
• _____ = regarding the surrounding area

• _____ = shine; brightness
• _____ = to reduce the intensity of

On account of the primate order of mammals including the closest relatives to humans in the animal kingdom, people have long wondered if primates can be taught to behave like humans. One area where there has been some success is in the field of **linguistics** as some humans have successfully taught primates to communicate by using language. As a general rule, primates cannot pronounce words since their tongues and vocal boxes do not permit speech. An early effort with a chimpanzee named Viki, who was raised like a human child, produced limited results with speech, but she required assistance to move her lips when making sounds and only learned a few words. As a result, in later experiments, scientists concentrated on trying to teach primates to use sign language and symbols called **lexigrams**, which represent human speech.

In the 1960s, researchers worked with a female chimpanzee named Washoe, and she eventually learned around 250 signs. Later, a baby chimpanzee named Louis was placed with her, and Louis learned how to sign by watching Washoe in what was the first example of a primate learning a human language by observing another. Another famed example of primate communication involved a female gorilla named Koko. She began training in sign language at Stanford University in 1972 and learned more than 1,000 signs. The scientists working with her believed that she could actually understand English, but other experts were skeptical of their claim.

A new direction in primate language learning was taken with Kanzi, a bonobo ape. In the 1980s, scientists at Georgia State University were attempting to teach Kanzi's mother how to use lexigrams when Kanzi picked up on what they were doing and learned to use them while his mother did not. They then decided to focus their efforts on Kanzi rather than his mother in a decision which proved to be insightful. Today, Kanzi can use up to 400 lexigrams with a specialized computer keyboard that, when pressed, makes speech in English. He can also utilize sign language, and there is strong evidence that he is capable of understanding spoken English.

*linguistics: the science of language
*lexigram: a symbol or figure that represents a word

1 The word "which" in the passage refers to

(A) scientists

(B) primates

(C) sign language

(D) lexigrams

2 The word "she" in the passage refers to

(A) Louis

(B) Washoe

(C) a primate

(D) Koko

Vocabulary

- _____ = animals such as humans, apes, and monkeys
- _____ = to focus; to stress
- _____ = doubtful
- _____ = perceptive

C | Animal Packs

Many species of animals establish packs, which can be either large or small and may consist of members of the same family or unrelated animals. Lions and wolves typically roam in packs in which every animal is a family member while large herd animals in Africa, including wildebeests and zebras, do not contain only related animals. A typical pack contains both leaders and followers. The primary leader is the alpha, any subordinate leaders are betas, and the omega is at the bottom of the pack's **hierarchy**.

Depending upon the species, the alpha could be male or female, but generally, the biggest, strongest, or oldest—or some combination of those three—is the alpha. For instance, the strongest and oldest male gorilla, called a silverback, is the alpha of its group. With regard to lion prides, the alpha is the strongest male capable of protecting the females and cubs. In most cases, the alphas receive preferential treatment from the other pack members, and they virtually always get first choice of any food acquired in addition to the largest portions. An alpha may, however, lose its status when it is challenged and defeated by another member of the pack, whereupon it is either killed or driven off so must live elsewhere.

The second in command of an animal pack is the beta, which, for dogs and wolves, is a strong male that is less powerful than the alpha. The majority of challenges to the alpha's position come from the beta, and when the alpha dies, the beta commonly takes over as the new alpha. At the opposite end is the omega, the animal deemed the weakest member by the rest of the pack. The omega is **subservient** not only to the alpha and the beta but also to every other pack member. Among dogs, for example, when the alpha approaches, the omega acts in a fawning manner by wagging its tail and lying down, so it exposes its belly. The omega is usually shy and avoids confrontations with the other pack members so is considered no threat to the alpha's position.

*hierarchy: a system in which people or things are ranked according to importance
*subservient: acting in a secondary or less important role

1 The word "they" in the passage refers to

- (A) lion prides
- (B) the females and cubs
- (C) the alphas
- (D) the other pack members

2 The word "it" in the passage refers to

- (A) the alpha
- (B) the omega
- (C) its tail
- (D) its belly

Vocabulary

- _____ = favorable; showing preference to another
- _____ = nearly; almost
- _____ = affectionate; servile
- _____ = a fight; hostility

▰ Mapping

The following chart shows the structure of the passage. Fill in the blanks with the appropriate words.

Animal Packs

Predators and prey both form ❶ _____
- may be family members or not related
- is pack hierarchy with ❷ _____ at the top

Alpha: can be male or female
- is usually the biggest, ❸ _____, and oldest member
- protects the others
- gets ❹ _____ treatment
- gets the best and most food

❺ _____ : is second in command
- may challenge alpha for leadership
- takes over pack if alpha dies
❻ _____ : is the weakest member
- is ❼ _____ to the others
- is no ❽ _____ to the alpha

▰ Summary

The following is a summary of the passage. Fill in the blanks with the appropriate words.

Many animals, including both ❶ _____ and prey animals, form packs that they travel in. Packs have both ❷ _____ and followers. The ❸ _____ is usually the biggest, strongest, and oldest male in the group. The alphas get preferential treatment from the other pack members and get the ❹ _____ choice of food and the largest portion. Alphas can lose their ❺ _____ if they are challenged and ❻ _____ by another member of the pack. The beta is the second in command and the most likely to ❼ _____ the alpha for leadership. The omega is the ❽ _____ member of the pack and is subservient to the alpha, the beta, and the other members.

A | **Adam Smith's Views on Economics** 🎧 CH02_3A

Scottish economist Adam Smith (1723-1790) is widely considered the father of modern economics. His 1776 work *An Inquiry into the Nature and Causes of the Wealth of Nations*, more commonly shortened to *The Wealth of Nations*, has had an enormous influence on economic theory and policy from the time it was published to the present day. Smith is particularly noted for his argument that free market economies are superior to controlled economies as well as his writing on the division of labor. He was a leading figure in the Scottish Enlightenment, and his work is often cited as being among the most influential in history.

Smith was educated at the University of Glasgow, where he studied philosophy, and he later did postgraduate work at Oxford University. He became an instructor at the University of Glasgow and taught rhetoric, logic, and philosophy. Smith's **mentor**, Francis Hutchinson, a professor at the University of Glasgow, had a major effect on Smith's career path and later writings. It was during Smith's tenure there that he began formulating his theories on economics which would later bring him worldwide fame.

The Wealth of Nations is an examination of the economic forces at work in early industrial Britain as well as a study of the forces influencing economics as a whole. In the work, Smith records his belief that the government should play a minimal role in the economy. This is the concept of the free market, in which people act in their own self-interest with as little governmental interference as possible. Smith describes the "invisible hand" of self-interest that acts as a guiding force in a free market economy. He argues that people do not manufacture and sell goods because they are benevolent but instead because they are eager to make a profit. As each person works to earn money, that individual provides goods and services others require. When people work together in this manner, they drive the economy and create wealth for their nation.

Another important idea about which Smith wrote was the concept of the division of labor. Smith pointed out that it required eighteen different steps for a man to make a single pin, so he could therefore make only a few pins each day. Yet if there were many workers, each of whom was doing either a single step or a few steps in the manufacturing process, Smith claimed that they could make a much larger number of pins in a single day. By dividing labor so that workers accomplished specialized tasks, production would become more efficient. It was from this idea that the now common practice of using assembly lines to manufacture products developed.

Today, Adam Smith's economic policies form the basis of what is deemed classical economics. While not all of his theories, especially those insisting upon less government control over the economy, have been widely **embraced**, Smith's influence in modern times is easy to see. In the past two centuries, the world has shifted from a land-based agrarian, rural society to a factory-based urban society. Whether this has been a change for good or not is arguable, but it cannot be denied that the world has been greatly influenced by what Adam Smith wrote during the eighteenth century.

*mentor: a teacher; a person who provides invaluable instruction
*embrace: to accept willingly

Vocabulary

- _____ = the art of using language effectively
- _____ = to create; to make
- _____ = kind
- _____ = relating to the land

1　In paragraph 1, the author's description of Adam Smith mentions which of the following?

　　(A) The thoughts of his that have had the greatest effect on the field of economics

　　(B) The manner in which he hoped that free market economies would be used by countries

　　(C) The role he played in influencing other members of the Scottish Enlightenment

　　(D) The arguments that he employed against the utilization of controlled economies

Rhetorical Purpose Question

2　The author discusses "Francis Hutchinson" in paragraph 2 in order to

　　(A) point out which of his theories had a lasting influence on the thoughts of Adam Smith

　　(B) credit him for being one of the leading intellectuals at the University of Glasgow

　　(C) name one of the people responsible for helping Adam Smith create his economic theories

　　(D) claim that he promoted the notion of free market economies before Adam Smith ever did

Reference Question

3　The word "they" in the passage refers to

　　(A) eighteen different steps

　　(B) a few pins

　　(C) many workers

　　(D) a few steps

Prose Summary Question

4　An introductory sentence for a brief summary of the passage is provided below. Complete the summary by selecting the THREE answer choices that express the most important ideas of the passage. Some sentences do not belong because they express ideas that are not presented in the passage or are minor ideas in the passage.

Adam Smith is one of the most noted economists in modern times and is particularly famed for his work on free market economies and the division of labor.

ANSWER CHOICES

1 The works of Adam Smith, in particular *The Wealth of Nations*, were once influential but are rarely read by people today.

2 According to Adam Smith, there is an "invisible hand" that helps guide people who are involved in a free market economy.

3 There was a major shift going on during Adam Smith's time as the economy changed from one dominated by agriculture to one ruled by factories.

4 Adam Smith taught classes in various subjects at the University of Glasgow, where he came into contact with Francis Hutchinson.

5 In Adam Smith's mind, controlled economies were inferior to free market economies since people always worked in their own self-interest.

6 The work that Adam Smith did on the specialization of tasks helped influence the later development of the assembly line.

B | The Eliminating of Dams

Dams are constructed for numerous reasons, the most common being to divert water for agriculture and to harness the power of flowing water to produce electricity. Nonetheless, while dams provide numerous benefits, they can harm the environment by disrupting the natural flow of water and therefore damage river ecosystems. They additionally hinder the passage of fish upriver and downriver and prevent people from using rivers for recreational purposes. Despite most dams having fish ladders, not all fish are capable of navigating them, so they die in large numbers. Furthermore, dams slow the water flow in rivers, and large amounts of silt, gravel, plant matter, and other debris accumulate behind them, and these combine to distort the characteristics of their rivers. These facts have led some people to conclude that certain dams should be eliminated and their rivers permitted to flow freely.

Removing a dam is not easily accomplished though as caution must be taken to avoid harming the river's fragile ecosystem further, and there exists the possibility of a sudden surge of water going downriver and flooding the land alongside the river, which could cause considerable damage. Thus great care must be taken when removing a dam. There are two primary methods used to eliminate dams: blowing them up or using machinery to break them apart. Destroying them with explosives is the quickest and simplest way yet has the most potential for trouble. This method is used only when a dam is located in a remote region where explosive devices will not damage any nearby dwellings. As for employing machinery, it is a more time-consuming and expensive process but is safer.

Whichever method is utilized, some preliminary steps must be taken. First, the water in the reservoir behind the dam must be drained. This can be accomplished slowly through the dam's own **spillways**, but, in some cases, such as the Glines Canyon Dam on the Elwha River, which was removed in Washington in 2011, the spillways are too high and cannot drain all the water. For that dam, holes had to be cut into its base to drain the water. When the water is gone, the silt and other debris behind the dam must next be removed. Occasionally, the silt is too deep and has too much mass to remove cheaply, so the river is simply diverted around the silt bed. Once the river is at a roughly equal level in front of and behind the dam—or if the water has been diverted around it—the destruction of the dam can proceed.

After a dam is destroyed, it may take a long time for the river system to rebound, and the removal of the dam itself may create additional problems. In 1973, the Fort Edwards Dam was removed from the Hudson River in New York, and a major environmental disaster **ensued**. Behind it was a huge mass of contaminated silt containing deadly chemical poisons. The dam had trapped the silt, but after it was gone, the polluted matter flowed downriver, and it soon destroyed part of the river's ecosystem by poisoning the fish in the water. Subsequent efforts to clean the river have lasted for decades and required the expenditure of a great amount of money.

*spillway: a passageway that allows excess water to escape from behind a dam
*ensue: to happen as a result of another action

Vocabulary

- _____ = to gather; to collect
- _____ = an artificial lake created by a dam
- _____ = the interacting of the organic and inorganic elements in a certain environment
- _____ = to come back; to return to one's original state

1   The word "these" in the passage refers to

   (A) fish ladders

   (B) fish

   (C) rivers

   (D) large amounts of silt, gravel, plant matter, and other debris

Negative Factual Information Question

2   According to paragraph 1, which of the following is NOT true about the negative effects of dams?

   (A) They cause some river life to die despite human efforts to prevent that from happening.

   (B) They change the nature of their rivers because of the matter that builds up behind them.

   (C) They prevent their rivers from flowing like normal and therefore alter their environments.

   (D) They cause some species to die out so much that they become extinct in those regions.

Factual Information Question

3   According to paragraph 4, the Hudson River suffered an environmental disaster because

   (A) the elimination of several dams that were built on it caused a disruption in its ecosystem

   (B) harmful chemicals that a dam had been holding back were released after it was removed

   (C) new spillways were drilled in one of its dams, which resulted in polluted silt being released

   (D) poisonous chemicals were released into it by people unconcerned about the environment

Prose Summary Question

4   An introductory sentence for a brief summary of the passage is provided below. Complete the summary by selecting the THREE answer choices that express the most important ideas of the passage. Some sentences do not belong because they express ideas that are not presented in the passage or are minor ideas in the passage.

   Since some dams harm their rivers, it becomes necessary to remove them through several different methods.

   ANSWER CHOICES

   ⬚1⬚ The Glines Canyon Dam was removed from the Elwha River when it was decided that it was causing harm to the environment.

   ⬚2⬚ One step necessary when removing a dam is to get the water levels on both sides of it to be roughly identical.

   ⬚3⬚ New spillways have to be drilled in some dams to get the water to a low enough level to facilitate the removal of the dams.

   ⬚4⬚ After dams are removed, they can still harm their rivers by releasing various pollutants that can require long amounts of time to clean.

   ⬚5⬚ The two most common ways to get rid of dams are to use explosives and to utilize machinery to take them apart.

   ⬚6⬚ Dams often prevent polluted silt from going downriver, and then people can easily remove the pollutants from behind the dam.

CH02_4A

City Design in Ancient Rome

A plan of Roman Cologne

The Romans were among the greatest builders in ancient times. Across their enormous empire, they constructed roads, amphitheaters, aqueducts, and numerous other structures, and the cities they founded were often the predecessors of modern ones. The Romans planned their cities carefully, and the design and construction of each reflected their social and economic needs while simultaneously showcasing their architectural style and engineering methods. It is a testament to their skill as builders that large numbers of their structures still exist in Europe, North Africa, and the Middle East today.

Some early Roman cities, including Rome itself, developed in a haphazard manner and featured various irregularities in their design, but most of the later ones were designed in a similar manner. As the Roman Republic—and the Roman Empire later—expanded, its soldiers marched through the countryside and established military camps, which were often the precursors of towns and cities. Each town and city was laid out in a standard pattern: a square with streets in a grid pattern that intersected at right angles. Oftentimes, two major streets bisected the town or city in a north-south and east-west direction and met in the center in a great square called a forum. The forum served as the economic and social center of the city. In addition, there were typically two diagonal streets that cut across the town or city that met in the center. The major streets were wider than the regular ones, which were of a uniform width. The majority of towns and cities had paved streets with large stones fit together and utilized concrete as the main construction material.

The grid pattern and the similarity of the street designs were necessary to enable soldiers easily to move anywhere in a city to defend it. Most Roman cities, especially those founded in the empire's later years, had walls and towers for defense. The walls had four main gates, one at each end of the two main roadways. While these defenses protected the people of the city, they had a negative effect by limiting how much it could increase in size. The Romans also built every city alongside a river or near a source of water. The river flowed through the city, and additional water was transported from nearby hills or mountains by large aqueduct systems. Most Roman cities had extensive piping systems to bring in water and to carry away sewage. While most people bathed and got drinking water from public facilities, wealthier citizens had water piped directly into their homes.

Urban life centered on a block enclosed by four streets. These blocks contained apartment buildings, called *insulae*, which stood several stories high. The blocks of *insulae* were the equivalent of modern-day urban neighborhoods, and the majority of the common people—the plebeians—lived in them. An *insula* lacked indoor water and sewage facilities, so its residents had to carry their water from nearby wells and cart their sewage to various dumping points. A larger type of home, known as a *domus*, was where wealthy individuals lived. They always resided in separate areas from the poorer citizens. Markets and businesses were established near *insulae*, so large cities had several commercial districts serving entire groups of blocks. However, the forum in each city was always the primary center of commerce and politics and was therefore constantly busy. In some cases, there was so much traffic in the busiest parts of the city that those areas became congested at certain times of the day. As a result, traffic could be restricted in some areas.

Every Roman city had several other common structures. Barracks for soldiers were standard as was a temple for religious functions. **1** Other buildings were theaters, amphitheaters, and basilicas, and the largest cities had a circus. **2** The theaters were utilized by actors putting on dramatic performances while the Romans used amphitheaters to watch games such as gladiatorial contests. **3** The basilicas served as places for people to engage in legal and business dealings, and the circuses were the equivalent of present-day horse racing tracks. **4** One last building that featured prominently was the *horreum*. A storehouse containing large amounts of grain, oil, wine, and other foodstuffs, this was a building necessary to keep urban dwellers fed and happy.

*Glossary

grid: a set of straight lines that intersect at right angles

sewage: waste matter

1   According to paragraph 1, which of the following is true about Roman cities?

    Ⓐ Only the largest ones contain amphitheaters, aqueducts, and other similar structures.

    Ⓑ They were always designed in the same way no matter what period of Rome's history it was.

    Ⓒ The ones that the Romans established were often inhabited by people living in later times.

    Ⓓ A majority of those that were built in the Middle East are still standing today.

2   The word "haphazard" in the passage is closest in meaning to

    Ⓐ stylized

    Ⓑ expected

    Ⓒ random

    Ⓓ traditional

3   Which of the sentences below best expresses the essential information in the highlighted sentence in the passage? Incorrect answer choices change the meaning in important ways or leave out essential information.

As the Roman Republic—and the Roman Empire later—expanded, its soldiers marched through the countryside and established military camps, which were often the precursors of towns and cities.

    Ⓐ Roman soldiers in both the times of the republic and empire made camps that often transformed into urban areas.

    Ⓑ During the Roman Republic and Roman Empire, there were soldiers stationed in camps located in many towns and cities.

    Ⓒ Most of the towns and cities in the times of the Roman Republic and Roman Empire were designed by soldiers.

    Ⓓ Camps full of soldiers were common sights in Roman towns and cities during the republic and empire days.

4   The word "uniform" in the passage is closest in meaning to

    Ⓐ exact

    Ⓑ reasonable

    Ⓒ miniscule

    Ⓓ appropriate

5 In paragraph 3, the author's description of Roman cities mentions all of the following EXCEPT:

   Ⓐ the types of defensive fortifications that were erected around them

   Ⓑ the types of weaponry that the soldiers employed to defend the cities

   Ⓒ the manner in which residents of the cities acquired their water

   Ⓓ the geographical locations that were considered ideal for them

6 In paragraph 4, the author implies that a *domus*

   Ⓐ had living facilities that were superior to those in an *insula*

   Ⓑ could sometimes be purchased by a person who was a plebeian

   Ⓒ was typically a multistory building much like an *insula* was

   Ⓓ contained quarters both for a family as well as the slaves they owned

7 Select the TWO answer choices from paragraph 4 that identify the purposes of forums in Roman cities. *To receive credit, you must select TWO answers*.

   Ⓐ To serve as the parts of the cities in which residents lived

   Ⓑ To facilitate business between various parties

   Ⓒ To be sites in which people were involved in politics

   Ⓓ To act as places where traffic could be redirected to

8 The word "this" in the passage refers to

   Ⓐ the *horreum*

   Ⓑ grain

   Ⓒ oil

   Ⓓ wine

9 Look at the four squares [■] that indicate where the following sentence could be added to the passage.

Those were places where the Romans held chariot races and other similar forms of entertainment.

Where would the sentence best fit?

Click on a square [■] to add the sentence to the passage.

10 **Directions:** An introductory sentence for a brief summary of the passage is provided below. Complete the summary by selecting the THREE answer choices that express the most important ideas of the passage. Some sentences do not belong because they express ideas that are not presented in the passage or are minor ideas in the passage. **This question is worth 2 points.**

> Drag your answer choices to the spaces where they belong. To remove an answer choice, click on it. To review the passage, click on VIEW TEXT.

Roman cities were designed in a similar manner during both the republic and empire years, and they often contained many of the same structures.

-
-
-

ANSWER CHOICES

1 Theaters, amphitheaters, and *horrea* were all structures that were considered standard in the majority of Roman cities.

2 Residents of Roman cities lived in *insulae* if they were plebeians and in *domi* if they were richer individuals.

3 The architectural style of the Romans changed over time, and this can be easily seen in the types of buildings they constructed.

4 Most Roman cities were designed identically, including the types of roads that they had and the various buildings located within them.

5 A large number of the cities that were founded by the Romans were never conquered militarily thanks to their heavy defenses.

6 Aqueducts carrying fresh water ran from the mountains all the way to the cities so that they could be used by their residents.

PASSAGE 2

Indo-European Languages

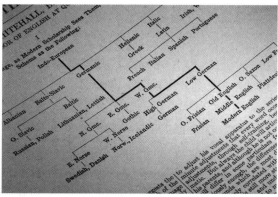

© Benoit Daoust

The root sources of modern languages are often difficult to determine because of a lack of written records. Only by comparing different languages can scholars understand their relationships with one another. This is particularly true of the Indo-European language group. Containing more than 400 sublanguages spoken by approximately fifty percent of the world's people, this group consists of several major modern languages, including German, English, Russian, Italian, French, Spanish, and Greek.

For a long time, those interested in linguistics noted how some words in different languages were similar. One such example is the words for various numbers in Latin and Greek. ◼1 This led people to conclude that Latin must be a daughter language of Greek since Greek civilization was highly influential on the Latin-speaking Roman civilization that later developed in Italy. ◼2 Then, in the eighteenth century, English scholar William Jones traveled to India and began studying the Sanskrit language. ◼3 Already an expert in Latin and Greek, Jones noted some similarities between both languages and Sanskrit. ◼4 In a lecture given in 1786, Jones proposed the groundbreaking idea that all three languages had a common root source. Instead of being a daughter language of Greek, Latin was perhaps a sister language.

The subsequent search for the root language of Greek resulted in scholars eventually concluding that a group of people living in Eastern Europe in the land occupied by modern-day Ukraine may be the source of many modern languages. They called this source language Proto-Indo-European. Starting around 3500 B.C., these people began to migrate and intermingled with other groups. Over the next 3,000 years, various languages were born through this process. As this occurred, numerous language branches that have some similarities but also many differences arose. Modern scholars categorize these languages into ten major branches: Anatolian, Indo-Iranian, Greek, Italic, Celtic, Germanic, Balto-Slavic, Armenian, Albanian, and Tocharian.

The Anatolian branch was spoken in parts of Turkey and Syria. In ancient times, the most significant of the languages in it was Hittite. All of the languages in the Anatolian branch are dead languages today. The evidence for them existing rests on some archaeological finds with writing on stone in cuneiform. The same cannot be said for the Indo-Iranian language branch, whose many sublanguages are spoken throughout parts of Iran, Pakistan, and India. They include Farsi, Pashto, Kurdish, Hindu-Urdu, Punjabi, and Bengali. Of the ancient languages in this branch, the most noteworthy is Sanskrit.

Linguistic scholars consider ancient Greek a group of dialects rather than separate subbranches. The emergence of Athens as the predominant Greek city-state in the fifth century B.C. led to its form of Greek, called Attic, to become widely used for both writing and speaking. Even before this time, the Italic language branch was transported to the Italian peninsula by migrating tribes from Central Europe. By 600 B.C., that group's main language, called Latin today, had spread across the peninsula. While Latin is still studied and spoken by individuals in academic and religious circles, it is no longer considered a living language; however, from Latin evolved the widely used subset of Romance languages that includes French, Italian, Spanish, Portuguese, and Romanian.

The Celtic language branch spread throughout Europe thanks to the efforts of many different tribes. They later became involved in a losing conflict with the Roman Empire, so Latin and its children, the Romance languages, came to dominate Western Europe. Nevertheless, the Celtic branch spawned sublanguages in parts of England, Ireland, Wales, Scotland, and the Breton peninsula in France. The Germanic branch survived Roman incursions into Central Europe and, over time, would branch into other modern-day languages centered in Germany, the Netherlands, England, Iceland, and Scandinavia. The Balto-Slavic language branch emerged as the dominant branch in Eastern Europe. Today, Balto-Slavic languages such as Russian, Polish, Czech, and Bulgarian dominate Eastern Europe.

Armenian and Albanian are distinct enough to be considered major Indo-European branches, but they are spoken in limited geographic locations and by fewer people than the other Indo-European languages. Additionally, less is known about their roots than the other languages. The last major Indo-European language is Tocharian, a dead language. It was used by people living near a desert located in western China. They left behind some writings in their distinct language before vanishing from history.

*Glossary

sublanguage: a variety of a language with its own distinct vocabulary that is used by a group of people

cuneiform: an ancient type of writing that had triangular or wedge-shaped characters

11 According to paragraph 1, which of the following is true about the Indo-European language group?

- Ⓐ Most of the languages that are in it are spoken in Europe and Africa today.
- Ⓑ It contains hundreds of sublanguages spoken by a large number of people.
- Ⓒ The majority of the languages in it are no longer spoken by most people.
- Ⓓ One of the languages in it is spoken by nearly half the world's population.

12 The word "groundbreaking" in the passage is closest in meaning to

- Ⓐ impressive
- Ⓑ influential
- Ⓒ revolutionary
- Ⓓ constructive

13 The word "They" in the passage refers to

- Ⓐ Scholars
- Ⓑ A group of people living in Eastern Europe
- Ⓒ Many modern languages
- Ⓓ These people

14 In stating that these people began to migrate and "intermingled with other groups," the author means that the people

- Ⓐ avoided others
- Ⓑ made war on others
- Ⓒ mixed with others
- Ⓓ taught others

15 According to paragraph 4, which of the following is NOT true about the Indo-Iranian language branch?

- Ⓐ It has sublanguages that are spoken in both India and Pakistan.
- Ⓑ Some of the languages in it are considered dead languages today.
- Ⓒ It includes Sanskrit, a language that was created in ancient times.
- Ⓓ Farsi, Bengali, and Pashto are some of the languages in it.

16 In paragraph 5, the author implies that Attic Greek

(A) served as a major influence on the development of the Latin language

(B) was introduced to Greece by tribes migrating there from Eastern Europe

(C) is no longer studied in the present day as knowledge of it has been lost

(D) was the major dialect that was spoken during the time of ancient Greece

17 What is the author's purpose in paragraph 6 of the passage?

(A) To focus on the effects the Roman Empire had on language development

(B) To explain why the Germanic branch has fewer languages than the Celtic branch

(C) To describe the language branches that developed throughout Europe

(D) To stress which languages are dominant in Eastern Europe today

18 In paragraph 7, the author implies that the Armenian language branch

(A) is the most frequently used language belonging to the Indo-European language groups

(B) features mostly dead languages that few people are capable of speaking today

(C) has more people that can speak its language than the Tocharian branch does

(D) was highly influential on people living in some parts of western China in the past

19 Look at the four squares [■] that indicate where the following sentence could be added to the passage.

This notion was considered the truth for a number of centuries.

Where would the sentence best fit?

Click on a square [■] to add the sentence to the passage.

20 **Directions:** An introductory sentence for a brief summary of the passage is provided below. Complete the summary by selecting the THREE answer choices that express the most important ideas of the passage. Some sentences do not belong because they express ideas that are not presented in the passage or are minor ideas in the passage. **This question is worth 2 points.**

> Drag your answer choices to the spaces where they belong. To remove an answer choice, click on it. To review the passage, click on VIEW TEXT.

The Indo-European language group contains several branches that have numerous languages spoken by around half of the world's population.

-
-
-

ANSWER CHOICES

1. The languages in the Anatolian branch as well as Latin and Tocharian are all considered dead languages today.

2. William Jones did some research on the origins of Greek and Latin after he started to study Sanskrit.

3. The Celtic, Germanic, and Balto-Slavic language branches contain many languages spoken in various parts of Europe.

4. Proto-Indo-European from 3,500 years ago is believed to be the source language that produced those languages in the Indo-European language group.

5. French, Italian, and Spanish are just three of the Romance languages that evolved from Latin.

6. Anatolian and Armenian are languages that are spoken by people from a number of different countries.

■ Vocabulary Review

A Complete each sentence with the appropriate word from the box.

emergence	dialect	noteworthy	primates	ambient

1 The sudden _____ of Mr. Watson as a powerful businessman surprised almost everyone.

2 Monkeys and chimpanzees are _____, and so are humans.

3 The members of that tribe speak a _____ known only to a few people.

4 Thanks to the sun's heat, the _____ temperature began to rise steadily.

5 Her most _____ accomplishment in her career was discovering a vaccine for a virus.

B Complete each sentence with the correct answer.

1 The country will **rebound** in the next year as its economy _____.

   a. remains the same   b. improves

2 The museum plans to **showcase** the ancient artifacts by _____ them to the public.

   a. exhibiting   b. selling

3 Janet's **insightful** questions at the conference showed how _____ she really is.

   a. inattentive   b. perceptive

4 A big pile of trash began to **accumulate** as volunteers _____ garbage in the park.

   a. gathered   b. scattered

5 The researchers will **bisect** the specimen by _____.

   a. cutting it in half   b. looking at it with a microscope

6 They intend to _____ by **formulating** it over the next few days.

   a. pack a box   b. make a plan

7 The _____ created a **glare** that made it hard to see.

   a. brightness of the sun   b. darkness in the room

8 The **confrontation** between the two men eventually led to a big _____ between them.

   a. discussion   b. fight

9 The **benevolent** ruler often showed off his _____ to the poor people of his country.

   a. cruelty   b. kindness

10 Mr. Smith shows **preferential** treatment to some employees by _____.

   a. favoring them over others   b. firing them at any time

Chapter **03**

Factual Information

◢ About the Question

Factual Information questions focus on the facts that are included in the passage. You are asked to answer a question asking about the facts or information that are covered in the passage. These questions may ask about details, definitions, explanations, or other kinds of information. The information asked about in these questions is always included in a small section of the passage. There are 1-3 Factual Information questions for each passage. There is an average of 2 of these questions per passage.

Recognizing Factual Information questions:

- According to paragraph 1, which of the following is true about X?

- The author's description of X mentions which of the following?

- According to paragraph 1, X occurred because . . .

- According to paragraph 1, X did Y because . . .

- According to paragraph 1, why did X do Y?

- Select the TWO answer choices from paragraph 1 that identify X. *To receive credit, you must select TWO answers.*

Helpful hints for answering the questions correctly:

- Most of these questions indicate the paragraph in which the correct answer is found. When trying to answer one of these questions, only look for the information in the paragraph mentioned in the question itself.

- Read carefully so that you understand what the facts are and what the author's opinions or thoughts are.

- Many answer choices for these questions are misleading or contain partially correct information. Make sure that the entire answer is accurate. Be especially careful of absolute words such as *always* and *never*.

- Some answer choices may contain accurate information that does not appear in the passage. Do not select these answer choices. Make sure the answer you select has information that appears in the passage.

- Some Factual Information questions require test takers to understand the entire paragraph, not just one part of it, to find the correct answer.

How Volcanoes Are Created

➡ Deep beneath the Earth's surface in the mantle, many rocks exist in liquid form on account of the extreme heat and pressure. This melted rock, called magma, sometimes heads toward the surface when there are cracks in the crust. These cracks tend to be located in places where the tectonic plates comprising the crust meet one another. In some instances, the magma ascends into the crust and remains there in large pools, but on other occasions, the magma reaches the surface and erupts. The place where the lava, as magma is known when it is on the surface, emerges from, often in a violent manner, is a volcano. While there are numerous volcanoes around the Earth, the majority exist along fault lines. The infamous Ring of Fire, which covers much of the eastern part of Asia along the Pacific coast and the western part of North and South America, again along the Pacific coast, has the most active volcanoes in the world.

According to paragraph 1, which of the following is true about volcanoes?

Ⓐ They can only be found in great numbers in the areas covered by the Ring of Fire.

Ⓑ Active volcanoes outnumber both extinct and dormant volcanoes on the planet.

Ⓒ Magma finds its way from the mantle to the surface by erupting from them.

Ⓓ The most violent ones are usually found in places where tectonic plates meet.

Paragraph 1 is marked with an arrow (➡).

| **Answer Explanation** |

Choice Ⓒ is the correct answer. The passage reads, "In some instances, the magma ascends into the crust and remains there in large pools, but on other occasions, the magma reaches the surface and erupts. The place where the lava, as magma is known when it is on the surface, emerges from, often in a violent manner, is a volcano." Thus magma emerges from the mantle to the surface by going through a volcano.

Practice with **Short Passages**

A | Totem Poles

🎧 CH03_2A

The Native American tribes in the Northwest Pacific region of North America are famed for their impressive totem poles, each of which is elaborately carved and painted and may tell a tale about a tribe or family or describe the deeds of a person or people. Constructing totem poles falls under the purview of specialized **artisans**, who spend hours selecting the right tree, felling and carving it, and finally painting it the proper hues before erecting it outdoors.

Every totem pole begins with a plan. The people who desire to make one meet with the artisan and decide on the design they want. Based on these **parameters**, the artisan then searches for and selects the best tree. Cedar trees are the most commonly used to make totem poles mostly because they are tall, have large diameters, have fewer branches than other trees, and have soft wood in relatively straight grains. These properties combine to make cedar trees ideal for carving into large, wide totem poles. An additional benefit is that they are durable so are thus less likely to rot and to fall into pieces than other trees. Some totem poles made from cedar are still standing more than a century after being carved and raised.

Once the selected tree has been felled and had its branches stripped, it must be carted back to the artisan's workshop, which is usually an indoor shop. The artisan and his assistants then strip the bark from the tree and smooth the large trunk that remains, whereupon the planned design is then etched into the tree trunk. A typical totem pole is designed in three sections: the bottom, middle, and top. Following the completion of the design stage, the artisan carves the designs by starting at the bottom. The top section often requires extra labor since many totem poles have protrusions such as the wings of birds attached to their tops, so it is the final part to be done. After the carving is finished, the totem pole is painted the desired color scheme. Finally, the individuals who commissioned it take possession and raise it during an elaborate ceremony.

*artisan: a craftsperson; a person who is skilled at a particular art
*parameters: guidelines; boundaries

1 Select the TWO answer choices from paragraph 2 that identify the reasons that totem poles are frequently made from cedar trees. *To receive credit, you must select TWO answers.*

Ⓐ Their ability to remain sturdy for periods lasting many years

Ⓑ Their pleasant aromas and the appearances of their wood

Ⓒ Their presence in abundance in the Northwest Pacific region

Ⓓ Their height and relative lack of branches

2 According to paragraph 3, the top section of a totem pole is typically made last because

Ⓐ it requires the most detailed work of all three parts of a totem pole

Ⓑ it is subject to change based upon the desire of the person commissioning the work

Ⓒ it contains parts sticking out from it that need more work done on them

Ⓓ it is tradition for Native American artisans to work from the bottom to the top

Vocabulary

- _____ = ornately; decoratively
- _____ = a range of quality, control, or concern
- _____ = a color
- _____ = something that sticks out or projects

60

B | The Formation of the Solar System

Astronomers estimate that the solar system is somewhere around five billion years old and have several theories regarding its creation. The most common—and most widely accepted—one is the nebular hypothesis. According to this theory, the solar system developed from an enormous cloud of gas and dust. First proposed in the eighteenth century, the nebular hypothesis was not widely accepted until the late twentieth century, when observations of newborn stars and their solar systems appeared to confirm many aspects of it.

The nebular hypothesis **posits** that a huge cloud of gas and dust began collapsing on itself due to the force of gravity. As it collapsed, the conservation of angular momentum caused the gas and dust to contract further and to spin rapidly. This spinning created a central core of elements—primarily helium and hydrogen—which formed a new star, or protostar, that would eventually become the sun. The contracting elements heated up, and nuclear fusion in the protostar soon occurred. Around the protostar, a large flat disc of dust, rock, and ice, which would become the planets, moons, and asteroids in the solar system, collected. This initial stage in the formation of the solar system lasted approximately 100,000 years.

Next, the planets formed through the process known as **accretion**. In the spinning disc of material surrounding the protostar, dust, rock, and ice started slamming into one another and clumping into bigger and bigger masses. As they increased in size, their gravitational fields attracted more material, so they grew even larger. Over the course of several million years, this process formed the planets. Those planets closest to the sun formed into balls of rocky material because only elements with high melting points, such as iron, nickel, and various silicates, could endure the sun's heat.

The outer planets, on the other hand, formed into giant balls of gas since in the colder region, which is called the frost line by astronomers and which starts between Mars and Jupiter, more of the spinning disc's material survived the sun's growing heat. This material mostly existed in the form of gas and ice crystals. The spinning outer planets captured large amounts of this material and subsequently grew into massive balls of gas that contained some frozen elements.

*posit: to state as a fact
*accretion: an increase in size due to the gradual accumulation of material

---

1 The author's description of the protostar in paragraph 2 mentions which of the following?

Ⓐ The manner in which it formed according to the nebular hypothesis

Ⓑ The size that it attained before the planets, moons, and asteroids formed

Ⓒ The way that nuclear fusion happened and caused it to become the sun

Ⓓ The amount of time that it spun until its central core was formed

2 According to paragraph 4, which of the following is true about the frost line?

Ⓐ The planets that are located within it travel around the sun from beyond Mars.

Ⓑ Astronomers believe that it is too cold for any forms of life to survive in it.

Ⓒ All of the planets in it took longer to create than the planets closer to the sun.

Ⓓ Elements such as iron and nickel are found on planets there in their gaseous forms.

Vocabulary

- _____ = to decrease in size
- _____ = to be completely around someone or something
- _____ = any mineral compound containing silicon
- _____ = next; later; afterward

C | Earthquake Prediction

CH03_2C

   Earthquakes rank among the most devastating of all natural disasters, and unlike many others, such as hurricanes and volcanic eruptions, they virtually always strike with no warning. This prevents people from evacuating the earthquake zone to save themselves. There have been some efforts to predict earthquakes, but they are rife with problems and have resulted only in limited successes.

   One method is to study the long-term history of earthquake patterns. Around the world, there are certain areas, such as Japan and the Pacific coast region of the United States, where earthquakes are frequent. These zones are located along fault lines, which mostly occur where the **tectonic plates** comprising the Earth's crust meet. By examining the historic record, seismologists can make general predictions regarding future earthquakes. Additionally, an increase in seismic activity in these zones may indicate the possibility of larger earthquakes in the near future. For example, when a minor earthquake ranking 3.0 on the **Richter scale** occurs, there is a roughly ten-percent chance of a larger one happening in the same area within a few days. This is too small a margin to justify the mass evacuation of people from a potential earthquake zone though.

   Making more specific predictions of when and where earthquakes will occur is extremely difficult. One area that has seen some small success is the studying of animal behavior as animals tend to be sensitive to sudden changes in their environments. Prior to an earthquake in Italy in 2009, the population of male toads in a region suddenly moved to new territories. This was later cited as an example of animals foreseeing an earthquake. Unfortunately, using animals to predict earthquakes is unfeasible at this time as it would require an enormous effort continuously to observe and report on animal populations in earthquake zones.

   Radon gas emissions may enable scientists to predict earthquakes in the future. There has been a notable rise in radon gas emissions coming from underground prior to many earthquakes. A paper published in 2009 showed that since 1966, almost ninety earthquakes were preceded by radon emission spikes. Some of these earthquakes, however, took place months after the emissions occurred, so it may not be possible accurately to state when tremors will happen. Based on current technology, it appears as though it is not possible to predict earthquakes with any measure of accuracy.

*tectonic plate: a large mass of land that is a part of the Earth's crust
*Richter scale: a scale that goes from 1 to 10 and measures the intensity of earthquakes

---

1 According to paragraph 2, why do earthquakes often take place in some parts of the planet?

   Ⓐ The past occurrence of earthquakes makes a region more susceptible to them in the future.

   Ⓑ They often happen in areas where large bodies of land meet the Earth's oceans.

   Ⓒ They occur near fault lines that exist where the plates making up the crust meet.

   Ⓓ The presence of volcanoes can weaken the Earth's crust and cause earthquakes to happen.

2 According to paragraph 3, one problem with relying upon animals to predict earthquakes is that

   Ⓐ scientists are not sure which types of animals they need to observe the closest

   Ⓑ watching groups of animals would require the expenditure of numerous resources

   Ⓒ there are not enough people who are trained to watch how animals behave

   Ⓓ how specific groups of animals behave prior to earthquakes is not yet known

Vocabulary

- _____ = abundant; plentiful
- _____ = a person who studies earthquakes
- _____ = impractical
- _____ = to happen before something else

◪ Mapping

The following chart shows the structure of the passage. Fill in the blanks with the appropriate words.

Earthquake Prediction

Can be devastating but are hard to predict
- attempts to predict earthquakes have problems and have only been somewhat successful

---

Study ❶ _____ patterns
- certain places get frequent earthquakes
- can examine ❷ _____ record and predict where earthquakes will happen
- if a 3.0 quake happens, is 10% ❸ _____ a large one will occur soon

---

Study animal ❹ _____
- are sensitive to changes in their environments
- male ❺ _____ moved to new territories before earthquake in Italy in 2009
- would be hard to do since must observe many groups

Radon gas ❻ _____
- rise in radon gas emissions from ground prior to many earthquakes
- since 1966, almost 90 earthquakes saw ❼ _____ in emissions
- some emissions happened ❽ _____ before earthquakes though

◪ Summary

The following is a summary of the passage. Fill in the blanks with the appropriate words.

Earthquakes can be devastating natural disasters, but it is very difficult to ❶ _____ them, unlike hurricanes and volcanic eruptions. Some ❷ _____ study the long-term history of earthquake patterns. Certain places in the world get ❸ _____ earthquakes, so they can predict where some earthquakes will occur. Additionally, when a 3.0 quake on the ❹ _____ scale happens, there is a 10% chance a larger one will occur soon. Animal ❺ _____ may also help predict earthquakes. In Italy in 2009, male toads moved to new territories ❻ _____ to an earthquake. And radon gas ❼ _____ often increase before many earthquakes. However, all of these methods have problems, so predicting earthquakes may not be ❽ _____ .

A The Formation of the Global Atmosphere CH03_3A

In modern times, the Earth's atmosphere is comprised of 78% nitrogen, 21% oxygen, a small amount of carbon dioxide, and **trace** amounts of several other elements. To reach this state, the atmosphere has undergone several transformations in its long history. In the beginning, the planet had no atmosphere, but, as the Earth began cooling, large amounts of gases were vented from the interior, primarily through volcanic activity. This marked the start of the planet's first atmosphere. During this stage, the atmosphere contained mostly water vapor, methane, carbon dioxide, and nitrogen, a mixture which could never be safely breathed by virtually all lifeforms on the planet today.

As the Earth cooled even more, the water vapor in the atmosphere fell from the sky as rain and began collecting on the surface roughly three billion years ago. It was in this water that the first forms of life appeared in the form of cyanobacteria, which is more commonly called blue-green algae. These algae fed off the huge amounts of carbon dioxide in the atmosphere and, through the process of **photosynthesis**, emitted oxygen back into the atmosphere. Over the next 300 million years, the level of oxygen in the atmosphere rose in small amounts and attained a level sufficient enough to begin combining with iron in rocks to oxidize and to produce rust. Through the study of such rocks, geologists have been able to pinpoint the early rise of the level of oxygen in the atmosphere. In fact, rocks absorbed so much of the oxygen produced at that time that the creation of an oxygen-rich atmosphere was forestalled.

It was approximately 750 million years ago that an oxygen boom began on the planet. A tipping point of sorts was reached, so the oxygen level started outpacing the carbon dioxide level by climbing to around a fifth of what it currently is. This was a significant enough change that lifeforms depending on carbon dioxide started dying out while those favoring oxygen started thriving. At that time, all life was in the oceans since it could not survive on land on account of the high levels of ultraviolet radiation produced by the sun. However, with the increase in the oxygen level of the atmosphere, some oxygen molecules hit by the sun's energy began splitting into single oxygen atoms. These single atoms then formed with airborne oxygen molecules, which have two atoms, to form ozone, which has three oxygen atoms. This process gradually formed the ozone layer, which protects life on the planet from high doses of ultraviolet radiation.

Once the ozone layer was established, the world's lifeforms, most of which were oxygen breathing, gradually emerged from the oceans and migrated onto the land. A balance between the carbon dioxide-breathing plants and oxygen-breathing animals slowly asserted itself. At the same time, carbon dioxide was being absorbed not only by plants but also by the oceans and rock formations in processes that continue to this day. As a result, the level of carbon dioxide declined to less than one percent of the atmosphere while the amount of oxygen rose. The end result of this entire process, which took billions of years, is the current state of the atmosphere.

*trace: tiny; miniscule
*photosynthesis: the process through which plants use the sun's energy to convert water and carbon dioxide into oxygen and sugar that they use for nourishment

Vocabulary

• _____ = a colorless, odorless, and flammable gas • _____ = to combine with oxygen
• _____ = a small aquatic organism that contains chlorophyll • _____ = to move from one place to another

1   The word "forestalled" in the passage is closest in meaning to

    Ⓐ   anticipated

    Ⓑ   hindered

    Ⓒ   produced

    Ⓓ   occasioned

Factual Information Question

2   According to paragraph 2, the oxygen level in the atmosphere increased because

    Ⓐ   certain lifeforms extracted carbon dioxide from the air and released oxygen into it

    Ⓑ   oxygen that had been previously contained in rocks escaped and moved into the atmosphere

    Ⓒ   the light from the sun caused compounds to break apart and to release free-standing oxygen

    Ⓓ   volcanic activity around the planet released large amounts of oxygen into the air

Negative Factual Information Question

3   In paragraph 3, all of the following questions are answered EXCEPT:

    Ⓐ   What caused the ozone layer to form in the Earth's atmosphere?

    Ⓑ   Why did no life exist on the planet's surface more than 750 million years ago?

    Ⓒ   When did the oxygen level in the atmosphere begin to exceed the carbon dioxide level?

    Ⓓ   How did ultraviolet radiation limit the size of the life that lived in the planet's oceans?

Prose Summary Question

4   An introductory sentence for a brief summary of the passage is provided below. Complete the summary by selecting the THREE answer choices that express the most important ideas of the passage. Some sentences do not belong because they express ideas that are not presented in the passage or are minor ideas in the passage.

The composition of the Earth's atmosphere has undergone several changes over the course of the planet's history.

ANSWER CHOICES

1   The creation of the ozone layer in the atmosphere enabled lifeforms to emerge from the oceans and to live safely on land.

2   Despite the fact that nitrogen dominates the planet's atmosphere, it cannot be safely breathed by most forms of life.

3   The sun's ultraviolet rays are harmful to all forms of life and would kill it in a relatively short period of time if it were exposed to the rays.

4   The early atmosphere contained a large amount of carbon dioxide, nitrogen, and other elements toxic to modern lifeforms.

5   The process of photosynthesis that was practiced by algae was what prompted oxygen to begin entering the atmosphere in large amounts.

6   There was a great amount of volcanic activity on the Earth in the early years after the planet was formed.

B | Movies and Theatrical Performances

Until the creating of motion pictures in the late nineteenth century, live theatrical performances were among the main ways people entertained themselves. Nowadays, the reverse is true as movie ticket sales and box office receipts far exceed those of live theater. While the two types of performances have some similarities, they are vastly different in many ways, and which is the better of the two depends on each person's individual taste and opinion.

Movies have several advantages over live theatrical productions, among them being of much greater scope, having casts of thousands in some cases, and using sophisticated special visual and sound effects to enhance the stories their directors want to tell. The stunning presentations created are a key reason that so many people worldwide enjoy watching movies. There are also a large number of genres, so there are love stories, detective stories, and even stories about superheroes, which means there is something for nearly everyone to enjoy. Movies cost less to attend than most live theatrical performances as tickets average around ten dollars a show while live theater is much more expensive, with tickets for Broadway productions costing hundreds of dollars or more. Finally, movies can be viewed at home on televisions or computer monitors, thereby eliminating the need to go out to be entertained.

Live theater, however, is not without **merits** of its own. For one thing, it is a more intimate presentation, with the audience and performers being in the same room at the same time, so there is a more intense connection than the one people get from watching actors on films. Theatrical performances and performers also tend to be of higher quality acting wise since the performers get no second chance if they make a mistake; movie actors, on the other hand, can do as many takes as necessary to get their lines or scenes right. If theater performers **flub** their lines, the audience will notice, and the performance as a whole will suffer. As a result, the best actors can be found in live theatrical performances. Finally, in live theater, no two performances are ever alike. Each time a play, opera, ballet, or musical is staged, it may utilize the same words, songs, and dance routines, but there is always something fresh for the audience to appreciate.

From a business point of view, movies tend to be more profitable than live theater. Movies can be copied and viewed worldwide by millions of people at the same time and thereby earn their producers and studios enormous returns on their investments in a relatively short amount of time. In recent years, for instance, some movies have grossed more than one billion dollars at the global box office. Live theater, however, is staged on one night in one place at one time, so its earning potential is limited by the number of seats in the theater. While some more popular performances are put on in different cities at the same time, there are still far fewer simultaneous shows than movies can achieve. Mainly on account of the wider accessibility of movies over theatrical performances, movies will likely continue to grow in popularity despite the fact that they are of poorer quality than theatrical productions.

*merit: value; excellence
*flub: to err; to make a mistake

Vocabulary

- _____ = to make better; to improve
- _____ = a kind or type
- _____ = strong with regard to feelings or emotions
- _____ = happening at the same time

1 Which of the following can be inferred from paragraph 1 about theatrical performances?

   Ⓐ They are sometimes performed by a small cast of only two or three actors.

   Ⓑ They make less money than movies but are still able to be profitable for their producers.

   Ⓒ They lost some of their popularity in the twentieth century due to the appearance of movies.

   Ⓓ They are considered better than movies by the majority of people in many countries.

2 In paragraph 2, why does the author mention "tickets for Broadway productions"?

   Ⓐ To note the difficulty of acquiring them for some of the most popular performances

   Ⓑ To stress how expensive they are in comparison to tickets for movies

   Ⓒ To explain the process that one needs to go through to purchase them

   Ⓓ To claim that they are inaccessible to the majority of people who seek entertainment

3 According to paragraph 4, which of the following is true about movies?

   Ⓐ Some of them have earned more than one billion dollars in a single country recently.

   Ⓑ A lot of them fail to earn money, but the ones that are profitable earn huge sums of money.

   Ⓒ Theatrical performances frequently earn much more money than movies do.

   Ⓓ They can produce large amounts of money for their backers very quickly.

4 Select the appropriate statements from the answer choices and match them to the type of entertainment to which they relate. TWO of the answer choices will NOT be used.

Movies (Select 3)	Live Theatrical Performances (Select 2)
•	
•	•
•	•

STATEMENTS

☐1 Tend not to be performed by the best actors and actresses

☐2 Are many different types of stories that can be presented to audiences

☐3 May have slight differences each time that they are seen by audiences

☐4 Require performers to spend long amounts of time rehearsing their lines

☐5 Have much larger casts than the other type of performance

☐6 Can be shown to a smaller number of people at the same time than the other

☐7 May take several months of preparation before audiences can see them

⌒ CH03_4A

White-Crowned Sparrow Vocalizations

The white-crowned sparrow is a songbird native to North America that breeds in Alaska and Canada in summer and winters in the continental United States and the northern part of Mexico. It is noted for its distinctive plumage consisting of a gray breast and a white crown with black streaks. The sparrow is also easily recognized by its unique song and call patterns. These vocalizations have been at the center of some intense studies by zoologists, the primary purpose of which was to recognize when the bird learns how to make songs and calls. A secondary purpose of the studies was to understand variations in the songs and the calls that occur in different geographical regions.

There are distinctive songs and calls produced by the sparrow, but only males of the species produce these vocalizations. There are regional varieties in the songs, but all follow a similar pattern. First, the sparrow makes a high, piercing whistle as an introduction. This is followed by more whistles in different patterns, and then the bird ends the song with an almost buzzing trilling sound. Every song lasts for only two to three seconds, and the bird sings songs in groups that are separated by pauses of up to eight or nine seconds between each one. As for its calls, the bird has around ten distinctive calls. They may sound similar to the songs, but they are not. Instead, the calls are composed of sharp whistles and chirps made in groups or as individual noises separated by pauses. The purposes of the calls vary, but the most common are alarm calls to warn others of nearby danger and harsh, rasping noises when the birds are having disputes with other males of the same species.

Zoologists are very interested in how male white-crowned sparrows come to learn their songs and calls. Experiments conducted indicated that the vocalizations are of an instinctive nature engrained in the birds from birth. However, the studies also showed that chicks need a teacher—an adult male—to assist them in properly learning the songs and the calls. In one experiment, zoologists took a male sparrow chick eight days old and isolated him from all others of his species. The bird produced songs and calls, but they were abnormal in comparison to those chicks raised together with others of the same species. In the same set of experiments, another male chick was raised with an adult male, and, over time, the chick seemed to pick up the correct vocalizations by listening to the adult male. The chick began learning with what the zoologists called subsongs, which were weaker versions of the adult's songs. Over time, the subsongs became more similar to the adult's songs and eventually matched them perfectly.

The studies further reinforced what zoologists already knew about other songbirds: They have a short window in which to learn their songs and calls. ■1 The sparrows had to learn them in a window ranging anywhere from fifteen to fifty days after hatching. ■2 After fifty days, males could not learn properly even if they were placed with adult males of their species. ■3 It is suspected that most male chicks in the wild learn the songs and calls directly from their fathers since adult white-crowned sparrows form strong pair bonds. ■4 This results in the males spending a lot of time with their chicks after they hatch since adult males defend the nest and help adult females feed the chicks.

A discovery of even greater interest from the studies was that white-crowned sparrows from the same regions have distinctive dialects in their vocalizations. For example, in a study performed on three different groups in three separate regions in California, zoologists learned there was a difference in the songs from each region as well as distinctive patterns in the songs of most of the sparrows in each area. The main theory on why this occurs is that male chicks learn the songs from their fathers and, in later years, become adults and then return to the same breeding and nesting grounds. They therefore pass on the songs they learned to the next generation, so regional distinctions in vocalizations develop among the sparrows in particular places.

*Glossary

plumage: the entire collection of feathers on a bird

trilling: having a singing sound that alternates tones rapidly

1 According to paragraph 1, zoologists studied the white-crowned sparrow in order to

Ⓐ understand why the bird lives in certain geographical areas

Ⓑ learn about some of the vocalizations that the bird makes

Ⓒ determine why its songs and calls sound different from those of other birds

Ⓓ find out more about the bird's unique mating habits

2 In paragraph 2, the author's description of the songs of the white-crowned sparrow mentions all of the following EXCEPT:

Ⓐ the amount of time that each of its songs typically lasts

Ⓑ the length of the pause between each song that it makes

Ⓒ the first sound that the bird makes when it starts to sing

Ⓓ the number of different songs that the bird sings

3 According to paragraph 2, which of the following is true about the white-crowned sparrow's calls?

Ⓐ Males sometimes make them when they are fighting with other males of their species.

Ⓑ They are made only in groups in the same way that the bird sings its songs.

Ⓒ The bird makes them for many reasons, but mating calls are made the most frequently.

Ⓓ A typical white-crowned sparrow is capable of making fewer calls than songs.

4 The author discusses "subsongs" in paragraph 3 in order to

Ⓐ describe the manner in which chicks learn to sing songs from adult male sparrows

Ⓑ differentiate between the songs that chicks can sing and the songs that adult males can sing

Ⓒ state that chicks with no male influence can only learn subsongs rather than regular ones

Ⓓ point out that they lack the proper vocalizations required since only chicks sing them

5 The word "reinforced" in the passage is closest in meaning to

Ⓐ defended

Ⓑ approved

Ⓒ armored

Ⓓ strengthened

6 In paragraph 4, the author implies that the white-crowned sparrow

(A) is capable of learning multiple songs and calls in the first two weeks after it hatches

(B) has a greater number of songs and calls to learn than most other species of birds

(C) may sometimes learn songs and calls from its mother if there is no adult male around

(D) requires more than two months to learn all of the songs and the calls it must know properly

7 Which of the sentences below best expresses the essential information in the highlighted sentence in the passage? Incorrect answer choices change the meaning in important ways or leave out essential information.

For example, in a study performed on three different groups in three separate regions in California, zoologists learned there was a difference in the songs from each region as well as distinctive patterns in the songs of most of the sparrows in each area.

(A) Zoologists conducted a study on sparrows in California and learned that the birds in each region sang different songs with their own unique patterns.

(B) In a study done on birds in three different places in California, zoologists confirmed that the sparrows in each place taught their young how to sing songs.

(C) There are three different places in California that zoologists have confirmed contain sparrows which sing unique songs and teach them to their chicks.

(D) Zoologists learned that the sparrows in three distinct regions in California sing songs that are identical to one another despite a lack of contact between each group.

8 According to paragraph 5, there are variances in the songs that different groups of white-crowned sparrows sing because

(A) every adult male teaches a slightly different variation of its songs to each of its chicks

(B) related birds continually visit the same breeding grounds and pass on unique songs to their chicks

(C) the songs that the birds sing are not engrained in their minds from birth, so they can have some differences

(D) the birds have an instinctual need to vary the songs they sing to differentiate themselves from other groups of birds

9 Look at the four squares [■] that indicate where the following sentence could be added to the passage.

Attempts were made by putting chicks with adult males, but as the birds neared two months of age, they were unable to learn their songs and calls properly.

Where would the sentence best fit?

Click on a square [■] to add the sentence to the passage.

10 Directions: An introductory sentence for a brief summary of the passage is provided below. Complete the summary by selecting the THREE answer choices that express the most important ideas of the passage. Some sentences do not belong because they express ideas that are not presented in the passage or are minor ideas in the passage. **This question is worth 2 points.**

> Drag your answer choices to the spaces where they belong. To remove an answer choice, click on it. To review the passage, click on VIEW TEXT.

The white-crowned sparrow is a bird noted for the songs and the calls it vocalizes, so many studies have been conducted on it.

-
-
-

ANSWER CHOICES

1. The white-crowned sparrow has a specific pattern in the songs that it sings and learns it from an adult male.

2. There are at least three different places in California that have white-crowned sparrows which have their own unique songs.

3. Zoologists have learned that white-crowned sparrow chicks require an adult male influence to learn how to vocalize different sounds properly.

4. Studies have revealed that white-crowned sparrow chicks must learn how to make songs and calls at an early age, or they will never be able to do so.

5. There are large groups of white-crowned sparrows that live in Canada, the United States, and Mexico at different times during the year.

6. Some of the calls that white-crowned sparrows make are to alert other birds of danger while others are for mating purposes.

The Origins of Salt in the Oceans

A salt evaporation pond in Sicily, Italy

The world's oceans have an average salinity of 3.5%, which means that a liter of seawater contains approximately thirty-five grams of salt. This is not a uniform amount, however, as the level of salinity varies from place to place. For instance, where fresh water enters the ocean through the onrushing flow from river mouths, the salinity level is much less. In contrast, some areas, such as the North Sea, have higher salinity levels. In the case of the North Sea, the flowing of the Gulf Stream Current is mostly responsible for its higher salinity level. Other places may be saltier if they get lower amounts of precipitation and a smaller influx of fresh river water. The average salinity of the oceans is lower in the polar regions and at the equator but higher at the mid-level latitudes.

The main source of ocean salinity is the inflow of fresh water containing mineral ions from land rocks. Water in the form of precipitation has an acidic quality that erodes rocks. This characteristic comes mainly from carbon dioxide in the atmosphere. When rocks erode, they release mineral ions that eventually make their way to the oceans in the form of runoff. While some of the ions are absorbed by marine lifeforms, over time, many are not absorbed, thereby increasing the oceans' salinity. The two most common mineral ions in the oceans are chloride and sodium, which comprise approximately eighty-five percent of the salt content in ocean water. Other mineral ions in ocean water include smaller amounts of magnesium, sulfur, calcium, and potassium.

The theory of rock erosion creating the oceans' salinity was first proposed by English scientist Edmund Halley in 1715 in a process he termed continental weathering. However, Halley was only partially correct as modern scientists further theorize that some ocean salinity originated in the ocean floors. This comes from hydrothermal vents at the bottoms of the oceans. As magma under the ocean floors heats up, it puts pressure on the floors and creates cracks. These cracks allow mineral ions to seep into the water, which further enhances its salinity. In addition, when the cracks become very large, undersea volcanoes begin to form. As these underwater volcanoes become bigger over time, they release plenty of mineral ions into the surrounding water, thereby contributing to the salinity of the water. There is another theory claiming that when the oceans formed billions of years ago, a great amount of sodium was leeched from the ocean floors, and that contributed to the water's salt content.

All of this buildup of salinity occurred over millions of years. The oceans did not become oversaturated with mineral ions due to the delicate balance of the hydrological cycle. ■ While the ongoing process of evaporation creates a greater percentage of salinity, the influx of fresh water from flowing rivers and precipitation counters this increase. ❷ Many marine lifeforms evolved during this process, so they adapted to living in salt water by forming the ability completely to eliminate salt from their bodies. ❸ Unfortunately, humans lack this capability. ❹ The kidneys are responsible for removing salt in humans' bodies, but they cannot cope with high amounts of it. Even the low level of salinity in seawater makes it unfit for human consumption. While consuming a small amount of seawater will not cause any detrimental effects, drinking large amounts will result in internal injuries and, eventually, death. Too much salt in the blood will cause renal failure because the kidneys become overworked and shut down, leading to death unless fresh water is consumed to flush out the salt in the system.

Despite being unfit for human consumption, it is possible to purify ocean water by desalinizing it. This is usually done through a distillation process, during which seawater is heated to a certain temperature. This allows the water to evaporate and become a gas that is later condensed to form fresh liquid water. Since ninety-seven percent of all the water on the Earth is found in the planet's oceans, it is no surprise that people are working to come up with multiple ways to remove the salt from water to provide water for crops and for people to consume.

*Glossary

renal: relating to the kidneys

desalinize: to remove the salt from

11 In paragraph 1, why does the author mention "the North Sea"?

  Ⓐ To explain the reason why relatively few rivers flow into it

  Ⓑ To claim that it receives a fairly low amount of precipitation annually

  Ⓒ To point out that the Gulf Stream Current flows to its waters

  Ⓓ To explain the reason that its waters are saltier than those in other places

12 According to paragraph 1, a place that the salinity level of an ocean may be lower than normal is where

  Ⓐ minerals are found on the ocean floor in great quantities

  Ⓑ there is a river bringing fresh water into the ocean

  Ⓒ large numbers of plants are growing on the ocean floor

  Ⓓ small amounts of rain or snow fall into the ocean

13 According to paragraph 2, what happens to some of the runoff from precipitation that reaches the oceans?

  Ⓐ It harms many marine lifeforms because of the mineral ions it is carrying.

  Ⓑ It evaporates and rises into the atmosphere in the form of water vapor.

  Ⓒ It carries mineral ions that enter the water and increase its salinity.

  Ⓓ It erodes large amounts of rock and carries small pieces to the ocean shore.

14 Which of the sentences below best expresses the essential information in the highlighted sentence in the passage? Incorrect answer choices change the meaning in important ways or leave out essential information.

As these underwater volcanoes become bigger over time, they release plenty of mineral ions into the surrounding water, thereby contributing to the salinity of the water.

  Ⓐ When undersea volcanoes erupt, they become bigger in size and also put large amounts of salt into the ocean water.

  Ⓑ If a volcano erupts under the ocean's surface, it can release a large number of mineral ions into the water around it.

  Ⓒ Volcanoes located underwater can make the ocean saltier by putting mineral ions into the water while they grow larger.

  Ⓓ Some volcanoes are known to erupt underneath the ocean's surface, which can make them grow bigger at times.

15 What is the author's purpose in paragraph 3 of the passage?

   Ⓐ To question the accuracy of a theory that was created by Edmund Halley

   Ⓑ To describe some possible reasons why the Earth's oceans became salty

   Ⓒ To emphasize that modern scientists know more now than people did in the past

   Ⓓ To argue that volcanoes are the primary reason for the oceans' high salinity levels

16 In paragraph 3, all of the following questions are answered EXCEPT:

   Ⓐ How might hydrothermal vents on the ocean floors contribute to the salt content of the oceans?

   Ⓑ Which person came up with the theory that the Earth's oceans became full of salt billions of years in the past?

   Ⓒ What is the connection between continental weathering and Edmund Halley?

   Ⓓ How is it possible for undersea volcanoes to have made the salinity level of the oceans higher?

17 The word "detrimental" in the passage is closest in meaning to

   Ⓐ advantageous

   Ⓑ periodic

   Ⓒ unexpected

   Ⓓ harmful

18 According to paragraph 5, which of the following is true about desalinization?

   Ⓐ There are so far only a couple of ways that it can successfully remove salt from water.

   Ⓑ It is a difficult process that only removes ninety-seven percent of the water's salt content.

   Ⓒ The most common way it is done is by heating ocean water to make it change its form.

   Ⓓ Most people around the world get their drinking water by using this process.

19 Look at the four squares [■] that indicate where the following sentence could be added to the passage.

Biologists assume the reason is that people, unlike many marine creatures, did not live in the oceans and therefore did not evolve to adapt to conditions there.

Where would the sentence best fit?

Click on a square [■] to add the sentence to the passage.

20 **Directions:** An introductory sentence for a brief summary of the passage is provided below. Complete the summary by selecting the THREE answer choices that express the most important ideas of the passage. Some sentences do not belong because they express ideas that are not presented in the passage or are minor ideas in the passage. **This question is worth 2 points.**

Drag your answer choices to the spaces where they belong. To remove an answer choice, click on it. To review the passage, click on VIEW TEXT.

There are several theories regarding why the Earth's oceans have salt water, which has various effects on both humans and animals.

-
-
-

ANSWER CHOICES

1. Scientists believe that some natural phenomena, including undersea volcanic eruptions, have added salt to the oceans.

2. Many ocean animals have developed ways to remove salt from their bodies, but humans are not able to do that.

3. A lack of precipitation in a part of an ocean can help reduce the average amount of salt in that area.

4. Most of the oceans' salinity comes from fresh water containing mineral ions that finds its ways into the Earth's oceans.

5. People are interested in desalinizing methods because the vast majority of the water on the Earth is found in its oceans.

6. Edmund Halley came up with one theory about why the Earth's oceans have such a high salt content.

◢ Vocabulary Review

A Complete each sentence with the appropriate word from the box.

ingrained	purview	seismologist	oxidize	delicate

1 Iron begins to _____ when exposed to air, which is what makes it rust over time.

2 This ecosystem is very _____, so if it becomes unbalanced, it could collapse easily.

3 Many animals have instincts that are _____ in them since birth.

4 The _____ predicts that a powerful earthquake could hit this area at any time.

5 His _____ is marketing, so he is not familiar with any other aspects of the project.

B Complete each sentence with the correct answer.

1 Enemy soldiers **surrounded** the city by covering _____ of the city's walls.

   a. every side   b. the front and back parts

2 Once Greg learned to **cope with** the pain, he was able to _____ it without medicine.

   a. appreciate   b. handle

3 The **piercing** sound was so _____ that it hurt many people's ears.

   a. soft   b. shrill

4 The data has slight **variations**, and those _____ resulted in the men's opposite opinions.

   a. differences   b. errors

5 **Rife** with wildlife, the forest has a _____ of animals living in it.

   a. small number   b. large number

6 The **intense** storm was so _____ that it dropped rain on the region for ten days.

   a. powerful   b. large

7 Alicia paints with dark **hues** as she prefers _____ that show cool emotions.

   a. images   b. colors

8 You must use a **uniform** amount of each ingredient, so be sure they are all _____.

   a. fresh   b. equal

9 Wendy's performance **precedes** John's, so she will play the piano _____ he does.

   a. before   b. after

10 The thriller **genre** of books is the _____ that Brian prefers to read the most.

   a. type   b. author

Chapter 04

Negative Factual Information

◢ About the Question

Negative Factual Information questions focus on information that is not included in the passage. You are asked to answer a question asking about facts or information that is NOT covered in the passage. Three of the four answer choices contain accurate information appearing in the passage while the correct answer choice has either incorrect information or information that does not appear in the passage. The information asked about in these questions is always included in a small section of the passage. There are 0-2 Negative Factual Information questions for each passage.

Recognizing Negative Factual Information questions:

- According to paragraph 1, which of the following is NOT true about X?

- The author's description of X mentions all of the following EXCEPT:

- In paragraph 2, all of the following questions are answered EXCEPT:

Helpful hints for answering the questions correctly:

- The question identifies one or two paragraphs where the correct answer can be found. Focus only on that part of the passage when looking for the correct answer.

- The correct answer may contain information that is factually correct but does not appear in the passage.

- The answer choices often restate the information mentioned in the passage but use different words and phrases. Be careful of slight deviations that can make these restatements become the correct answer.

The Silurian Period

The Silurian Period began roughly 443 million years ago and concluded approximately 416 million years ago. It is one of the most notable periods in the Earth's history for the primary fact that the first evidence of life existing on land has been dated to it. Fossils of land creatures from the Silurian Period include those of fungi, arachnids, and centipedes, and there is also evidence that vascular plants developed then. While it is possible there were both plants and animals on land in prior periods, such as the Ordovician, that has not been proven by the fossil record. Another notable aspect of this period was that fish evolved to a great extent during it. For instance, the first known freshwater fish as well as the first fish with jaws come from this time. Finally, the first coral reefs have been dated to the Silurian Period. This is most likely due to the tremendous changes the Earth underwent then, particularly the melting of enormous glacial formations, which caused the levels of the planet's seas to rise considerably.

The author's description of the Silurian Period mentions all of the following EXCEPT:

(A) the types of animals that began living on the land

(B) the likely reason that coral reefs appeared in some of the Earth's waters

(C) the manner in which water-dwelling creatures underwent changes

(D) the places where fossils of the first land creatures from this time were found

| Answer Explanation |

Choice (D) is the correct answer. The passage mentions that fossils of land creatures dating from the Silurian Period have been found. However, there is no mention in the passage of where those fossils were discovered.

A | The Migration of the Indigo Bunting

🎧 CH04_2A

The indigo bunting is a small sparrow-like bird noted for its vivid blue plumage. It is typically found living in forested areas alongside rivers and streams as well as at the edges of fields and on paths going through forests where trees have been cleared for power lines. In these places, the female of the species builds a nest in low brush located no more than a meter above the ground.

Zoologists have carefully studied the **migration** patterns followed by the indigo bunting. It mostly dwells in the eastern parts of Canada and the United States during the summer breeding season, and it flies south to Mexico as well as to Central America and the northern part of South America during the winter months. While it was once confined to the northern region of the United States in the summer, its territory expanded several decades ago. For instance, in the 1970s, the indigo bunting was discovered living in eastern Canada during the summer months for the first time. Zoologists believe that this change in its range was a result of Canada having warmer summers than it had enjoyed in previous decades.

The total amount of distance covered by the indigo bunting when it migrates is approximately 1,900 kilometers each way. The bird usually migrates in a straight path due south. Those animals living in the east move to wintering grounds in the east while those residing in the west migrate to wintering grounds in the west. Intensive studies of the indigo bunting have proven that it has excellent **navigational** skills, which permit the bird to migrate at night since it can use the stars for guidance. Experiments with the indigo bunting have shown that it has an internal system allowing it to adjust its flight path as the angles of the stars change while they move through the night sky. This ability allows the bird to fly south to the same wintering grounds every year and then to return north to the same summering grounds.

*migration: the movement from one place to another, often on a temporary basis
*navigational: relating to the planning or guiding of a course

1   According to paragraph 2, which of the following is NOT true about the indigo bunting?

Ⓐ Some of the behavior that it exhibits is thought to have been affected by warm weather.

Ⓑ The area in which it dwells in the summertime has gotten larger in recent decades.

Ⓒ It breeds in regions that are located both in the United States and Mexico.

Ⓓ Its behavior concerning where it flies throughout the year has been studied by scientists.

2   In paragraph 3, all of the following questions are answered EXCEPT:

Ⓐ What experiments did scientists do to learn about the indigo bunting's navigational skills?

Ⓑ Why is the indigo bunting able to migrate to new lands by flying at night?

Ⓒ What is the average distance the indigo bunting flies when it migrates?

Ⓓ How can the indigo bunting manage to fly to the same places on an annual basis?

Vocabulary

- _____ = bright
- _____ = dense growth of plants such as bushes and shrubs
- _____ = around; about
- _____ = focused

The Circulation of Water in the Oceans

Water in the Earth's ocean is in a constant state of **flux** as it moves in both the horizontal and vertical planes. In the horizontal plane, water mostly circulates because of the wind acting on the ocean's surface in what is called wind-driven circulation. As for the vertical plane, water circulates on account of fluctuations in the salinity and temperature of the ocean itself in what is known as thermohaline circulation. This kind of circulation typically makes water move more slowly than wind-driven circulation.

Wind-driven circulation, as its name indicates, results from the action of the wind on the water's surface. It is possible for this circulation to affect the water at a tremendous depth underneath the surface; nevertheless, the greatest effect the wind has on water circulation lies in the 200 meters closest to the surface. Interestingly, the surface of the water moves at a rate of only two to three percent of the wind's speed. The water also does not move directly as the wind blows, but it instead moves at an angle diagonal to the wind's direction because of the Coriolis force caused by the Earth's rotation. The upper layer of the ocean, where the wind and Coriolis force act in concert, is named the Ekman layer after the scientist who discovered it.

Thermohaline circulation is much slower than wind-driven circulation. Changes in the ocean's salinity and temperature, which both affect the density of the water, are the primary causes. As water becomes more or less dense, its **buoyancy** changes: Less buoyant water sinks whereas more buoyant water rises. When ocean water cools, it becomes denser, and when the water in the ocean evaporates, the remaining water becomes saltier and therefore denser. Dense water is less buoyant, so it sinks toward the bottom. While that water is sinking, equilibrium must be established, so less dense water rises toward the surface. This process establishes a loop of rising and falling water, which is the main cause of the thermohaline circulation pattern in the oceans.

*flux: constant change
*buoyancy: the ability of something to float or rise in a fluid

1 In paragraph 2, the author's description of wind-driven circulation mentions all of the following EXCEPT:

 Ⓐ the name of the layer of the ocean where its effects can be found

 Ⓑ the reason the water does not move in the same direction as the wind

 Ⓒ the part of the ocean where it is the most powerful

 Ⓓ the reason the water does not move as fast as the wind blows

2 According to paragraph 3, which of the following is NOT true about thermohaline circulation?

 Ⓐ It is most affected by the salinity of the water as well as its temperature.

 Ⓑ It happens when dense water sinks and causes less dense water to rise.

 Ⓒ It is the slower of the two types of circulation in the planet's oceans.

 Ⓓ It is more powerful deep beneath the surface rather than closer to it.

Vocabulary

- _____ = slanting
- _____ = compactness
- _____ = a state of balance
- _____ = a pattern that behaves in a circular manner

Herman Melville and His Work

American writer Herman Melville (1819-1891) is renowned for his novels describing adventures on the high seas such as those featured in his **magnum opus** *Moby-Dick*. While Melville lived a long life, the bulk of his work was written and published between 1846 and 1857. During his lifetime, he was actually considered a failed author, and it was only following his death that people recognized the genius of his writing and gave him the praise he justly deserved. Since the early twentieth century, however, his writings have taken their place alongside the other classics of American literature.

Melville's life at sea and his disillusionment with his strict religious upbringing heavily influenced his work. His travels began in 1839, when he shipped out as a seaman on a voyage to Liverpool, England. Later, he went on a whaling voyage to the South Pacific Ocean and spent some time living amongst the natives there. His personal adventures sometimes featured in his writing, and his first two novels, *Typee* (1846) and *Omoo* (1847), were based on his voyage south of the equator. In addition, *Moby-Dick* (1851) was influenced by his time on the whaler.

In his writing, Melville often criticized the strict Calvinist lifestyle his parents raised him with. In *Typee* and *Omoo*, he is sharply critical of Christian missionaries in the Pacific islands and claims they did more harm than good. Some of Melville's biographers believe he became a **humanist** at that point, cast aside religion, and came to believe that man alone was responsible for his life and fate, especially on the vast, lonely, open ocean. This theme prevailed in his later works, in which his characters frequently openly doubt God and religion.

Another novel, *Pierre* (1852), deals directly with Melville's feelings of doubt. In the book, he writes harshly about organized religion and claims it is hypocritical since it lacks a correlation between its pious creeds and the actual deeds of its followers. Melville further points out that trying to fill one's soul with religion is futile since God does not respond, and thus the soul is left void. Melville writes that this void must be filled by people communicating with and coming into contact with others. By that time in his life, Melville had truly abandoned his religious beliefs and thoroughly embraced humanism.

*magnum opus: a masterwork
*humanist: a person who believes that human interests and values are of the greatest importance

1 In paragraphs 1 and 2, the author's description of Herman Melville's writing mentions all of the following EXCEPT:

Ⓐ the years during which most of his books were completed

Ⓑ what caused him to express his feelings about religion in his works

Ⓒ how his own personal experiences influenced some of the novels he wrote

Ⓓ the manner in which people's opinions of his written works changed over time

2 According to paragraph 3, which of the following is NOT true about Herman Melville?

Ⓐ He wrote negatively about the actions of some Christians in his works.

Ⓑ He most likely abandoned his religious beliefs while he was writing.

Ⓒ He wrote frequently about his feelings regarding God and religion.

Ⓓ He included a great deal of religious imagery in both *Typee* and *Omoo*.

Vocabulary

• _____ = famous	• _____ = disappointment; disenchantment
• _____ = majority	• _____ = pretending to possess virtues or beliefs one does not really have

◢ Mapping

The following chart shows the structure of the passage. Fill in the blanks with the appropriate words.

```
                    ┌─────────────────────────────────┐
                    │   Herman Melville and His Work   │
                    └─────────────────────────────────┘
                                   │
        ┌──────────────────────────────────────────────────┐
        │ Wrote novels set on the high ❶ _____    │
        │                                                   │
        │  – wrote most of his works between 1846 and 1857  │
        │  – many of his writings are considered            │
        │    ❷ _____                              │
        └──────────────────────────────────────────────────┘
                    │                          │
```

Wrote stories based on his life at sea	Criticized ❺ _____ in his works
– shipped out as a seaman and spent time on a ❸ _____	– was critical of Christian ❻ _____ in *Typee* and *Omoo*
– personal ❹ _____ are featured in *Typee*, *Omoo*, and *Moby-Dick*	– became a ❼ _____
	– writes harshly about religion in ❽ _____

◢ Summary

The following is a summary of the passage. Fill in the blanks with the appropriate words.

While Herman Melville was considered a ❶ _____ writer during his life, people have considered many of his works ❷ _____ of American literature since the twentieth century. Melville spent time at sea, and his experiences are ❸ _____ in his works. *Typee*, *Omoo*, and *Moby-Dick* were all ❹ _____ by his time at sea. Melville's works often criticize ❺ _____. Many people believe Melville was a ❻ _____ and abandoned religion. He writes very harshly about religion in his novel *Pierre* as he claims that religion is ❼ _____. He writes that people should fill the voids in their lives by communicating with others.

A | Mausoleums in Ancient Societies

🎧 CH04_3A

Since the dawn of time, mankind has sought to deal with the dead in a respectable manner. One way people in ancient times handled that was to inter bodies in large tombs, or mausoleums. The term was first used to refer to the enormous tomb of King Mausolus in Halicarnassus, which was located in the land occupied by the modern-day nation of Turkey and was a structure so impressive that it was deemed one of the seven wonders of the ancient world. In the distant past, mausoleums were almost always built for leaders, such as the Egyptian pharaohs, for whom the pyramids were erected, but over time, it became standard to construct simpler structures for deceased individuals of more modest standing and wealth.

Unlike the Egyptians, who constructed their pyramids thousands of years ago, the Greeks came late to mausoleum building. **1** In the initial years after they became civilized, they preferred to bury their dead in the ground with just stone markers, often with **bas-relief carvings** on them. **2** Only after the conquests of Alexander the Great in the fourth century B.C. brought the Greeks into contact with more exotic cultures did their mausoleums become more elaborate. **3** Greek mausoleums from that time were mostly square shaped, had peaked roofs, and featured columns either in a frontal façade or surrounding the entire structure. **4** The Greeks also often painted **frescoes** inside their mausoleums, and pottery was placed inside them along with the corpses.

The Romans practiced burial from their earliest days but later introduced cremation and put people's ashes into urns. Nevertheless, even when they burned a body, they saved a small part of it and buried it after conducting certain rites. Roman cemeteries were located outside urban centers. The poor were simply buried in plots while the wealthy were interred in large mausoleums, some of which can still be seen lining the roadways in places outside Rome and other urban regions. Roman mausoleums imitated the Greek style in that they were square with peaked roofs and included columns and elaborate entrances. The mausoleums of famous and wealthy families traditionally housed several generations of dead in urns. The largest of these crypts even included dining rooms and kitchens for family members to use when they were making visits to honor their deceased ancestors. Most featured bas-relief carvings and paintings both inside and outside, and the richest families had gardens outside the main entrance.

The ancient Chinese also constructed large, ornate mausoleums for their dead leaders. The styles of their mausoleums varied over time, but they frequently featured both an aboveground structure and subterranean chambers. A long road—a spirit way—usually led to the tomb and was lined with statues of animals and people. The surface structure of the mausoleum was mostly just an elaborate entrance to the underground tombs. The tombs of members of the imperial family tended to be inside mountains while those of lesser standing were buried beneath large mounds. Burial chambers could be one level or many depending upon the sizes of the structures and how many individuals were buried within them. The burial chambers themselves contained large numbers of statues and had murals painted on the walls.

*bas-relief carving: a sculpture in which the figure projects from the background
*fresco: artwork that involves painting on moist plaster

Vocabulary

- _____ = to bury
- _____ = a vase used to hold the ashes of a cremated individual
- _____ = foreign; unusual
- _____ = underground

1 According to paragraph 1, which of the following is true about mausoleums?

   Ⓐ No mausoleums were ever constructed that were bigger than the one located in Halicarnassus.

   Ⓑ The first mausoleums that were ever constructed for leaders were the pyramids built in ancient Egypt.

   Ⓒ They were once made only for the leaders in certain places but were later built for many people in ancient societies.

   Ⓓ Both the pyramids and the tomb of King Mausolus were among the seven wonders of the ancient world.

Negative Factual Information Question

2 In paragraph 3, the author's description of Roman burial practices mentions all of the following EXCEPT:

   Ⓐ the style that was preferred by the people who constructed mausoleums

   Ⓑ what kinds of artwork were displayed both on the inner and outer parts of mausoleums

   Ⓒ the time in their history when the Romans began interring people in mausoleums

   Ⓓ how the Romans treated the bodies of people after they passed away

Insert Text Question

3 Look at the four squares [■] that indicate where the following sentence could be added to the passage.

All of these styles have been adopted by people in many countries in the Western world in more modern times.

Where would the sentence best fit?

Fill in a Table Question

4 Select the appropriate statements from the answer choices and match them to the ancient civilization to which they relate. TWO of the answer choices will NOT be used.

Greece (Select 3)	Rome (Select 2)	China (Select 2)
•		
•	•	•
•	•	•

STATEMENTS

1 Had some burial chambers that contained multiple levels beneath the ground

2 Made some mausoleums so big that they contained rooms such as kitchens

3 Constructed mausoleums that still exist in places located outside cities

4 Took years to construct mausoleums due to the great size of them

5 Had columns outside their mausoleums and frescoes inside them

6 Built tombs for some members of royal families within mountains

7 Preferred to build tombs in the form of pyramids to make them more imposing

8 Began making ornate mausoleums after the fourth century B.C.

9 Initially buried their dead in the ground and marked the gravesites with stones

The History of Venice

The city of Venice lies on a group of islands in the northern part of the Adriatic Sea off the coast of Italy. During its lengthy history, it served as a principal port of trade on the Adriatic, and its people grew rich and powerful from their commercial lifestyles. At one time, Venice was one of the leading powers in the entire Mediterranean world as it was the center of a great republic with several overseas possessions. However, during the fifteenth century, both the city and its entire empire fell into a decline from which it never recovered.

There exists archaeological evidence that people lived on the islands occupied by Venice long before the Roman era. During the decline of Rome in the fifth century, the islands got their first permanent settlers, who moved there in search of a refuge as they fled the barbarian invaders on the mainland. The islands of Venice provided a safe haven primarily because the barbarians lacked the ability to navigate well on sea and could not wage naval warfare. According to tradition, the city was founded in the year 421, yet it had no substantial population for many years afterward. Gradually, the population increased, and the people living there amassed wealth thanks to the fish and salt the sea provided.

Isolated from events transpiring on the Italian peninsula, the Venetians turned their attention to the sea and the lands by the Adriatic and eastern Mediterranean seas. They constructed a great fleet of trading ships to ply these waters as well as naval vessels to protect them. Immense wealth from the east flowed into Venice and made its people rich and powerful. Venice also served as a port of departure for the Crusaders during the Crusades, which earned the Venetians money. In addition, during the Fourth Crusade in 1204, a Venetian fleet assisted in the sacking of Constantinople, the capital of the Byzantine Empire, and subsequently brought home a phenomenal amount of **plundered** treasure. Due to its trading contacts, Venice became a cosmopolitan community with people from many eastern lands, including Muslims, Jews, and Greeks, all living in it. With their wealth, the Venetians constructed a great city with impressive works of architecture during the city's heyday in the Middle Ages.

In 1348, the Black Death devastated the population of Venice and initiated the city's decline. The city's residents struggled to retain their position of power in the eastern world for the next century. In 1453, the fall of Constantinople to the Ottoman Turks resulted in Venice becoming involved in ruinous warfare on a nearly constant basis, which sapped the city's wealth and power. Then, when the **New World** was discovered in 1492, the center of European power shifted from the Mediterranean to nations such as Spain, France, England, and Portugal, all of which bordered the Atlantic Ocean. Venice's position was further eroded in the 1500s by wars with its neighbors and plagues.

Gradually, Venice's power diminished until it was conquered by Napoleon in 1797. The city switched hands between the French and Austrians several times until it became a part of the Austrian Empire in 1815 following Napoleon's ultimate defeat. In 1848 and 1849, Venice briefly attained independence during the revolutions that swept through Europe, but the Austrians soon regained control. Finally, during the Italian wars of unification in the 1860s, Venice became a permanent part of Italy. Today, it exists primarily as a tourist spot and is world renowned for its canals and architecture.

*plundered: stolen; looted
*New World: North and South America

Vocabulary

- _____ = to practice; to engage in
- _____ = a safe place
- _____ = apart from others; alone
- _____ = the time when someone or something is at its peak

1 The word "refuge" in the passage is closest in meaning to

   (A) township

   (B) sanctuary

   (C) fortress

   (D) utopia

Inference Question

2 In paragraph 3, the author implies that Venice

   (A) reached the height of its greatness during the Middle Ages

   (B) erred in sacking the city of Constantinople during the Fourth Crusade

   (C) fought battles against some of the other cities on the Italian mainland

   (D) made people from foreign lands live in their own sectors in the city

Negative Factual Information Question

3 In paragraph 4, all of the following questions are answered EXCEPT:

   (A) What caused the nations by the Atlantic Ocean to become more powerful in the 1400s?

   (B) Which event resulted in Venice starting to lose power?

   (C) How were Venice's relationships with the other European powers in the Mediterranean area?

   (D) Why did Venice get into many battles with the Ottoman Turks?

Prose Summary Question

4 An introductory sentence for a brief summary of the passage is provided below. Complete the summary by selecting the THREE answer choices that express the most important ideas of the passage. Some sentences do not belong because they express ideas that are not presented in the passage or are minor ideas in the passage.

The city of Venice rose to a position of great power during the Middle Ages but steadily lost power and influence in the centuries following that period.

ANSWER CHOICES

[1] Many Europeans who were heading east to fight in the Crusades found passage there by ships sailing from Venice.

[2] Even though Venice is said to have been founded in 421, few people lived there for a long period of time in its early years.

[3] The plundering of many treasures from Constantinople during the Fourth Crusade helped Venice become wealthier.

[4] Both plagues and constant warfare with the Ottoman Turks resulted in Venice losing power after the middle of the 1400s.

[5] When the people of Venice turned their attention to shipping, they became wealthy and helped increase the power of the city.

[6] After Venice was conquered by Napoleon in 1797, it was controlled by France, Austria, and Italy at various times during the next century.

Deep-Sea Marine Life

An illustration of an angler fish

The region deep beneath the ocean's surface is inhospitable on account of the absolute darkness, the freezing temperatures, the relative lack of food, and the crushing pressure. At first glance, it seems a virtually impossible place for life to exist, yet, as exploratory missions to the deepest parts of the ocean have discovered, it does. When the first excursions thousands of meters beneath the surface were made, explorers were shocked to find creatures living at depths previously thought to be uninhabitable. Over time, the marine lifeforms that dwell in these places adapted to their circumstances and proved that life can survive in the harshest and most unforgiving places.

To deal with the lack of light so far beneath the surface, many deep-sea creatures utilize a form of bioluminescence, a chemical reaction in their bodies that produces light but not heat. Marine biologists believe bioluminescence serves several functions. First, for some fish, it acts like a flashlight by enabling them to see as they swim while in others, it helps them attract mates. And some animals, such as the angler fish, use their light to draw in prey, which they attack and consume. **1** However, bioluminescence is a poor substitute for sunlight, so many deep-sea creatures have developed extra sensors to assist them in finding their way. **2** The stout blacksmelt has very large eyes with sensors enabling it to pick up low amounts of light. **3** Other lifeforms have evolved a stronger sense of smell to detect chemical scents emitted by members of the same species, which enables them to find mates. **4**

As one descends deeper beneath the surface, the enormous amount of water places intense pressures on everything. To avoid being crushed, many deep-sea creatures have evolved by becoming smaller and by having more gelatinous bodies and bones as opposed to the more inflexible body structures of animals living near the surface or on land. Deep-sea creatures additionally lack swim bladders and other cavities which inflate and deflate because they would be easily crushed by the high pressure. Instead, some creatures have specialized molecular structures that help them better withstand the water pressure. The molecules comprising them are common in all fish and are responsible for the distinct smell most fish have, but fish living at great depths have more of them and therefore have an even more intense smell.

The water temperature thousands of meters under the surface hovers between minus one degree Celsius and four degrees above zero, which is cold enough to freeze most life. Deep-sea marine lifeforms have adapted their bodies to withstand this severe cold though. Some have special enzymes while others have high levels of unsaturated fats, both of which allow animals' bodies to handle the cold, and other deep-sea creatures move at slow speeds to conserve energy, thereby protecting them from the cold as well. In some spots on the ocean floor, thermal vents release energy from the Earth's interior. Around these hot vents, numerous lifeforms reside, and they have established their own unique ecosystems in the cold ocean depths.

Another problem for creatures living so deep is food. Most marine lifeforms survive by consuming other marine life, yet thousands of meters beneath the surface, there is a distinct lack of prey for predators to catch. Some, including the angler fish, have evolved to become successful predators, but many others depend on marine snow, the remains of dead fish falling from levels above the deepest parts of the ocean. When creatures die in the ocean, they start sinking. As their bodies fall apart, they create marine snow, which is the continual dropping of small particles of flesh that creatures underneath it then consume. Deep-sea creatures frequently have slower metabolisms that enable them to survive for long periods of time on small amounts of food. They also have large mouths with jaws that can open very wide and teeth that point inward. This ensures that they can easily catch falling food and also lets them grab prey and hold on to it if the opportunity ever arises. Since many creatures living deep in the ocean have multiple adaptations, they not only survive but also thrive despite residing in an environment that would instantly kill most other creatures.

*Glossary

gelatinous: viscous; jellylike

thermal vent: an area where heat from the inside of the Earth is released

1   According to paragraph 1, which of the following is true about the bottom of the ocean?

   (A) It appears to have as much life as does the area that is nearest the surface of the ocean.

   (B) It contains lifeforms that have changed so that they can survive in the harsh conditions there.

   (C) The first time people visited the bottom of the ocean, they saw virtually no life there.

   (D) The relative lack of food is the main reason there is little life in that part of the ocean.

2   In paragraph 2, the author uses "the angler fish" as an example of

   (A) one of the top predators that lives at the bottom of the ocean

   (B) a creature that uses bioluminescence to help it attract a mate

   (C) a fish that has developed large eyes to improve its ability to see

   (D) an animal that is capable of creating light from its own body

3   In paragraph 2, the author's description of bioluminescence mentions all of the following EXCEPT:

   (A) some of the ways that animals can create light from their bodies

   (B) the area of the ocean where this capability is beneficial to animals

   (C) the manner in which some marine animals utilize this capability

   (D) the name of one of the fish that is able to create its own light

4   The word "inflexible" in the passage is closest in meaning to

   (A) formidable

   (B) unique

   (C) rigid

   (D) opaque

5   According to paragraph 3, fish that live near the bottom of the ocean have no swim bladders because

   (A) they do not work well when fish are more gelatinous in form and have fewer bones

   (B) there is no need for fish living there to use swim bladders to rise toward the surface

   (C) the molecules that comprise them cannot stay together so deep under the water

   (D) their existence would cause the fish to be crushed by the intense water pressure

6 According to paragraph 4, which of the following is NOT true about how creatures survive in the cold temperatures deep in the ocean?

(A) They make use of enzymes which enable their bodies to handle the cold conditions.

(B) They save energy by moving at speeds slower than those animals normally swim at.

(C) They reside near places at the bottom of the ocean where hot water is spewed.

(D) They consume large amounts of food to build up layers of fat in their bodies.

7 Which of the sentences below best expresses the essential information in the highlighted sentence in the passage? Incorrect answer choices change the meaning in important ways or leave out essential information.

Since many creatures living deep in the ocean have multiple adaptations, they not only survive but also thrive despite residing in an environment that would instantly kill most other creatures.

(A) Animals living deep beneath the ocean's surface must learn to adapt quickly, or they will be killed by the severe conditions.

(B) Because so many creatures have been killed by the conditions deep in the ocean, only a few of them actually live there.

(C) The adaptations of some animals let them do well in their environment despite the fact that most other animals would die there.

(D) Numerous new species have evolved in the deep ocean thanks to their ability to adapt to an environment that kills most creatures.

8 Which of the following can be inferred from paragraph 5 about deep-sea creatures?

(A) They eat less often than creatures that live near the ocean's surface do.

(B) They are capable of swimming at great speeds even in the dark.

(C) They prefer to consume marine snow rather than to hunt for food themselves.

(D) They can grow to become some of the largest creatures in the world's oceans.

9 Look at the four squares [■] that indicate where the following sentence could be added to the passage.

Others use this ability to sniff out prey, which makes them dangerous hunters deep underneath the surface.

Where would the sentence best fit?

Click on a square [■] to add the sentence to the passage.

10 Directions: An introductory sentence for a brief summary of the passage is provided below. Complete the summary by selecting the THREE answer choices that express the most important ideas of the passage. Some sentences do not belong because they express ideas that are not presented in the passage or are minor ideas in the passage. **This question is worth 2 points.**

Drag your answer choices to the spaces where they belong. To remove an answer choice, click on it. To review the passage, click on VIEW TEXT.

The creatures that live deep in the ocean rely upon various adaptations in order to survive in the extreme environment there.

-
-
-

ANSWER CHOICES

1. The very cold temperatures and the relative lack of food are two difficulties that animals living near the bottom of the ocean must overcome.

2. Many creatures living deep beneath the surface rely on bioluminescence to create their own light to provide benefits to themselves.

3. The first humans to venture down to the bottom of the ocean were surprised by how much life was actually thriving there.

4. The bodies of some deep-sea fish are more gelatinous, enabling them to withstand the crushing water pressure.

5. Marine snow, which is the decomposing remains of dead fish, falls to the bottom of the ocean and provides fish there with a source of food.

6. The large jaws and teeth and strange body shapes of some deep-sea creatures give some of them terrifying appearances.

Star Clusters

The Pleiades cluster   Omega Centauri

Throughout the universe, stars in galaxies can be found by themselves or in groups known as star clusters. They come in two main types—open and globular clusters—with a few other subsidiary types. The stars in a cluster are held together with powerful gravitational forces and move in the same direction around a common central point. Each cluster contains stars that most likely formed simultaneously from the same cloud of interstellar dust, thereby making each star have a similar age. Due to these characteristics, the study of star clusters is important because they can help provide astronomers with an easy way to learn more about star formation and how stars age.

Open star clusters are grouped in loose formations in which individual stars can be observed through a telescope. They typically form in the disk or in spiral arms of galaxies, so they are sometimes called galactic star clusters. Thousands of these clusters are known to exist in the galaxies which astronomers have studied closely, including the Earth's own Milky Way Galaxy. Open star clusters are normally fewer than thirty light years in diameter and include anywhere between fifty and approximately 1,000 stars. Most open star clusters are a few hundred million years old; however, some may be more than one billion years old. The formation of an open star cluster is occasionally spherical, and they have been seen taking a wide variety of different shapes. A few nearby open star clusters can be seen from the Earth with the naked eye and have been known to humans since ancient times. Among them are the Pleiades cluster, which is around 440 light years away from the solar system, and the much closer Hyades cluster, which is only about 150 light years away.

Open star clusters may be broken up by external gravitational forces. As they move through a galaxy, they encounter giant molecular clouds of stellar matter whose strong gravity causes individual stars to break formation with the open cluster. Astronomers believe that the Earth's sun may have once been part of an open cluster and that it broke off in this manner. The fact that the sun exists in a wide area of space with few close stars as neighbors lends credence to this theory. Even though stars in an open cluster may break formation, they still move in the same direction. Astronomers call these moving groups stellar associations.

Globular star clusters differ from open star clusters in several ways. They have a great deal more stars with some clusters containing millions of them. They are also much broader as they range from fifty to 450 light years in diameter. Additionally, globular star clusters take on a more spherical shape than open star clusters. They have greater luminosity and are much older, including some billions of years old. Globular star clusters are usually found close to the center of a galaxy and move around the central halo. **1** While open star clusters close to the solar system were known since ancient times because the individual stars in some could be observed with the naked eye, globular star clusters appeared to people to be masses of cloudy dust. **2** It was only when the telescope was invented in the seventeenth century that astronomers became able to distinguish individual stars located in globular star clusters. **3** An example of a globular star cluster is Omega Centauri, which is located approximately 16,600 light years away from the Earth. **4** It is comprised of several million stars, making it the largest globular star cluster in the Milky Way.

Observing star clusters allows astronomers to learn more about star formation, age, and luminosity. Because every star in a star cluster formed at roughly the same time from the same nebula cloud of stellar dust, the light from each star in the formation travels nearly the same distance to the Earth and reaches the planet at roughly the same time. Therefore, by observing just one star in the cluster, astronomers can utilize the readings of that single star to make inferences about the other stars in the same cluster. For example, by measuring the luminosity of one star, they do not have to waste any effort on observing that feature of the other stars in the cluster.

*Glossary

naked eye: the eye without any visual enhancements such as telescopes or binoculars
molecular cloud: a large cloud of molecules and dust in space that stars form from

11 In paragraph 1, which of the following is NOT true about star clusters?

    (A) The majority of the stars they contain were formed around the same time.

    (B) The stars that are found in them are joined by the force of gravity.

    (C) There are several types of them, but two kinds are the major ones.

    (D) They are difficult for astronomers to study and to learn information about.

12 In paragraph 2, why does the author mention "the Pleiades cluster"?

    (A) To state that people can only see it by using a powerful telescope

    (B) To point out that people have been aware of it for thousands of years

    (C) To note that it is closer to the Earth than any other open star cluster

    (D) To compare it to the Hyades cluster with regard to its size

13 According to paragraph 2, open star clusters are often referred to as galactic star clusters because

    (A) they have been known to be as large as a small galaxy

    (B) they usually have the characteristics of a spiral galaxy

    (C) they are normally located in specific parts of galaxies

    (D) they have gravitational forces equal to those of a galaxy

14 The word "credence" in the passage is closest in meaning to

    (A) respect

    (B) appearance

    (C) example

    (D) belief

15 In paragraph 3, the author implies that stellar associations

    (A) include both stars in open clusters as well as stars no longer in them

    (B) appear more commonly in the Milky Way Galaxy than do open star clusters

    (C) have weaker gravitational fields than open star clusters do

    (D) tend to be destroyed by having all of their stars break formation over time

16 The word "luminosity" in the passage is closest in meaning to

- (A) size
- (B) brightness
- (C) gravity
- (D) heat

17 Which of the sentences below best expresses the essential information in the highlighted sentence in the passage? Incorrect answer choices change the meaning in important ways or leave out essential information.

While open star clusters close to the solar system were known since ancient times because the individual stars in some could be observed with the naked eye, globular star clusters appeared to people to be masses of cloudy dust.

- (A) Viewing star clusters with the naked eye was possible in ancient times, but people were unaware of the composition of globular star clusters then.
- (B) People in ancient times were aware of the unique compositions of both open star clusters and globular star clusters.
- (C) It was only possible for people to see the stars in open star clusters in ancient times because nobody had invented the telescope yet.
- (D) A long time ago, people saw globular star clusters as masses of dust whereas they were able to see certain stars in some open star clusters.

18 According to paragraph 5, why do astronomers only need to study one star in a cluster on some occasions?

- (A) All of the dust in the cluster makes getting accurate readings on stars difficult to do.
- (B) The brightness of a single star makes observing others in the cluster nearly impossible.
- (C) Most of the stars in a cluster are nearing their end, so there is little need to study them.
- (D) The stars in the cluster have similar characteristics due to the nature of their formation.

19 Look at the four squares [■] that indicate where the following sentence could be added to the passage.

This enabled the people who were observing them to realize just how many stars could be found in some clusters.

Where would the sentence best fit?

Click on a square [■] to add the sentence to the passage.

20 **Directions:** Select the appropriate statements from the answer choices and match them to the star cluster to which they relate. TWO of the answer choices will NOT be used. **This question is worth 3 points.**

Drag your answer choices to the spaces where they belong. To remove an answer choice, click on it. To review the passage, click on **VIEW TEXT**.

STATEMENTS

1.   May be located in the central part of the galaxy it is in
2.   Is not affected when it encounters a molecular cloud
3.   Includes the Hyades cluster, which is relatively close to the Earth
4.   Is the larger of the two main types of star clusters
5.   Loses gravitational power as it becomes older and smaller
6.   Is known to exist in the spiral arms of various galaxies
7.   Could contain as few as around fifty stars in it

STAR CLUSTER

Open Star Cluster (Select 3)

-
-
-

Globular Star Cluster (Select 2)

-
-

■ Vocabulary Review

A Complete each sentence with the appropriate word from the box.

| deceased | intensive | heyday | mass | subsidiary |

1 George has a(n) _____ look on his face since he is concentrating very hard.

2 There is a huge _____ of pollution in the river that is slowly moving toward the ocean.

3 The bodies of the _____ were taken to a funeral home to be prepared for burial.

4 The _____ companies must all file reports with the firm's headquarters in Lisbon.

5 In the actor's _____, he was one of the most popular people in the country.

B Complete each sentence with the correct answer.

1 **Approximately** half of the class showed up, so _____ fifteen students went to the event.

   a. Around   b. Exactly

2 The **bulk** of the population agrees with lowering taxes, so a _____ voted in favor of it.

   a. minority   b. majority

3 The artist draws with **diagonal** lines as he prefers _____ lines instead of circular ones.

   a. straight   b. slanted

4 As a **principal** stakeholder, Carol is one of the _____ owners in the business.

   a. minor   b. major

5 Tom can _____ a lot of pain, so he could **withstand** the agony from his broken leg.

   a. endure   b. appreciate

6 The **exotic** art on display in the art gallery comes from a _____ region.

   a. foreign   b. nearby

7 When **equilibrium** is achieved, there is _____ between the two sides.

   a. chaos   b. balance

8 The **excursion** into the jungle was considered a successful _____ by the researchers.

   a. expiration   b. expedition

9 Nobody wants to _____ a tiger in the jungle again after **encountering** one a while ago.

   a. meet   b. fight

10 The **disillusionment** they felt was obvious from the looks of _____ on their faces.

   a. disappointment   b. glee

Chapter 05

Sentence Simplification

Question Type | Sentence Simplification

◤ About the Question

Sentence Simplification questions focus on a single sentence. You are asked to choose a sentence that best restates the information in the sentence that is highlighted in the passage. You need to note the primary information that is found in the sentence and make sure that it is included in the answer choice that you select. The words, phrases, and grammar in the answer choices vary from those in the highlighted sentence. There are 0-1 Sentence Simplification questions for each passage.

Recognizing Sentence Simplification questions:

- Which of the sentences below best expresses the essential information in the highlighted sentence in the passage? Incorrect answer choices change the meaning in important ways or leave out essential information.

  [You will see a sentence in bold.]

Helpful hints for answering the questions correctly:

- The highlighted sentence typically contains at least two separate clauses. Make sure that you know what the main point or idea of each clause is.

- The answer choice you select must contain all of the important information that is in the highlighted sentence.

- Do not select answer choices that contain incorrect information or that omit important information.

- The answer choices for these questions are approximately half the length of the sentences being asked about. Therefore, you should consider how to summarize information in long sentences.

Early American Coppersmiths

While most people living in the English American colonies in the 1600s and 1700s were engaged in farming, there were also individuals who plied various trades. Coppersmiths were some of the most esteemed of these people. Although copper does not have the intrinsic value that gold and silver possess, it was still prized by the American colonists. The reason is that copper's relative softness permitted it to be shaped easily by coppersmiths. As such, coppersmiths were responsible for shaping copper into a wide variety of tools and pieces of equipment. They made candlesticks, pots, kettles, and utensils for the home, and they additionally used copper to make nails, hoops to place around barrels, and horseshoes, all of which were of immense value to the farmers living in their regions. Since copper was fairly cheap, coppersmiths saw much more business than did silversmiths as many of the American colonists lived frugal lives and had little interest in spending large sums of money.

Which of the sentences below best expresses the essential information in the highlighted sentence in the passage? Incorrect answer choices change the meaning in important ways or leave out essential information.

Since copper was fairly cheap, coppersmiths saw much more business than did silversmiths as many of the American colonists lived frugal lives and had little interest in spending large sums of money.

- (A) The American colonists did not like spending a lot of money, so coppersmiths were busier than silversmiths because of the inexpensive nature of copper.
- (B) Coppersmiths working in the American colonies were typically a lot busier than silversmiths were even though silver was more valuable than copper.
- (C) While both coppersmiths and silversmiths were busy, coppersmiths were the busier of the two since most Americans preferred buying cheaper copper items.
- (D) The frugal nature of the American colonists led them to save their money, so they did not purchase items made from silver with great frequency.

| **Answer Explanation** |

Choice (A) is the correct answer. The highlighted sentence emphasizes the cheapness of copper and the fact that American colonists did not want to spend much money, so they preferred coppersmiths to silversmiths. Those themes are included in answer choice (A), which makes it the correct answer.

A | The Archaeological Study of Pottery

🎧 CH05_2A

While digging at sites of interest, archaeologists often unearth **shards** of pottery, which provide a great amount of information. Archaeologists study pottery for three main reasons. First, it was common in most civilizations and was used by people in all levels of society. Next, it easily broke and was not always repaired. Thus pottery shards are among the most common items found at dig sites. Lastly, pottery is more durable than other materials, such as wood and cloth, and shards can last for thousands of years.

Making pottery required special materials and skills, so the presence of pottery indicates that a civilization had attained a certain level of technology. Early pottery was made in open pits from simple red clays, which produced brittle pottery. Later, more advanced pottery makers used clay mixed with substances such as sand, crushed shells, bones, and even other pieces of broken pottery, which resulted in stronger creations. Only at later times was pottery made with potter's wheels and fired in **kilns**, which both produced better final products. The earliest pottery was unglazed, so the discovery of stronger kiln-fired, glazed pottery shows that a people attained a higher level of knowledge. As archaeologists dig, they can determine the different periods of a civilization by the pottery found in each level. The most advanced pottery is usually at the top while the more primitive types are located deeper underground.

People in ancient civilizations made pottery from nearby deposits of clay. Different kinds of clay produce different types of pottery, so when archaeologists know where pottery was made and where shards of it have been found, they can discover ancient trade routes and connections between various tribes. For example, the Chinese had excellent clays that produced the ancient world's best pottery. Therefore, the discovery of Chinese pottery shards at a site far away indicates that trade between the Chinese and another group occurred.

*shard: a sliver; a splinter; a small broken piece of something
*kiln: an oven used for baking pottery

Which of the sentences below best expresses the essential information in the highlighted sentence in the passage? Incorrect answer choices change the meaning in important ways or leave out essential information.

Different kinds of clay produce different types of pottery, so when archaeologists know where pottery was made and where shards of it have been found, they can discover ancient trade routes and connections between various tribes.

Ⓐ Since each type of clay makes unique pottery, archaeologists can learn a great deal about the past if they know where pottery was produced and where pieces of it have been unearthed.

Ⓑ When archaeologists dig up shards of pottery in different places, they can figure out what parts of the world the people of a certain area were in contact with.

Ⓒ There are many things that archaeologists can learn about the pottery shards that they dig up and study, including where the clay that the pieces were made from came from.

Ⓓ Unless archaeologists know exactly what kind of clay was used to make a certain type of pottery, they cannot learn about ancient trade routes or how tribes contacted one another.

Vocabulary

- _____ = to dig up; to excavate
- _____ = easily breakable; fragile
- _____ = long-lasting; strong
- _____ = to cook; to heat

104

The Origins of the Chinese Han Dynasty

China's Han Dynasty (206 B.C.–220 A.D.) was one of the longest-lasting Chinese dynasties and unified the majority of the land comprising modern-day China into a single empire. Before this period, China was divided into different states battling for **supremacy** for roughly two centuries. The Warring States Period ended, however, when the powerful Qin conquered six major states by 221 B.C. and brought China together under the country's first strong dynasty. Nevertheless, the Qin Dynasty lasted only a short time as its harsh rule resulted in a rebellion breaking out in 208 B.C., a few years following the death of Emperor Qin Shi Huang.

This rebellion involved most of the conquered states, including the central Han state. The Han's foremost general was Liu Bang, who had previously served as a policeman. One day prior to becoming a general, a group of prisoners Liu Bang was escorting while working as a lawman escaped his custody, so, fearing he would be executed, he fled to the countryside, formed an outlaw band, and rebelled against Qin authority. His power and status increased, and the Han leaders eventually installed him as their head general during their rebellion against the Qin. Liu Bang captured the Qin capital of Xianyang in 207 B.C. and ended the Qin's rule, whereupon he was hailed as a hero and became the leader of the Han.

The Han state attempted to dominate affairs in China, but other states, such as the Chu, had assisted in overthrowing the Qin and were unwilling to **acquiesce** without a fight. The leader of the Chu, Xiang Yu, therefore challenged Liu Bang for leadership of China. The two states and their allies warred for four years. Finally, in 202 B.C., the opposing armies met at the decisive Battle of Gaixia, during which some of the Chu's allies betrayed them, and the Chu forces were surrounded. Attacked by the Han and with its supply lines cut, the Chu army became demoralized, many soldiers surrendered, and Xiang Yu committed suicide to avoid capture. Following the Chu defeat, Liu Bang crowned himself emperor of China and established the Han Dynasty.

*supremacy: power; leadership
*acquiesce: to comply; to give up

Which of the sentences below best expresses the essential information in the highlighted sentence in the passage? Incorrect answer choices change the meaning in important ways or leave out essential information.

One day prior to becoming a general, a group of prisoners Liu Bang was escorting while working as a lawman escaped his custody, so, fearing he would be executed, he fled to the countryside, formed an outlaw band, and rebelled against Qin authority.

- (A) Liu Bang began to rebel against the Qin after he realized that he should not be working as a lawman but should instead be leading outlaws fighting against the government.
- (B) While Liu Bang was escorting some prisoners, they convinced him to escape with them, which he did, and then he became their leader and helped them battle the Qin.
- (C) When Liu Bang was working as a lawman, an incident occurred that caused him to fear for his life, so he escaped, founded a gang, and began to fight against the Qin.
- (D) The Qin promoted Liu Bang to general when they realized that he should not be escorting prisoners but should instead be fighting outlaws in the countryside.

Vocabulary

- _____ = cruel; difficult
- _____ = a revolution; a revolt
- _____ = to rule over; to control
- _____ = deprived of spirit or hope

The Mid-Atlantic Ridge

The longest mountain range on the Earth is not easily visible because it lies deep underneath the Atlantic Ocean. The Mid-Atlantic Range extends from Iceland to an area deep in the South Atlantic Ocean. It rises around three kilometers above the ocean floor and is 1,500 kilometers wide in certain areas. Its exact length is difficult to determine since the Mid-Atlantic Range is part of an extensive, globally connected ridge of underwater mountains approximately 40,000 kilometers in length.

The Mid-Atlantic Ridge was formed at the boundary of four of the tectonic plates comprising the crust. In the north are the Eurasian and North American plates while the southern boundary is formed by the African and South American plates. These plates are drifting apart from one another, which is resulting in the geological process known as seafloor spreading. As they separate, magma from beneath the crust wells up and cools, which helps create the mountain range. In the center of the Mid-Atlantic Range is a lengthy and deep rift valley in the precise place where the plates pull apart and where new magma is collecting. In a few places, islands, the most notable of which is Iceland, have formed along the mountain range where the tectonic forces have pushed the land above the water's surface.

Once the existence of the Mid-Atlantic Ridge was proven in the 1950s, the fact that the seafloor was spreading apart lent credence to the theory of **continental drift**, which was then in dispute. Samples of basalt taken from the Atlantic Ocean floor helped prove the theory. Basalt is an **igneous rock** produced by cooling lava, and it possesses unique magnetic properties that maintain the magnetic polarity that existed at the time it was formed. Since the Earth's polarity has changed over time, with the north and south magnetic poles reversing on occasion, by examining the polarity of different groups of basalt rocks from the Mid-Atlantic Ridge, geologists could date them. The conclusion they reached was that the oldest rocks were the farthest from the central rift valley while the youngest were the closest to it.

*continental drift: the notion that the continents are in constant motion and are slowly moving on the Earth's surface
*igneous rock: rock formed when magma cools and becomes solid

---

Which of the sentences below best expresses the essential information in the highlighted sentence in the passage? Incorrect answer choices change the meaning in important ways or leave out essential information.

In a few places, islands, the most notable of which is Iceland, have formed along the mountain range where the tectonic forces have pushed the land above the water's surface.

(A) Islands such as Iceland exist in certain places all over the undersea mountain range.

(B) When some of the mountains in the ridge become high enough, they break the surface of the ocean to form islands.

(C) The actions of the tectonic plates have created numerous islands, including Iceland, in places around the world.

(D) Forces inside the Earth have created islands such as Iceland in various spots in the mountain range.

Vocabulary

- _____ = great in size
- _____ = a border
- _____ = exact
- _____ = believability; credibility

◪ Mapping

The following chart shows the structure of the passage. Fill in the blanks with the appropriate words.

The Mid-Atlantic Range

Is the Earth's ❶ _____ mountain range

- runs underwater from ❷ _____ to South Atlantic Ocean
- rises up to 3km and is 1,500km wide in places

Formation: formed at the ❸ _____ of four tectonic plates

- plates are drifting apart
- ❹ _____ rises and cools to create mountains
- some islands created by movement

---

❺ _____ drift: theory given credence because of mountain range

- examine basalt
- has unique magnetic properties
- ❻ _____ rocks farthest from central valley and ❼ _____ ones closest to it

◪ Summary

The following is a summary of the passage. Fill in the blanks with the appropriate words.

The Mid-Atlantic Range is the Earth's longest mountain range and ❶ _____ from Iceland all the way down to the South Atlantic Ocean. The range was formed at the boundary of four ❷ _____ plates on the crust. The plates are moving ❸ _____, which results in seafloor spreading. While separating, ❹ _____ rises and cools, which has created the mountain range. There is a long, deep ❺ _____ where the plates are pulling apart. The existence of the range has helped lend ❻ _____ to the theory of continental drift. ❼ _____ samples have been examined, and they have shown that the oldest rocks are the ❽ _____ from the valley while the youngest ones are the closest to it.

A | The Origins of Oil Painting

🎧 CH05_3A

Prior to the fifteenth century, artists commonly used water-based paints or employed egg yolks as a **binding agent** in a style known as egg tempera. Since then, however, oil paints have gained widespread use and popularity. Oil paints are a mixture of a pigment with an oil base, typically linseed oil, and a thinner. The oil is a binding agent, which holds the pigment to the surface upon which the paint is applied and serves as a drying agent that allows the paint to oxidize, turn into a gel, and then harden. Compared to water-soluble paints, which dry in one to three days, and egg tempera, which dries faster, most oil paints dry much more slowly—usually two to three weeks after being applied. This feature lets artists work with the paint for longer periods of time, thereby permitting more layering as well as more details and richer tones than water paints.

It is unknown when oil paints were first used, but recent discoveries in Afghanistan indicate mural artists there utilized oil paints as early as the seventh century. However, as yet, there is little evidence that knowledge of oil paints spread from there to other lands. There are some instances of oil being employed as a drying medium in artwork created in the Byzantine Empire, but art historians are not sure whether the technique originated there or came from Afghanistan. A Benedictine monk named Theophilus claimed to have mixed pigments with oils to make paints in a treatise written in the twelfth century, which indicates that the Byzantines may have discovered the process by themselves.

Extensive use of oil paints in Europe was uncommon until the early fifteenth century, when European artists, who primarily used egg tempera as their binding agent, started seeking something that would give them more flexibility when painting and would permit them to paint in more detail and with more vibrant colors. Artists during that time experimented with different oils, including linseed oil, as binding agents. Most art historians agree that Dutch artist Jan van Eyck was the first individual to develop a way properly to prepare linseed oil and pigments so that they produced fine oil paints. They are uncertain precisely when and how he did so though since, although his career as an artist spanned many years, large numbers of his early works have been lost. His earliest surviving paintings—from the 1430s—were done with oil paints. The new style of painting quickly spread, and most Dutch artists were soon experimenting with oil paints.

Simultaneously, experiments with mineral and biological agents produced more vibrant colors, therefore improving the quality of the new oil paints. Oil paints swiftly spread around Europe—they were especially popular in Italy—and that had a major influence on artwork produced during the Renaissance. Oil replaced egg tempera as the preferred binding agent for pigments since it had several advantages. For example, works done with egg tempera had to utilize a **gesso** that the paint could adhere to. Then, the paint had to be applied in thin layers that dried quickly and could not easily be changed. On the other hand, oil paints dried more slowly, permitting changes to be made. They could also be applied with more delicate brushstrokes to permit more detail. Oil paints were much livelier than those done with egg tempera as well. All those advantages resulted in oil paints becoming the dominant painting medium once they were perfected.

*binding agent: an ingredient that lets a mixture hold its shape or stay together
*gesso: a prepared surface such as plaster that artists paint on

Vocabulary

* _____ = a semi-rigid solid
* _____ = a painting done on a wall or ceiling
* _____ = to cover a certain amount of time
* _____ = fine; gentle

1 In paragraph 1, all of the following questions are answered EXCEPT:

(A) How does the oil base that is added affect the paint itself?

(B) How quickly do oil paints dry in comparison to other types of paint?

(C) Which kinds of paints were used by artists before the 1400s?

(D) How many layers of paint can artists apply when using oil paints?

Sentence Simplification Question

2 Which of the sentences below best expresses the essential information in the highlighted sentence in the passage? Incorrect answer choices change the meaning in important ways or leave out essential information.

A Benedictine monk named Theophilus claimed to have mixed pigments with oils to make paints in a treatise written in the twelfth century, which indicates that the Byzantines may have discovered the process by themselves.

(A) There is a treatise that was written in the twelfth century by a Byzantine monk named Theophilus which records the manner in which he added oil to the paint that he made.

(B) Some people believe that the Byzantines were the first to make oil paints on account of a description written in the twelfth century by a monk named Theophilus.

(C) In a document written in the twelfth century, Theophilus wrote about making oil paints, which shows that the Byzantines might have learned how to make them by themselves.

(D) The process of making oil paints is described in great detail by a Theophilus, who was a monk living in the Byzantine Empire during the twelfth century.

Reference Question

3 The word "They" in the passage refers to

(A) Binding agents
(B) Most art historians
(C) Linseed oil and pigments
(D) Fine oil paints

Prose Summary Question

4 An introductory sentence for a brief summary of the passage is provided below. Complete the summary by selecting the THREE answer choices that express the most important ideas of the passage. Some sentences do not belong because they express ideas that are not presented in the passage or are minor ideas in the passage.

Oils paints have many advantages over water-based paints and egg tempera, so they became very popular with European artists starting in the fifteenth century.

ANSWER CHOICES

1 The ability to apply oil paints with fine brushstrokes appealed to many artists, so they adopted the use of oil paints.

2 Oil paints dry much more slowly than other types of paints, which made them more attractive to artists since that let them make changes to their work.

3 There is a debate amongst art historians as to whether oil paints were first used by artists in Afghanistan or in the Byzantine Empire.

4 Jan van Eyck was a big supporter of oil paints, but many of his early paintings have not survived until the present day.

5 Linseed oil was one of the first types of oil to be used by people who experimented with adding oil as a binding agent to their paints.

6 During the Renaissance, the usage of oil paints began with the Dutch but then spread elsewhere in Europe when artists recognized their advantages.

Friedrich Froebel and Kindergarten

Friedrich Froebel (1782–1852) was a German educator who focused on children's learning. His life as an instructor began in 1805 after he accepted a post at a secondary school in Frankfurt, Germany. During his lifetime, he worked in both Germany and Switzerland and was strongly influenced by Swiss educator Johann Heinrich Pestalozzi. Froebel additionally wrote and published numerous pamphlets and books on his educational theories and is best remembered today as the creator of kindergarten.

Froebel's childhood was the primary influence on his desire to see the establishing of a place for young children to play and grow. As a young boy, Froebel grew up near the Thuringia Forest in Germany and had a devout Christian upbringing, which instilled in him a love of nature and a belief in the interconnectedness of all living things. Froebel was a poor student as a child, which may have inspired him to desire to assist others like him. He had great difficulty with languages and writing but excelled at math, especially geometry. That inspired him to find employment first as a forest land surveyor and later in the field of architecture, but, in 1805, he abruptly decided to switch careers and accepted a teaching position in Frankfurt.

Fortunately for Froebel, the school at which he was employed was one of the first outside Switzerland to utilize the methods of Johann Heinrich Pestalozzi. This famed individual, who helped Switzerland become one of the first nations in Europe to achieve nearly 100% **literacy**, believed that children had an enormous capacity and desire to learn. His style allowed children to explore their natural curiosity rather than having them sit for hours while listening to lectures and learning by **rote** methods. After concluding his tenure at the school, Froebel would later spend two years in Switzerland, where he worked closely with Pestalozzi. There, Froebel came up with the theory that would influence him for the remainder of his career. He concluded that all children needed to play so that they could be educated by using physical movements and imaginative powers. In 1816, he opened a school in Thuringia to put his theories into practice.

At that time, there was no formal education for German children younger than seven, so Froebel's school was revolutionary. By taking young children and developing their minds and bodies, Froebel hoped to plant the seeds for future success in education and life in them. At Froebel's school, singing and dancing were used to encourage healthy activities in children. He also developed a series of geometric building blocks—today called Froebel Gifts—that the children played with and used to understand geometry and to develop spatial awareness. A third aspect of his educational style was to allow the children to work in a garden, where they could watch plants grow and learn to care for them.

In 1837, Froebel created a new school in Bad Blankenburg in Thuringia, which, in 1840, he began calling a *kindergarten*, or children's garden. The term developed from his notion that a school should be a place for children to learn and grow, much like a garden is. The success of Froebel's school won him countless admirers, who spread his ideas following his death in 1852. Today, the necessity of early childhood education is believed by people throughout the world, thereby showing how influential Froebel's theories have become over time.

*literacy: the ability to read and write
*rote: a fixed or mechanical way of doing something

Vocabulary

- _____ = pious; sincere
- _____ = an ability; a capability
- _____ = suddenly; at once
- _____ = new; groundbreaking; radical

1   Which of the sentences below best expresses the essential information in the highlighted sentence in the passage? Incorrect answer choices change the meaning in important ways or leave out essential information.

As a young boy, Froebel grew up near the Thuringia Forest in Germany and had a devout Christian upbringing, which instilled in him a love of nature and a belief in the interconnectedness of all living things.

   (A) Froebel came to love the outdoors and believed that all creatures are connected to one another on account of where he grew up and the beliefs he held.

   (B) Because Froebel lived by a forest, he spent a lot of his time outdoors and enjoyed being in nature.

   (C) Froebel thought all living things are interconnected, and that made him become a devout Christian.

   (D) After growing up near a forest in Germany, Froebel abandoned his Christian beliefs and came to believe that all things in nature are related to one another.

2   The author discusses "Johann Heinrich Pestalozzi" in paragraph 3 in order to

   (A) contrast his theories on teaching children with those of Friedrich Froebel

   (B) provide some examples of how he assisted children in reaching their full potential

   (C) explain his beliefs regarding the ability of young children to learn

   (D) claim that his influence on Friedrich Froebel was not as great as was once thought

3   Select the TWO answer choices from paragraph 4 that identify the methods Friedrich Froebel used to teach children at his school. *To receive credit, you must select TWO answers.*

   (A) Both singing and dancing were taught to students.

   (B) Children were encouraged to do hands-on activities.

   (C) There was an emphasis upon rote learning methods.

   (D) Students were taught practical skills from textbooks.

4   An introductory sentence for a brief summary of the passage is provided below. Complete the summary by selecting the THREE answer choices that express the most important ideas of the passage. Some sentences do not belong because they express ideas that are not presented in the passage or are minor ideas in the passage.

Friedrich Froebel's beliefs on educating children led him to become the founder of kindergarten.

ANSWER CHOICES

1 Froebel called his school a kindergarten since he wanted it to be a place for children to learn and grow, which would help them as adults.

2 Froebel wanted to develop the minds and bodies of children, so he had them do physical activities as well as mental exercises.

3 While many people support the work Froebel did, there are others who dislike the notion of children attending school at very young ages.

4 Froebel got into the field of education by accident as he had done other work prior to becoming a teacher.

5 His belief that children needed to play and to develop their imaginations was the driving force behind Froebel's ideas on childhood education.

6 Froebel and Pestalozzi worked together to perfect their theories on the best ways to go about educating young children.

🎧 CH05_4A

Olmec Civilization Art

An Olmec stone head

The first <u>Mesoamerican</u> culture was the Olmec civilization, which rose in the southeastern region of the modern-day nation of Mexico. Established sometime between 1400 and 1200 B.C., it did not decline until roughly 400 B.C. It began as a farming culture in the Tabasco region, which is crossed by an extensive river system that provided irrigation and a means of transportation for the Olmecs. As the population in the area increased, the trappings of civilization, including a leadership class, organized religion, great building projects, extensive trade networks, and the development of art, accompanied it. Today, little of the Olmecs remains except for some remnants of their cities and numerous works of art, the majority of which consists of cave paintings, sculptures, pottery, jade masks, jewelry, and colossal stone heads.

While a few wooden artifacts have been unearthed, most Olmec art that has survived to the present day was done in stone, which is better able to endure the hot, tropical climate in the Olmec homeland. Human figures are typical representations in Olmec art and often have cleft heads, thick lips, almond-shaped eyes, and downturned mouths. Animals, especially fish and snakes, are common figures in Olmec art, but jaguars held a special place in Olmec beliefs. According to Olmec mythology, they reproduced with human females and produced a hybrid being that modern archaeologists call a were-jaguar. Showing how popular jaguars were to the Olmecs, numerous pieces of Olmec art depict humans holding what appear to be were-jaguar babies.

Among the most renowned of all Olmec art objects are the enormous stone heads that have been discovered at numerous ancient sites. **1** The largest stand up to three meters high, weigh twenty tons, and are made from basalt. **2** Their bottoms are flat, and their heads rest on the ground with nothing to support them. **3** They have the classic Olmec almond-shaped eyes, downturned mouths, and fleshy lips, and the heads also seem to be wearing helmets similar to those that the Olmecs wore in a ballgame they once played. **4** The purpose of the heads is uncertain, but some archaeologists have speculated that they represent various rulers of the Olmecs, so the statues were made to honor them.

Other major Olmec artwork includes statues and <u>steles</u>, some of which have carvings on their faces, as well as extremely large carved stone thrones. On a smaller scale, the Olmecs were adept at creating tiny stone figurines, typically from jade. They were particularly skilled at making masks, also from jade. Some masks were small and might have served as decorations while others were life sized and were likely worn on people's faces during ceremonies. Cave paintings are among the rarest extant examples of Olmec art as there are merely a few examples. The Olmecs believed in a god called the earth dragon, who was said to dwell inside caves, so it is likely that caves found with paintings on their walls served as places of worship. Many cave paintings portray the common motif of humans and animals living together, with jaguars being the most prominent animals.

The Olmec people additionally made exquisite pottery from the numerous fine clays found in their homeland. Most of the pottery was painted in rich hues of red, orange, green, and blue, and designs were frequently etched into the clay. Examples of Olmec pottery have been found in areas all around Central America, which shows how extensive their trade contacts and influence in the region were. Archaeologists have proved that the clay used in the pottery came from nearby major Olmec cities, and they can also date the pottery to the time that the Olmec civilization reigned supreme in the area. The conclusion they have reached is that the pottery was a major trade item for the Olmecs. Clues regarding the influence of the Olmecs in their geographical region can be found in other works of art as well. For example, the jade they utilized in masks and figurines was taken from a valley in Guatemala, which is far from their homeland. Without a doubt, the Olmecs' trade system and desire for material to construct art with brought them into contact with other people and helped them attain a great amount of influence on various Mesoamerican civilizations.

*Glossary

Mesoamerican: relating to Mesoamerica, the region stretching from Central Mexico southward to Honduras and Guatemala

stele: an upright stone pillar that contains an inscription or design and which serves as a monument

1 In paragraph 1, which of the following can be inferred about the Olmecs?

   (A) They are considered among the top artists in Mesoamerican history.

   (B) They relied on warfare to defeat their enemies and to expand their territory.

   (C) Precisely when their civilization was founded is not known to historians.

   (D) Most of the art that they created was made to honor the deities they worshipped.

2 According to paragraph 2, which of the following is true about Olmec art?

   (A) Most Olmec wooden artifacts show images of humans instead of animals.

   (B) It features not only humans but also a variety of species of animals.

   (C) There are more representations of jaguars than any other types of animals.

   (D) The humans that appear in it do not resemble the actual Olmec people.

3 Which of the sentences below best expresses the essential information in the highlighted sentence in the passage? Incorrect answer choices change the meaning in important ways or leave out essential information.

The purpose of the heads is uncertain, but some archaeologists have speculated that they represent various rulers of the Olmecs, so the statues were made to honor them.

   (A) Archaeologists are not sure, but they think the heads represent Olmec rulers who were honored by the people.

   (B) The heads that the Olmecs created were used to worship some of the past rulers that they had.

   (C) Nobody knows why the Olmecs carved gigantic heads of some of the rulers that they had in the past.

   (D) In an attempt to honor their past rulers, some Olmec artists carved very large heads that were made out of stone.

4 In paragraph 3, the author's description of the stone heads the Olmecs made mentions all of the following EXCEPT:

   (A) the facial characteristics which they feature

   (B) the places at which they have been unearthed

   (C) the objects that they appear to be wearing

   (D) the heights and the weights of the biggest ones

5 The word "motif" in the passage is closest in meaning to

    (A) pattern

    (B) theory

    (C) theme

    (D) vision

6 In paragraph 4, the author's description of Olmec jade art mentions which of the following?

    (A) How the jade that the Olmecs used was acquired

    (B) The appearances of the jade figurines the Olmecs made

    (C) The reason the Olmecs used jade as opposed to other rocks

    (D) The purpose of some of the jade art the Olmecs created

7 The word "hues" in the passage is closest in meaning to

    (A) images

    (B) shades

    (C) shadows

    (D) strokes

8 According to paragraph 5, how did the Olmecs use the pottery they made?

    (A) They stored the grain that they grew in their fields inside it.

    (B) They conducted commerce with other nearby tribes by trading it.

    (C) They painted pictures on it and then placed it in places of worship.

    (D) They used it as containers of certain possessions of value.

9 Look at the four squares [■] that indicate where the following sentence could be added to the passage.

La Venta and San Lorenzo are particularly noted for the colossal heads that were unearthed there.

Where would the sentence best fit?

Click on a square [■] to add the sentence to the passage.

10 **Directions:** An introductory sentence for a brief summary of the passage is provided below. Complete the summary by selecting the THREE answer choices that express the most important ideas of the passage. Some sentences do not belong because they express ideas that are not presented in the passage or are minor ideas in the passage. **This question is worth 2 points.**

> Drag your answer choices to the spaces where they belong. To remove an answer choice, click on it. To review the passage, click on VIEW TEXT.

The Olmec people of Mesoamerica created various types of art that had both human and animal representations.

-
-
-

ANSWER CHOICES

1. A great deal of Olmec art, such as the giant stone heads, depicts humans, but jaguars were also popular topics in their art.

2. It was not until the Olmecs achieved a high level of civilization that they had both the time and the ability to produce any art.

3. The pottery that the Olmecs created was not only decorated and of high quality, but it was also used as a trade item with other people.

4. The Olmecs mostly avoided working with wood to create art as they were aware that it would decompose and not last very long.

5. The Olmecs worshipped several deities, including the earth dragon, so they dedicated some of their art to their gods.

6. Jade was utilized to create both small figurines and also masks, some of which were likely worn during some ceremonies.

The Post-World War II American Economy

Suburban development in Colorado Springs, Colorado
© David Shankbone

The Great Depression in the 1930s struck the American economy a severe blow which nearly proved fatal. Then, boosted greatly by the entry of the United States into World War II in 1941, it slowly began recovering. ∎ Constructing machines of war and feeding, arming, and cladding millions of soldiers gave the economy a much-needed shot in the arm. ❷ Following the war's end in 1945, Americans feared a return to poor economic conditions, but this did not happen as the economic momentum of the war carried over into peacetime. ❸ The country's gross national product grew from 200 billion dollars in 1940 to 300 billion dollars in 1950 and, eventually, to 500 billion dollars by 1960. ❹

The economy was assisted by the United States' new position as a world leader. The onset of the Cold War between the U.S. and the Soviet Union resulted in an arms race as each side sought to develop massive and powerful military forces. The American government funneled enormous sums of money to its military forces, allowing them to grow to a tremendous size for a peacetime military. These funds were paid for with income tax dollars taken from the growing American workforce, which had been aided by the return to the country of millions of soldiers, many of whom entered universities paid for by the G.I. Bill. It provided educational supplements to soldiers and allowed more people to attend universities than at any previous time in American history. University graduates then entered the workforce and became taxpayers.

Growth in peacetime industries and transportation additionally stimulated the economy. The development of the television, radio, and music industries opened new fields of entertainment and profit for the economy. Factories also started resuming manufacturing civilian products that people could afford since so many jobs were being created. Automobile factories retooled from making tanks and jeeps to manufacturing cars again. President Eisenhower signed the Federal Aid Highway Act of 1956, which began the interstate highway building program, thereby greatly enhancing automobile production. This interstate highway system also contributed to economic growth as large parts of the nation became connected by the more than 60,000 kilometers of roads that were constructed. During the war, many industries—particularly the aircraft industry—developed in the southwest and Pacific coast regions. Wartime innovations involving aircraft resulted in peacetime advances in civilian aircraft production. By the 1960s, civilian air transportation became common.

A housing boom fueled in part by low-interest-rate loans to returning soldiers, allowing them to be able to afford to purchase new homes, also occurred after the end of the war. New houses were constructed using techniques such as having **prefabricated** sections of houses built in factories and then assembled onsite. The convenient housing market in turn resulted in numerous marriages and higher birthrates—the so-called baby boom—because more people felt that they had enough money to start families and to have homes of their own. Many of these homes were constructed in locations outside cities in what soon became suburbs. Denizens of suburbs were frequently people fleeing inner cities to find peace and quiet in the safety and comfort of their new homes.

There was also expansion of large conglomerates as big companies swallowed smaller ones, which led to consolidation in both industry and services. This had an effect on the workforce as more individuals became white-collar office-going employees. Innovations in factory production led to more machines doing work, thereby shrinking the size of the blue-collar workforce. One other area where the economic boom had a negative impact was on small farmers. Large numbers of farms were purchased by corporations when the food industry started expanding and becoming more streamlined. Small family-owned farms could not compete with large food corporations, so this, in turn, resulted in more people abandoning their farms to find work in urban centers.

The end result of everything was a booming national economy by the 1960s. Urban populations expanded while rural populations declined. A large number of Americans became educated, well-paid, homeowning suburbanites. This growth happened virtually unabated until 1973, when a recession tied to growing world oil prices and rising inflation resulted in a decline that stagnated the economy for several years.

*Glossary

gross national product: the total value of all the goods and services produced in a country in one year
prefabricated: constructed beforehand

11 The word "boosted" in the passage is closest in meaning to

(A) arranged

(B) improved

(C) transported

(D) altered

12 In paragraph 2, why does the author mention "the Cold War"?

(A) To explain some of the reasons that it took place right after World War II ended

(B) To note that it was not an actual war involving fighting but was based on economics

(C) To point out that the Soviet Union was eventually defeated by the United States

(D) To describe how it contributed to the improvement of the post-war American economy

13 According to paragraph 2, which of the following is true about the G.I. Bill?

(A) It helped increase the population of American university students to record highs.

(B) It only provided funds for American soldiers who had fought in World War II.

(C) It became law because a more educated workforce was needed in the United States.

(D) It was a direct result of the Cold War that started as soon as World War II ended.

14 Which of the sentences below best expresses the essential information in the highlighted sentence in the passage? Incorrect answer choices change the meaning in important ways or leave out essential information.

President Eisenhower signed the Federal Aid Highway Act of 1956, which began the interstate highway building program, thereby greatly enhancing automobile production.

(A) The Federal Aid Highway Act of 1956 was what caused a large number of interstates to be built throughout the country.

(B) The result of a bill regarding roads that was signed into law by the president was that more cars were manufactured.

(C) Because of the American president, more cars were able to be built in the United States than ever before in 1956.

(D) President Eisenhower was responsible for building the interstates that connected cities all throughout the entire country.

15 In paragraph 3, the author implies that the interstate highway system

(A) was not considered positively by most Americans when construction on it began

(B) took nearly a decade to be completed once work on it started in the 1950s

(C) made it much easier for people to drive though the country after 1956

(D) was the largest public works project ever engaged in by the American government

16 In paragraph 4, all of the following questions are answered EXCEPT:

(A) How did the new construction techniques for homes result in lower housing prices?

(B) Why did many Americans decide to leave the cities and to move to the suburbs?

(C) What enabled the baby boom in the United States to take place?

(D) How were so many American soldiers able to afford to purchase new homes?

17 According to paragraph 5, small farmers were harmed in the postwar economy because

(A) food prices declined since farming methods improved crop yields by a great amount

(B) banks often refused to provide them with loans to keep their farms from going bankrupt

(C) many of their farms were uncompetitive in comparison to large corporation-owned farms

(D) too many people decided to find jobs that paid them more money in large urban centers

18 The word "unabated" in the passage is closest in meaning to

(A) undetected

(B) nonstop

(C) opposite

(D) unopposed

19 Look at the four squares [■] that indicate where the following sentence could be added to the passage.

In fact, the American national economy began growing at an unprecedented rate during this period.

Where would the sentence best fit?

Click on a square [■] to add the sentence to the passage.

20 Directions: An introductory sentence for a brief summary of the passage is provided below. Complete the summary by selecting the THREE answer choices that express the most important ideas of the passage. Some sentences do not belong because they express ideas that are not presented in the passage or are minor ideas in the passage. **This question is worth 2 points.**

> Drag your answer choices to the spaces where they belong. To remove an answer choice, click on it. To review the passage, click on VIEW TEXT.

After World War II ended, the American economy became very powerful for a number of reasons.

-
-
-

ANSWER CHOICES

1. Soldiers returning home from the war benefitted by getting more educated and also entered the workforce in great numbers.

2. The American economy went into a recession in 1973 due to rising oil prices in places such as the Middle East.

3. The blue-collar workforce began to decline, and lots of Americans also decided to enter the farming industry.

4. A lack of people in the workforce meant that companies had to pay their workers much higher wages than normal.

5. Many people could afford cheap housing, which resulted in increased marriage and childbirth rates.

6. Factories began manufacturing many products, and they were shipped on the tens of thousands of kilometers of new highways built.

■ Vocabulary Review

A Complete each sentence with the appropriate word from the box.

> boundary   spanned   fired   funneling   momentum

1 The car's _____ let it move forward a bit after it ran out of gas.

2 The potter _____ the ceramics in the kiln to harden them.

3 The reign of the king _____ a period of more than four decades.

4 Future Technology, Inc. is _____ money into research on nanotechnology.

5 There is a wall all along the _____ between the two countries.

B Complete each sentence with the correct answer.

1 This bridge is **durable**, so it is _____ enough to last for more than a hundred years.

   a. strong
                    b. long

2 With a **capacity** of 10,000 people, the stadium _____ a large crowd.

   a. cannot host
                    b. has the ability to host

3 There are only five **extant** copies of that manuscript that _____ the present day.

   a. people remember in
                    b. have survived to

4 The _____ was a success as the people who started the **rebellion** won against the tyrant.

   a. revolution
                    b. battle

5 A **devout** believer in her religion, Gina prayed _____ all the time.

   a. happily
                    b. sincerely

6 The company plans to **resume** operations by _____ its main factory next month.

   a. opening
                    b. closing

7 Lucy's favorite painting is the **mural** that she created on _____ in her home.

   a. a wall
                    b. an easel

8 _____, the concert **abruptly** ended when the singer left the stage.

   a. Eventually
                    b. All of a sudden

9 Several tiny _____ were the only **remnants** of the house after the explosion.

   a. fragments
                    b. nails

10 Everyone was so **demoralized** by what had happened that they _____.

   a. expected to win
                    b. gave up hope

Chapter **06**

Inference

Question Type | Inference

◪ About the Question

Inference questions focus on the implications that are made in the passage. You are asked to analyze the information presented in the passage and then to come to logical conclusions about it. The answers to these questions are never explicitly written in the passage. Instead, you need to infer what the author of the passage means. These questions often require you to understand cause and effect and also to compare and contrast various events, people, or ideas. There are 0-2 Inference questions for each passage. Most passages have at least 1 Inference question though.

Recognizing Inference questions:

- Which of the following can be inferred about X?

- The author of the passage implies that X . . .

- Which of the following can be inferred from paragraph 1 about X?

Helpful hints for answering the questions correctly:

- Inference questions often focus on various cause and effect relationships. Think about the possible unstated effects of various events, ideas, or phenomena that are presented in the passage.

- You need to be able to read between the lines to answer these questions properly. Focus not only on what the author is overtly writing but also on what the author is hinting at in the text.

- Avoid selecting answer choices because they contain words that are found in the passage. These are frequently misleading.

- The correct answer will never contradict the main point of the passage. Avoid answer choices that go against the main point or theme of the passage.

- Some Inference questions use words such as *suggest* rather than *imply* or *infer*.

- The difficulty level of these questions has increased. In some cases, test takers must be able to understand an entire paragraph rather than only a part of it.

Organic Food

In recent years, organic food has increased in popularity so much that the organic farming industry has grown by more than thirty percent. Many individuals involved in the business claim that organic food provides more health benefits than nonorganic food does. Proponents state, for instance, that organic food can reduce the risks of getting certain types of cancer as well as heart disease and also that it can prevent premature aging while boosting the body's immune system. However, the results of numerous scientific studies are less than conclusive. Most of them show that there are no major benefits and that organic and nonorganic foods are equally as good for the body. Despite the lack of evidence organic food improves people's health, it is still strongly supported by numerous people because fertilizers, pesticides, and other chemicals are not used to grow it, which results in less harm to the environment. On the other hand, organic food is much more labor intensive than nonorganic food, and this is reflected in the prices charged for it at supermarkets.

The author of the passage implies that organic food

(A) takes a long amount of time to grow in farmers' fields

(B) costs a great deal more than nonorganic food does

(C) has a large number of supporters in the scientific community

(D) can sometimes be harmful to the health of the people consuming it

∣ Answer Explanation ∣

Choice (B) is the correct answer. The passage reads, "Organic food is much more labor intensive than nonorganic food, and this is reflected in the prices charged for it at supermarkets." In pointing out that organic food "is more labor intensive" and that "this is reflected in the prices charged for it," the author is implying that organic food is much more expensive than nonorganic food.

A | The Honeybee Waggle Dance

CH06_2A

Honeybees dwell in hives in colonies called swarms, each of which has a queen bee and a few male drones, which are used for reproductive purposes, while the bulk of the insects are female worker bees. Occasionally, a swarm becomes too large for its hive, so the honeybee colony divides into two as half the bees remain in their home whereas the other half leave to establish a new swarm. The departing bees find a nearby tree to stay at temporarily and then begin the process of searching for a new home, which may take several days.

This task is given to selected honeybees called **scouts**, which fly away in every direction to discover a suitable place to construct their hive. When a scout believes it has found a good location, it returns to the swarm and performs an elaborate series of motions that scientists call the waggle dance. The scout moves in a figure eight pattern on the side of the swarm that it wishes the rest of the bees to follow; however, the swarm will not move until most of the other scouts return and perform dances of their own.

Each scout performs the waggle dance, with some acting more aggressively than the others. Observations of this ritual indicate that the honeybee scouts dancing in the most aggressive manner believe they have found an optimal place for their hive. What happens next is something similar to a competition: Each scout **endeavors** to win over the swarm with its dancing prowess. The honeybees dance simultaneously, and there are frequently occasions during which two or more scouts dance on the same side of the swarm.

Gradually, the most aggressive dancers win over the less forceful ones, which abandon their places around the swarm and move to the side where the most aggressive dancers are flying. Eventually, every scout winds up doing the waggle dance on the same side. At that point, the swarm follows the scouts to the new location, where they begin constructing their hive.

*scout: one sent out to obtain information
*endeavor: to try hard; to do one's best

1 Which of the following can be inferred from paragraphs 1 and 2 about honeybees?

Ⓐ The male drones can sometimes outnumber the female bees.

Ⓑ They will die in great numbers if their home becomes overpopulated.

Ⓒ All of the bees that fly off to search for a new home are females.

Ⓓ Every honeybee in the hive is capable of doing the waggle dance if necessary.

2 In paragraph 4, the author implies that honeybees

Ⓐ must reach a consensus on the hive's new location before they start building it

Ⓑ may sometimes construct two new hives if the scouts cannot agree on one location

Ⓒ can take a couple of weeks to build their hive after determining where to make it

Ⓓ will react in an aggressive manner toward any animal interrupting the waggle dance

Vocabulary

- _____ = a male bee that is stingless and makes no honey
- _____ = the act of moving back and forth
- _____ = best; ideal
- _____ = ability; skill

B Interpreting Texts on Ancient Relics

   Relics are artifacts from ancient civilizations such as the Egyptians, Greeks, and Mayans. On many occasions, archaeologists discover relics containing text written in ancient languages. These items could be ancient books and scrolls, or they could simply be vases and coins with writing on them. Interpreting these texts can be difficult, particularly if the language is a previously undiscovered one, and the texts may additionally be hard to read if they are incomplete or if sections have worn away. Another complication is that interpreting them must be done without the reader introducing any bias based upon modern language and culture.

   Lost languages are among the numerous obstacles archaeologists must overcome to interpret texts on relics. One solution is to utilize a key, such as the Rosetta Stone, which was discovered in Egypt in 1799. It contains an ancient Egyptian decree written in three languages, one of which is in Egyptian **hieroglyphics**, an unknown language at the time of its discovery; however, another language on it is ancient Greek, which scholars understood. By comparing the text, scholars made great leaps in interpreting hieroglyphics. Unfortunately, other ancient languages, such as Minoan Linear A, have not been deciphered primarily because no key that can assist translation efforts has been discovered yet.

   The Rosetta Stone was mostly intact, but its missing parts exacerbated efforts to interpret its text, something which frequently happens with relics. The passage of time may result in carvings, paintings, drawings, and textual **inscriptions** getting worn away. For instance, the Tel Dan Stone, a stone with ancient Hebrew inscriptions that was found in Israel in 1993, is broken in places, and large portions of text are missing. The result is a long-standing controversy over the precise interpretation of the writing on it.

   How modern scholars view texts is another obstacle to interpreting them since translators have their own personal biases. Researchers must therefore keep the historical and cultural context of the period when the text was written in mind. This can be difficult when little is known of the people who wrote the text and when or why they wrote it though.

*hieroglyphics: a pictographic script used by the ancient Egyptians
*inscription: something written on brick, stone, or another surface, often in honor of a person or event

---

1 In paragraph 2, which of the following can be inferred about hieroglyphics?

   (A) There is a small group of people who use it for communication today.

   (B) The first recorded discovery of it was found on the Rosetta Stone.

   (C) It is read and understood by some individuals in the present day.

   (D) It is widely considered more difficult to read than Minoan Linear A is.

2 In paragraph 3, the author implies that the Tel Dan Stone

   (A) has a smaller percentage of its text intact than the Rosetta Stone does

   (B) contains not only ancient Hebrew text but also some drawings and inscriptions

   (C) has been useful to academics trying to understand ancient Hebrew society

   (D) has resulted in scholars rethinking their theories since its discovery in 1993

Vocabulary

· _____ = something difficult, complex, or problematic   · _____ = to discover the meaning of

· _____ = prejudice; hostile feelings toward a person or group   · _____ = to make worse or more difficult

C | The Roaring Twenties

Historians refer to the decade of the 1920s as the Roaring Twenties when describing the cultures of Europe and North America. That period has that moniker since the pace of life then was faster than it had been before. It was a time of great economic success and social change exemplified by the widespread use of modern technologies and the dramatic altering of the culture.

In many ways, the Roaring Twenties was a reaction to the death and destruction of World War I (1914–1918). Following the gloom and uncertainty of the war years, people sought good lives and pleasure, which fueled a desire to spend money and to acquire the best things. A brief recession followed the war's conclusion, but economic prosperity quickly became the norm as the desire for consumer goods resulted in the mass production of automobiles, refrigerators, telephones, and other electronic products. Urban centers increased in size as people moved away from the countryside. This initiated an urban building boom, epitomized by the architectural style called **art deco**. The Empire State Building and Chrysler Building, both in New York City, were designed in that style.

Culturally, the decade was defined by the rise of new genres of music, the beginning of mass entertainment, and greater freedom for women. Jazz music moved from the American South to large cities in the United States and Europe. Motion pictures, radio shows, and sports such as baseball provided entertainment for millions of people. This led to the rise of celebrities as the public followed intimate details of the lives of famous people such as actor Rudolph Valentino and baseball star Babe Ruth. During this time, women in many nations became eligible to vote and gained more freedom. Changes for them included the shedding of the confining clothing of the prewar years to more loose-fitting dresses, long necklaces, and floppy hats, which exemplified the **flapper** look. Sadly, much of the prosperity and change was built on a weak financial structure—the stock market—and when it collapsed in 1929, it brought the Roaring Twenties to a sudden halt.

*art deco: a decorative style of art that stresses geometric shapes and bold colors
*flapper: a young woman that behaved in an unconventional manner in the 1920s

1 In paragraph 2, the author implies that the Roaring Twenties

    Ⓐ was a time when the unemployment rate fell to record lows and most people had jobs

    Ⓑ saw most people getting electricity in their homes for the first time

    Ⓒ was an age during which the first skyscrapers were built in New York City

    Ⓓ was a period of relative peace in both Europe and North America

2 Which of the following can be inferred from paragraph 3 about women?

    Ⓐ A large number of them voted for the first time in their lives during the 1920s.

    Ⓑ During the Roaring Twenties, they encouraged men to let them design their own clothes.

    Ⓒ In the 1920s, large numbers of them became celebrities in the entertainment industry.

    Ⓓ Some women were elected to important political positions during the Roaring Twenties.

Vocabulary

- _____ = a name
- _____ = to serve as an example
- _____ = wealth; affluence
- _____ = very personal; private

▋ Mapping

The following chart shows the structure of the passage. Fill in the blanks with the appropriate words.

> **The Roaring Twenties**

> Was the ❶ _____ of the 1920s
> - was a faster pace of life
> - featured economic success and social changes

> Economy: people spent lots of money
> - was ❷ _____ prosperity
> - bought mass-produced consumer goods
> - ❸ _____ centers became larger

> Culture: ❹ _____ moved to large cities in U.S. and Europe
> - rise of celebrities
> - women could ❺ _____
> - women gained more ❻ _____

▋ Summary

The following is a summary of the passage. Fill in the blanks with the appropriate words.

The 1920s are often referred to as the ❶ _____ Twenties because of the ❷ _____ success and social change that took place then. Following World War I, the Roaring Twenties was a time when people spent money, so their ❸ _____ improved. They bought many consumer items such as automobiles, refrigerators, and telephones, and many people ❹ _____ from the country to cities. As for ❺ _____, jazz became prominent, and motion pictures, radio shows, and sports entertained millions of people. Women became ❻ _____ to vote and gained more freedom. However, the Roaring Twenties ended when the stock market ❼ _____ in 1929.

A | Pretend Play and Child Development

🎧 CH06_3A

When children play together, they commonly pretend by acting out games and scenarios in which they play different roles, such as monsters, superheroes, pirates, doctors, and princesses. The close observation of child play has led psychologists to regard it as an essential component of children's mental development. By participating in pretend play, children learn to develop reasoning and to anticipate possibilities from various scenarios, both of which assist them in decision making. They learn to separate plausible scenarios from implausible ones by understanding what is real and what is not, and they also learn to control their emotions in group situations, thereby permitting them to interact successfully with others.

According to some psychologists, there are two stages of pretend play: fantasy play and **sociodramatic** play. Fantasy play begins around the age of two, which is when children frequently enter day care and interact with their peers for the first time. This type of play includes children verbalizing when they are pretending to do something at various stages in their activities. For instance, a child might say, "I am swimming now," and then make swimming motions with his arms. As children age and spend more time with other children, fantasy play gradually transforms into sociodramatic play. At that point, children engage in pretend scenarios and go through them without explaining what they are doing at each stage. For example, a group of children pretending to be like pirates will act like buccaneers for a long time without having to say, "We're pirates," or, "We're attacking the ship now."

Both types of play can benefit children as they participate in social activities with others the same age. They learn many important aspects of social interaction, such as cooperation and appreciation of others' points of view and feelings. Furthermore, they make friends by including others in their games. As children progress from fantasy to sociodramatic play, they develop cognitive awareness by learning about the world. They comprehend that the world has rules and that actions have consequences. Children also learn what is possible and impossible as they use more realistic situations, such as playing doctor while someone pretends to be sick, when engaging in sociodramatic play. They partake in more real-life situations that are conceivable as opposed to pretending to be superheroes saving the world from aliens or some other menace.

Another advantage of pretend play is that children learn how to gain better control over their emotions. They develop and express more positive emotions, become more thoughtful, learn to engage with others in positive ways, and understand how others feel in various situations. At the same time, they start to become able to control negative emotions such as **selfishness** and anger. Finally, by playing in groups, children learn that they cannot be the center of attention at all times.

Some parents worry when their children engage in extensive amounts of pretend play as they believe their children are not learning about the real world. Yet psychologists emphasize that parents should not discourage pretend play as it is necessary for children's development. This is especially true for young children since, as they age, their time becomes restricted once school begins, and they have to engage in learning more structured in nature.

*sociodramatic: relating to the assuming and acting of various roles
*selfishness: self-centeredness; greed

Vocabulary

- _____ = an imagined sequence of events
- _____ = a specialist in the study of the human mind
- _____ = an equal; a person of the same status or age as another
- _____ = a threat

1   According to paragraph 1, which of the following is NOT true about pretend play?

   (A) Children need to participate in it in order to develop their minds.

   (B) The roles that children assume when doing it dictate their future careers.

   (C) It teaches children to learn about what is real and what is not.

   (D) Doing it enables children to be able to associate well with others.

2   Which of the following can be inferred from paragraphs 2 and 3 about sociodramatic play?

   (A) Children engaged in it do not feel the need to state aloud what actions they are doing.

   (B) It is considered the more useful type of pretend play for developing imaginations.

   (C) Most children participate in it by doing some kind of outdoor activity.

   (D) The majority of it involves children doing activities that are normally implausible.

3   Select the TWO answer choices from paragraph 4 that identify the advantages of pretend play. *To receive credit, you must select TWO answers.*

   (A) Children become more aware of others' emotions.

   (B) Children improve their athletic skills and abilities.

   (C) Children learn how to do activities together with others.

   (D) Children develop both positive and negative emotions.

4   Select the appropriate statements from the answer choices and match them to the type of pretend play to which they relate. TWO of the answer choices will NOT be used.

Fantasy Play (Select 3)	Sociodramatic Play (Select 2)
•	
•	•
•	•

STATEMENTS

1 Typically has children pretending situations that could happen in reality

2 Teaches children that what they do has specific results

3 Is the initial type of play that children engage in

4 Is recommended by psychologists that parents do it with their children

5 Often involves children acting out unrealistic scenarios

6 Requires children both to act and say what they are doing

7 May prevent children from learning about the world around them

Plant Distribution and Plate Tectonics

The theory of plate tectonics holds that the Earth's crust is comprised of numerous large sections, or plates, which are in constant movement and are pushing against or pulling away from one another. Related to plate tectonics is the theory of continental drift—the notion that millions of years ago, all of the world's continents were joined as one massive supercontinent and then later slowly drifted apart until they reached their present-day positions. Although continental drift is nearly universally accepted today, this was not always the case. When German scientist Alfred Wegener first proposed the theory in 1912, the idea was scoffed at by other scientists, especially since Wegener provided little proof of this theory at the time. Gradually, however, over the next few decades, more and more substantial evidence emerged that appeared to prove Wegener's theory.

Among this evidence is the fact that certain species of fossilized and living plants have been found on widely separate continents. This seems to be solid evidence that these continents were once joined sometime in the past. As an example, **fossils** of the fernlike plant glossopteris, which appeared roughly 300 million years ago, have been discovered in places in South Africa, Australia, South America, India, and even Antarctica. Geologists believe these places were all once connected as part of the supercontinent Pangaea. A seed-bearing tree, glossopteris was one of the dominant plants of its era and lived on the Earth for almost fifty million years.

Approximately 135 million years ago, when the first flowering plants appeared, Pangaea had already divided into two very large continents. The southernmost one, dubbed Gondwanaland, contained parts of all the lands that are in the **Southern Hemisphere** today. Modern plants common to these lands are descended from plants that existed 135 million years ago. The best example is the cycad plant family. Containing around 185 species, cycads are currently widely distributed in these southern lands.

For a long time, this widespread distribution of both glossopteris and plants belonging to the cycad family baffled botanists since these plants had no means of distributing themselves across vast regions of land. Plants typically move to new territories by distributing their seeds, which they accomplish in three primary ways. First, animals such as birds consume seeds, move to new lands, and defecate the seeds onto the ground. Next, the wind picks up seeds and carries them away. Last, seeds can float on water and drift to new lands. In all three cases, when the seeds reach a new spot, they get buried in the ground, whereupon they germinate and then grow into mature plants.

However, none of these methods seems possible for the cycad family. These plants produce large seeds that birds cannot consume and carry to other lands, nor can the wind easily pick them up and carry them through the air. In addition, most cycads grow far inland away from coastal regions, and, even if they grow near water, most of their seeds are too heavy and therefore cannot float on water and drift to new lands. The glossopteris' seeds were also quite large, so it appears unlikely that they could have been carried to so many regions located thousands of kilometers apart if the continents had been in the same positions 300 million years ago that they are in today. Therefore, most scientists have concluded that plate tectonics and continental drift are the only realistic explanations for the widespread distribution of these plants.

*fossil: the preserved remains of a plant or animal
*Southern Hemisphere: the half of the Earth that lies beneath the equator

Vocabulary

- _____ = large; considerable
- _____ = to confuse
- _____ = to name
- _____ = to begin to grow

1 In stating that the idea was "scoffed at," the author means that the idea was

(A) ridiculed　　　　　　　　　　　(B) considered

(C) shunned　　　　　　　　　　　　(D) proved

2 In paragraph 2, the author implies that glossopteris

(A) was one of the first plants ever to evolve on the planet

(B) has been found in fossilized forms on all of the Earth's continents

(C) went extinct sometime around 250 million years ago

(D) bore fruit that was consumed by a wide variety of animals

3 Which of the sentences below best expresses the essential information in the highlighted sentence in the passage? Incorrect answer choices change the meaning in important ways or leave out essential information.

In addition, most cycads grow far inland away from coastal regions, and, even if they grow near water, most of their seeds are too heavy and therefore cannot float on water and drift to new lands.

(A) Because cycads have large seeds that are incapable of floating on the water, they are rarely found near water but instead grow inland.

(B) The seeds of cycads rarely spread by means of water because they are very heavy, and the plant also tends to grow in dry places far from water.

(C) Cycads do not grow near large bodies of water, and even those living near water bear seeds that weigh too much, so they cannot float.

(D) One method of seed dispersal for cycads is water even though the seeds themselves are quite heavy and do not float well on it.

4 An introductory sentence for a brief summary of the passage is provided below. Complete the summary by selecting the THREE answer choices that express the most important ideas of the passage. Some sentences do not belong because they express ideas that are not presented in the passage or are minor ideas in the passage.

The dispersal of the fossils of some plants that lived millions of years ago has helped prove that the continents were once closely connected to one another.

ANSWER CHOICES

1 Plants in the cycad family grow around the world, but they rarely grow near water, and cycad seeds are too heavy to float.

2 The first plant to emerge on the planet was glossopteris, and it grew in all sorts of climates and ecosystems.

3 When Alfred Wegener came up with his theory of continental drift, virtually nobody believed what he claimed.

4 Scientists have concluded that a supercontinent must have existed since the remains of identical plants have been found in numerous places.

5 There are three primary methods of seed dispersal, which include transportation by animals and dispersal by the wind.

6 Fossils of glossopteris, a type of plant, have been found on numerous continents despite the fact that seed dispersal for it would have been difficult.

🎧 CH06_4A

Immigrating for Work

There are many reasons people move to new countries, but arguably the most common one is to find employment. Doing so is not simple though, primarily because many natives have no desire to see people from other countries moving to their shores. Additional problems for people immigrating for work concern socioeconomic factors, including immigrants' education levels, their inability to find suitable employment, and their medical history and criminal past. Many immigrants may also not assimilate into their new countries as they tend to suffer culture shock and cannot handle living in a new culture. Overall, moving to a new country to find work is at best a difficult proposition and at worst an impossible one for most individuals.

The main difficulty regarding immigrating is that most countries do not permit it to be accomplished easily. While the majority of nations allow foreign workers to come temporarily, being able to move to and live permanently in another nation is much more difficult to accomplish. Countries such as Canada and New Zealand have strict policies concerning how foreigners can become permanent residents. They have lists of preferred professionals, such as doctors and engineers, who receive priority. The main reason for this is that these nations have no desire for new arrivals to become burdens on their social services. Instead, they want newcomers to be hardworking, taxpaying, and productive members of society rather than unemployed deadbeats that consume large amounts of government funding while producing little in return.

As a result of policies such as these, most people wishing to emigrate should possess a high level of education. Yet even those with good educations may not have their degrees recognized in the countries they wish to move to. For example, most doctors moving to countries in North America and Europe from other parts of the world must take special exams to prove their medical skills and knowledge. And virtually anyone lacking a university degree will find it difficult to be accepted as a permanent resident. These individuals must also have a clean bill of health. ∎ People with serious preexisting medical problems, such as cancer and AIDS, will find it practically impossible to become permanent residents in most countries since those nations do not want sick people who will require expensive medical treatment. **2** This is especially true for countries such as Australia, Canada, and New Zealand as well as most countries in Europe, where health care is paid for by taxes. **3** Another impediment concerns people's criminal pasts as anyone who has ever been found guilty of a serious criminal offense will likely be prohibited from moving to a new land. **4**

Nevertheless, despite these barriers, many people manage to qualify for permanent residency and find themselves legally in foreign lands and with good jobs. For many, their problems are just beginning though. Language barriers are serious issues for people who lack fluency in their new country's language. If a new arrival does not fully understand the language in the new country, accomplishing basic tasks may present difficulties. While English is used as a first or second language in numerous countries, English speakers have trouble in some places since not everyone can speak the language. In some cases, the parents might have a grasp of the local language, but their children may have to enroll in schools despite not knowing the language well enough to study in it. In Toronto, Canada, the school board has to organize special English as a second language classes for the large number of foreign children who live there but do not possess the language skills necessary to be fully educated.

On top of all these problems is the strong likelihood that newly arrived permanent residents will suffer from culture shock. This term encompasses many things, but, in essence, it is a general negative reaction one has upon leaving one's own culture to live in another environment. Sensations such as homesickness, anxiety, depression, frustration, and fear frequently overwhelm new arrivals, who feel that they do not belong in their new land and wonder if they erred in moving to it. For some, the sentiment never goes away, so they wind up returning to their homelands to places that are more comfortable.

*Glossary

culture shock: negative feelings, such as stress and bewilderment, that a person gets when in an unfamiliar culture

deadbeat: a lazy person who does no work and contributes little or nothing to society

1 The phrase "assimilate into" in the passage is closest in meaning to

(A) adapt to

(B) partake in

(C) agree with

(D) approve of

2 In paragraph 1, the author's description of the problems immigrants face mentions all of the following EXCEPT:

(A) specific difficulties that they may encounter in trying to move to other lands

(B) the effect that getting used to a new culture can have on them

(C) ways they can overcome the issues they must deal with in their new countries

(D) how the people in the countries in which they move to feel about them

3 Which of the sentences below best expresses the essential information in the highlighted sentence in the passage? Incorrect answer choices change the meaning in important ways or leave out essential information.

While the majority of nations allow foreign workers to come temporarily—for several months to a year or two—being able to move to and live permanently in another nation is much more difficult to accomplish.

(A) Nearly every country permits foreign workers to be in them for brief amounts of time, but only a few nations permit these people to become permanent residents.

(B) In most countries, there are foreigners who only live there for short periods of time as well as those who have made those nations their permanent homes.

(C) Living permanently in a new country is almost as simple for foreigners to arrange as living in another nation for a year or so is.

(D) Most countries allow foreigners to work in them for abbreviated periods of time but make it harder for these people to reside in them full time.

4 In paragraph 2, the author implies that many people who want to move to new countries

(A) work much harder than most of the citizens of the countries they are moving to

(B) are believed to have little of benefit to offer by many foreign governments

(C) must pay a significant amount of money to accelerate the immigration process

(D) require extensive retraining since they are unqualified for most jobs

5   In paragraph 3, the author uses "cancer and AIDS" as examples of

(A) two of the most common medical problems suffered by emigrants from foreign lands

(B) medical conditions that health care in some countries does not provide full treatment for

(C) issues that could prevent people from being permitted to immigrate to new countries

(D) the two primary reasons that people applying for permanent resident status are rejected

6   According to paragraph 3, which of the following is true about people who want to emigrate from their homelands?

(A) The lack of a formal education decreases their chances of being able to move.

(B) A criminal record can be overlooked if a person has something of benefit to offer.

(C) They will not be allowed to enter most countries if they have any kind of sickness.

(D) They must pay for their medical care even in countries with government healthcare programs.

7   The word "grasp" in the passage is closest in meaning to

(A) respect

(B) knowledge

(C) hold

(D) approval

8   In paragraph 5, the author's description of culture shock mentions which of the following?

(A) The best ways that people can successfully overcome it

(B) Which people are the most likely to suffer from it

(C) The types of emotions it may cause people to have

(D) The times when it usually affects newcomers to foreign lands

9   Look at the four squares [■] that indicate where the following sentence could be added to the passage.

And even in other countries without government-run healthcare programs, it is uncommon for severely sick people to be granted entry on a permanent basis.

Where would the sentence best fit?

Click on a square [■] to add the sentence to the passage.

10 **Directions:** An introductory sentence for a brief summary of the passage is provided below. Complete the summary by selecting the THREE answer choices that express the most important ideas of the passage. Some sentences do not belong because they express ideas that are not presented in the passage or are minor ideas in the passage. **This question is worth 2 points.**

> Drag your answer choices to the spaces where they belong. To remove an answer choice, click on it. To review the passage, click on VIEW TEXT.

Individuals who wish to immigrate to new lands must deal with a number of issues in order to become permanent residents of those nations.

-
-
-

ANSWER CHOICES

1. Culture shock can affect people who have been in a new culture for a brief period of time or even many years.

2. Those people seeking permanent residency in foreign lands should be educated and healthy as well as good citizens.

3. Both foreign professionals and those individuals lacking job skills are desired for permanent jobs in some countries.

4. An individual with cancer or AIDs may not be permitted to live in countries such as Australia, New Zealand, and Canada.

5. After being approved to immigrate to a new country, people often have to deal with problems such as language barriers and culture shock.

6. Most countries resist admitting too many immigrants due to opposition from their citizens, who do not want too many foreigners living in them.

North American Pyramids

Monks Mound

Mesoamerican cultures in Mexico and Central America are renowned for their impressive architectural feats as they built enormous cities with a wide variety of structures, among them being those shaped like pyramids. What is less well known is that Native American cultures north of Mexico in North America also built pyramidlike structures of their own. In one small corner of British Columbia in Canada, a tribe built extensive small pyramidlike structures that served mainly as burial mounds. Even larger and more elaborate structures were built by the Mississippi culture near the location of the modern-day city of St. Louis in the United States.

Near the confluence of the Fraser and Harrison rivers and close to the city of Chilliwack, British Columbia, lies the Scowlitz archaeological site. Located there was a village belonging to the Scowlitz people, who first put roots down in that area approximately 3,000 years ago. Over time, their dead were placed in burial mounds lined with stone, covered with dirt, and built in shapes like pyramids. While these three-meter-high structures are tiny compared to Egyptian and Mesoamerican pyramids, they did serve similar functions as places of burial and worship. ■ Since 1992, archaeologists have been researching the site with care under the supervision of descendants of the ancient Scowlitz people. ■ They discovered approximately 200 burial mounds grouped in clusters in one ten-square-kilometer area. ■ Within many of the burial mounds, they unearthed tribal artifacts and the remains of the departed. ■ Scowlitz tribal lore stated that even after their people no longer permanently lived in the area, tribe members frequently returned to hunt, to fish, and to worship at these burial mounds.

Mounds of varying sizes were additionally a part of the Mississippi culture located in what is today the central United States. This culture originated around 500 A.D. and rose to prominence in central North America around the year 1000. Near where St. Louis is today, a magnificent city that at one point housed up to 30,000 people arose. It featured dozens of large pyramids, yet by the time European explorers reached the region in the seventeenth century, the city had been long abandoned. Historians were unaware of the city's proper name, so they called it Cahokia after a local tribe despite that tribe's own members admitting that their ancestors had nothing to do with the construction of the city. Today, the area is called the Cahokia Mounds State Historic Site and lies on the eastern side of the Mississippi River.

The ancient city of Cahokia included a huge central plaza with large pyramids and was surrounded by outlying areas containing numerous small homes with streets connecting every place to the others. There is evidence that the region once featured around 120 large mounds, but only eighty remain today. The pyramids were constructed of earth and were once covered in stone, but over time, locals removed many stones for modern building projects. Many of the pyramids were erected in tiers with structures built on individual floors as well as on the flat tops of the pyramids. These structures were built by using the wattle and daub method and had thatched roofs. Archaeologists believe people made the pyramids by digging up earth with stone hoes and by carrying the dirt in woven baskets to the building site. This activity required years of hard labor. There is evidence that the largest pyramids were built in layers with small mounds progressively evolving into larger, more elaborate pyramids over time. There is evidence of at least ten periods of building activity for the larger pyramids.

The largest pyramid around the central plaza is referred to as Monks Mound. It stands thirty meters high, covers more than five and a half hectares, and once had four stories with a flat top upon which there was a large structure that may have been a place of worship. Many of the smaller pyramids appear to have been elaborate burial mounds for the leaders of the people who founded the city while other pyramids contain the remains of numerous people buried in clusters. Evidence from these remains indicates to archaeologists that the people living in the region engaged in ritual human sacrifice, much like Mesoamerican tribes in the south such as the Aztecs.

*Glossary

wattle and daub method: a construction method using sticks, earth, and clay

hectare: a unit of land that covers 10,000 square meters

11 In paragraph 1, the author implies that the pyramids in North America

  Ⓐ can be found in a large number of places all throughout Canada and the United States

  Ⓑ are not nearly as well known as the pyramids constructed by Mesoamerican cultures

  Ⓒ often rival the pyramids built in Mexico and Central America with regard to their size

  Ⓓ were almost exclusively constructed by people belonging to the Mississippi culture

12 In paragraph 2, why does the author mention "the city of Chilliwack, British Columbia"?

  Ⓐ To provide the name of a place where some small pyramids have been found

  Ⓑ To claim that it was a village founded by the Scowlitz people 3,000 years ago

  Ⓒ To compare the pyramids that were found in it with those built in South America

  Ⓓ To explain how it had a major effect on the field of Native American archaeology

13 In paragraph 2, all of the following questions are answered EXCEPT:

  Ⓐ How were the pyramids that belonged to the Scowlitz people constructed by them?

  Ⓑ What do some of the stories told by the Scowlitz people say about their actions in the past?

  Ⓒ What was the importance of the ancient site found near Chilliwack by archaeologists?

  Ⓓ How did archaeologists manage to first discover the dig site located near Chilliwack?

14 Which of the sentences below best expresses the essential information in the highlighted sentence in the passage? Incorrect answer choices change the meaning in important ways or leave out essential information.

Historians were unaware of the city's proper name, so they called it Cahokia after a local tribe despite that tribe's own members admitting that their ancestors had nothing to do with the construction of the city.

  Ⓐ Nobody was sure what the name of the city was in the past, so some historians simply decided to call the city Cahokia.

  Ⓑ Historians called the city Cahokia, which was the name of a local tribe, but the members of the tribe claimed that their people did not build the city.

  Ⓒ Even though the Cahokia tribe was not located anywhere near the city, that was the name historians gave to the city.

  Ⓓ The members of the Cahokia tribe informed local historians that they were not involved in the construction of the city.

15 According to paragraph 3, the people belonging to the Mississippi culture

(A) had a period in which they dominated the local region for around 1,000 years

(B) constructed several large cities capable of housing 30,000 people near St. Louis

(C) had many interactions with European explorers who visited them in the 1600s

(D) built one large city that had a large number of pyramids in the St. Louis region

16 The word "tiers" in the passage is closest in meaning to

(A) levels

(B) methods

(C) repetitions

(D) phases

17 In paragraph 4, the author implies that some pyramids in Cahokia

(A) were constructed by using a method that was only known by the Mississippi people

(B) were completely dismantled by people who lived after the city was abandoned

(C) were used as burial mounds whereas others were meeting places for local residents

(D) took roughly ten years for people to make due to their very large sizes

18 According to paragraph 5, which of the following is true about Monks Mound?

(A) Some of the leaders of the Mississippi people are thought to be buried within it.

(B) Archaeologists believe that its construction was influenced by the Aztec tribe.

(C) The pyramid stood thirty meters high and had the remains of many people in it.

(D) It was a pyramid that had four stories and was located by the city's central plaza.

19 Look at the four squares [■] that indicate where the following sentence could be added to the passage.

The relics that archaeologists recovered have been instrumental in their ability to understand more about the Scowlitz culture.

Where would the sentence best fit?

Click on a square [■] to add the sentence to the passage.

20 **Directions:** An introductory sentence for a brief summary of the passage is provided below. Complete the summary by selecting the THREE answer choices that express the most important ideas of the passage. Some sentences do not belong because they express ideas that are not presented in the passage or are minor ideas in the passage. **This question is worth 2 points.**

Drag your answer choices to the spaces where they belong. To remove an answer choice, click on it. To review the passage, click on VIEW TEXT.

Both the Scowlitz and Mississippi people in North America built pyramids in the past.

-

-

-

ANSWER CHOICES

1. Some of the pyramids in Cahokia, such as Monks Mound, were tall, had multiple stories, and took many years to build.

2. Archaeologists consulted with the Scowlitz and Mississippi people while excavating the dig sites containing pyramids.

3. The pyramids built by the Scowlitz people were relatively small and were probably used as places of worship.

4. The Scowlitz people and the Cahokia people had already disappeared by the time the Europeans visited North America.

5. Some of the pyramids that were built by Native American tribes have various resemblances to those in Mesoamerica.

6. The pyramids found near St. Louis and Chilliwack had human remains in them, showing that they were burial sites.

◼ Vocabulary Review

A **Complete each sentence with the appropriate word from the box.**

intimate	germinate	complications	confluence	sentiment

1 Adam experienced some _____ from the operation he recently had.

2 There is a large city that was founded at the _____ of the two rivers.

3 Once the spring rains begin to fall, the seeds will _____, and plants will grow.

4 There is a lot of positive _____ toward the celebrity because of the charities she helps.

5 Some people provide _____ details of their lives to complete strangers.

B **Complete each sentence with the correct answer.**

1 His **prowess** on the tennis court is due to his great _____ the game.

   a. desire to play   b. skill at playing

2 Judges should show no **bias**, but some are still _____ defendants in the courtroom.

   a. prejudiced against   b. fair with

3 When a person has a **substantial** amount of money, that individual has _____.

   a. a lot of it   b. very little of it

4 The legal _____ set up are real **impediments** to doing business in that country.

   a. barriers   b. methods

5 The television program **features** many celebrities and also _____ some funny skits.

   a. attempts   b. shows

6 His online **moniker** is Captain Smith since he does not want others to know his real _____.

   a. address   b. name

7 To get **optimal** results, one should hire the _____ employees.

   a. best   b. most energetic

8 When a jury is made up of one's **peers**, everyone is said to be _____ one another.

   a. equal to   b. friends with

9 David is **renowned** for being a master pianist, which is why he is _____.

   a. ambitious   b. world famous

10 The looming **menace** that the coming asteroid poses is a _____ to the entire world.

   a. threat   b. boon

Chapter **07**

Rhetorical Purpose

Question Type | Rhetorical Purpose

◼ About the Question

Rhetorical Purpose questions focus on the reasons that certain information is included in the passage. You are asked to answer a question about why the author decided to write about something in the passage. The function of the material rather than its meaning is important for these kinds of questions. The information asked about in these questions is always included in a small section of the passage. There are 1-2 Rhetorical Purpose questions for each passage.

Recognizing Rhetorical Purpose questions:

- The author discusses "X" in paragraph 2 in order to . . .

- Why does the author mention "X"?

- The author uses "X" as an example of . . .

Other Rhetorical Purpose questions ask about the function or purpose of an entire paragraph. The questions are phrased like this:

- Paragraph 4 supports which of the following ideas about . . . ?

- Paragraphs 2 and 3 support which of the following ideas about . . . ?

- What is the author's purpose in paragraph 4 of the passage?

Helpful hints for answering the questions correctly:

- Read only the paragraph that is mentioned in the question itself. Then, think about how the topic mentioned in the question relates to that paragraph or the entire passage.

- The words that are used in the answer choices, particularly the verbs, are very important when you try to find the answer. Look for words such as *define, illustrate, explain, argue, compare, contrast, criticize, refute, note, example,* and *function.*

- There is a special emphasis on these questions. Some questions ask about entire sentences, not just words or phrases.

The Art of Frederic Church

In the nineteenth century, artists belonging to the Hudson River School produced some of the greatest American landscape art. One of these artists was Frederic Church. Despite having studied with Thomas Cole, who is widely acknowledged for having established the Hudson River School and for inspiring many of its artists, Church's works were different from his mentor's. Cole's art often featured religious allegories while Church's paintings focused more on synthesizing scenery from various places in New York and New England into single paintings. One such work—and one that gained him international fame—was the large painting entitled *Niagara*. Unlike many of the other members of the Hudson River School, Church did not remain in that region for the majority of his career as an artist. He painted landscapes of scenes he viewed in Columbia and Ecuador, and he even ventured to the North Atlantic Ocean to create pictures of icebergs. Later trips took him to Jamaica, Europe, and the Middle East, where he created some of the best American art of the nineteenth century.

The author uses "*Niagara*" as an example of

- Ⓐ a painting that was done in the typical style of Frederic Church
- Ⓑ a work of art that Frederic Church did late in his career
- Ⓒ an artwork made by Frederic Church that was influenced by Thomas Cole
- Ⓓ one of the paintings that made the Hudson River School very famous

| Answer Explanation |

Choice Ⓐ is the correct answer. The passage reads, "Cole's art often featured religious allegories while Church's paintings focused more on synthesizing scenery from various places in New York and New England into single paintings. One such work—and one that gained him international fame—was the large painting entitled *Niagara*." The author first explains Church's work and then writes "one such work" prior to mentioning *Niagara*. So the author is using the painting as an example of Church's typical style.

A | Poetic Justice in Literature

🎧 CH07_2A

Poetic justice can best be described by the phrase "you reap what you sow" as, essentially, good deeds are rewarded whereas bad deeds are punished. As a literary device, it provides readers with a sense of satisfaction that everything ultimately turns out properly since good emerges triumphant and evil is **vanquished**. Poetic justice appears throughout history in the literature in cultures around the world. There is a universal trend in which people sympathize with good characters who suffer and wish ill upon bad individuals who cause suffering. By employing poetic justice, an author can give the reading audience exactly what it wants.

Ancient Greek philosopher Aristotle did not entirely agree with its use since he believed tragedy's primary purpose was to evoke emotions of pity and fear in an audience, yet poetic justice was common in Greek poetry and drama. The classic example of it is found in the play *Oedipus Rex* by Sophocles. An oracle **prophesizes** that Oedipus will kill his father and marry his mother. Defying the gods and rebelling against his fate, Oedipus flees what he believes to be his homeland and heads for the kingdom of Thebes. During his journey, he quarrels with a stranger on a road and kills the man, and then he weds the king's widow. Unbeknownst to him, the stranger was his father and the woman his mother; they had abandoned him as a baby, and he had been raised in a foreign land. In the Greek mind, Oedipus was rightly punished for attempting to alter his destiny, which only the gods could determine.

The plays of William Shakespeare abound with examples of poetic justice as well. *Hamlet* has one instance in the guise of Hamlet's uncle, Claudius, who murders Hamlet's father, usurps the throne, and then marries Hamlet's mother. By the end of the play, Claudius receives his just reward when Hamlet kills him. In other Shakespearian plays, including *King Lear* and *Macbeth*, greed and the desire for power result in tragedy for those whose misdeeds trigger terrible events and subsequently receive their deserved fate by the end of the play.

*vanquish: to defeat, often in battle
*prophesize: to tell the future

---

1 The author discusses "*Oedipus Rex*" in paragraph 2 in order to

   Ⓐ claim that it was disliked by Aristotle because of its usage of poetic justice

   Ⓑ point out that it is the most famous example of poetic justice from ancient literature

   Ⓒ tell the story of Oedipus and explain why the Greek people enjoyed it so much

   Ⓓ describe the events that occur that result in Oedipus receiving poetic justice

2 In paragraph 3, why does the author mention "William Shakespeare"?

   Ⓐ To name him as an author who included many examples of poetic justice in his work

   Ⓑ To compare the manner in which he used poetic justice to the way Sophocles used it

   Ⓒ To describe the events in *Hamlet* and *King Lear*, two of the most famous plays he wrote

   Ⓓ To ascribe his continuing popularity to the fact that he made use of poetic justice

Vocabulary

• _____ = to feel compassion for		• _____ = destiny	
• _____ = to produce		• _____ = to take power by force	

B | The Structure of the Human Eye

Comprised of more than thirty major parts, the human eye ranks among the body's most intricately designed and complex organs. However, for simplicity's sake, this complicated body part can be reduced to its major **components**—the pupil, iris, lens, cornea, retina, and optic nerve—and their main functions. Each part plays a vital role in granting sight to a person.

The most familiar parts of the eye are the pupil and the iris because they are easily visible when looking at a person's eyes. The pupil is the central hole that allows light to enter the eye. It typically changes size to permit entry to more or less light by contracting in bright light and expanding in dim light. The iris is the colored area of the eye surrounding the pupil and is the part which controls the contracting and expanding of the pupil thanks to muscles connected to it that enable the iris to open and close.

The cornea and lens let the eye focus light in particular ways after it enters the eye. The cornea is located in front of the pupil and iris while the lens lies behind them. The cornea is a curved, transparent structure that bends light toward the pupil. On account of this function, the cornea has no blood vessels that could potentially **cloud** it, so it receives nutrients from the watery tears that cover the eye whenever a person blinks. As for the lens, it takes the light entering the pupil and focuses it toward the back of the eye in the direction of the retina. The lens has the ability to change shapes to focus on objects at various distances.

The retina is formed by sensitive photoreceptor cells called rods and cones, which form the images that a person sees through the pupil. The rods handle black and white images and are used mostly in situations involving dim light while the cones are responsible for images requiring colored light. As images form on the retina, they are instantaneously sent along the optic nerve to the brain, where they are interpreted as what a person sees.

*component: a piece or part of something larger
*cloud: to make blurry

---

1 The author discusses "the iris" in paragraph 2 in order to

   Ⓐ claim it is the most visible part of the eye

   Ⓑ explain the manner in which it works with the pupil

   Ⓒ compare its functions with those of the pupil

   Ⓓ focus on how it gives color to the eye

2 In paragraph 4, the author uses "sensitive photoreceptor cells" as an example of

   Ⓐ the parts of the eye connected to the optic nerve

   Ⓑ the most important parts of the human eye

   Ⓒ cells in the eye that can cause blindness when damaged

   Ⓓ the components of the eye that make up the retina

Vocabulary

- _____ = complexly
- _____ = to become smaller
- _____ = admitting light; clear
- _____ = instantly; at once

C | Bird Territoriality

Like most animals, birds possess the desire to control the territory in which they live. **Ornithologists** refer to this area, where the bird conducts its normal daily activities, as its home range. The size of the home range depends on the species. Large birds of prey, including eagles and hawks, may possess home ranges covering dozens of square kilometers while many seabirds defend only a small space found in the immediate vicinity of their nests. Some birds may be slack in defending their home ranges but may become quite aggressive during the breeding season and when eggs are in their nests. Birds typically defend their home ranges the most aggressively against other birds of the same species but may also react **belligerently** to transgressions made by other species of birds or other types of animals.

Birds normally defend their home ranges for three primary purposes: to protect their food sources, to compete for mates when breeding, and to defend nests full of eggs or chicks against predators. Hummingbirds, for instance, defend prime sources of nectar from other hummingbirds as well as insects that consume it. Male grouses defend the small patches of ground they use for breeding displays to attract females from other males of their species. And penguins aggressively defend the patches of seashore where they lay their eggs when predatory birds approach.

When defending territory, few birds actually make physical contact with one another but instead utilize warnings such as the songs of male birds. These songs inform other birds that a male has claimed a specific area of land. If, however, the songs are ineffective, a bird may make a prominent display of aggressive posturing, which may include spreading its wings and puffing up its body. Should this not work, the aggrieved bird may give chase, and actual fighting sometimes occurs. In most cases, fighting happens when birds are defending their nests against predators such as lizards, snakes, and small mammals intent on consuming their eggs or chicks.

*ornithologist: a person who studies birds
*belligerently: aggressively

---

1   In paragraph 1, the author uses "eagles and hawks" as examples of

   Ⓐ some of the birds that do not typically possess home ranges

   Ⓑ species of birds that protect their home ranges when other birds approach

   Ⓒ birds which frequently claim territories covering large amounts of land

   Ⓓ two types of birds that become aggressive during the breeding season

2   In paragraph 2, why does the author mention "Male grouses"?

   Ⓐ To explain the reason that they defend their home ranges from other birds

   Ⓑ To compare the manner in which they protect their territory with that of penguins

   Ⓒ To state that they do not usually attack other birds of their own species

   Ⓓ To describe the breeding displays that they use to attract female grouses

---

Vocabulary

- _____ = to be relaxed
- _____ = the act of trespassing
- _____ = noticeable
- _____ = distressed; upset

▌ Mapping

The following chart shows the structure of the passage. Fill in the blanks with the appropriate words.

Bird Territoriality

Birds ❶ _____ home ranges from others
- may have large or small home ranges
- aggressive during ❷ _____ season or when have eggs

3 reasons to defend home ranges
- to protect food ❸ _____
- to ❹ _____ for mates
- to defend nests full of eggs or chicks
- hummingbirds, grouses, and penguins all defend home ranges

Defending territory: rarely make
❺ _____ contact
- use ❻ _____ such as songs
- make prominent ❼ _____ by spreading wings and puffing up body
- may give chase and actually ❽ _____

▌ Summary

The following is a summary of the passage. Fill in the blanks with the appropriate words.

Birds want to control the ❶ _____ in which they live, so they protect their home ranges. Birds such as eagles and hawks have very large home ranges while ❷ _____ have very small ones. Birds are usually the most ❸ _____ defending their home ranges during the breeding season or when they have eggs in their nests. Birds defend their home ranges mostly to ❹ _____ food sources, to compete for ❺ _____ , and to defend nests full of eggs or chicks. Birds often do not make physical ❻ _____ when defending their territory. Instead, they use warnings such as ❼ _____ . However, they may ❽ _____ aggressively, chase other birds, and even fight if they have to.

A | Attila the Hun

CH07_3A

Attila the Hun was the leader of a tribe of Eurasian nomads that invaded the Roman Empire in the mid-fifth century. Around 370 A.D., the Huns appeared from east of the Volga River and settled in the land that is Hungary today. They warred against Rome and other tribes, and they overran parts of the Eastern Roman Empire before invading the Western Roman Empire while under Attila's command. They employed mounted archers to engage in mobile warfare, and they developed reputations for being fierce warriors from whom others fled in terror. Eventually, the Romans themselves branded Attila with the moniker "The Scourge of God."

Attila's birthdate is uncertain, but some historians place it around 406. Two of Attila's uncles ruled together as they followed a common practice of the Huns involving joint-rule by brothers. During that period, the Huns had a **cordial** relationship with the Eastern Romans, who employed the Huns as mercenaries for their wars with the barbaric tribes pushing against the empire's northern borders. In 434, both of Attila's uncles died, so Attila and his older brother Bleda became the co-rulers of the Huns.

After the initiation of some troubles with the Eastern Roman empire, the brothers negotiated a peace that brought the Huns a great amount of wealth in the form of tribute and the ransoming of Roman prisoners. But this peace only lasted until 440, when the Huns and the Eastern Roman Empire began battling each other again. **1** By 443, the Hun army had marched to the walls of Constantinople, the capital of the Eastern Roman Empire, but the soldiers could not get past the prominent defenses; however, they had defeated Roman field armies, so, once again, the Romans negotiated a peace requiring them to pay a much larger tribute of gold and higher ransoms for prisoners. **2** Satisfied, the Huns returned to their homelands. **3** Then, in 445, Bleda died, leaving Attila as the sole ruler. **4**

Attila then set out on his greatest campaign: the invasion of the Western Roman Empire. The impetus for the invasion was a marriage. In 450, Honoria, the sister of Valentinian, the emperor of the Western Roman Empire, had written to Attila and requested his assistance because she wished to avoid an arranged marriage to a Roman senator. Attila interpreted her plea as a marriage proposal, claimed Honoria as his bride and half her brother's empire as her **dowry**, and invaded the west. The Huns marched through the Germanic lands and invaded Gaul while allying with other tribes along the way.

Attila's vast host met the Romans and their Visigoth allies at the Battle of Chalons in 451. The battle ended in a stalemate but effectively terminated the Huns' invasion of Gaul. A year later, a problem with supplies resulted in a failed invasion of northern Italy, which led to a decline in the Huns' fortunes. Thwarted in his attempt to marry Honoria, Attila took a new bride from a Germanic tribe in 453. However, during his wedding night feast, Attila suffered a seizure and died. Some historians speculate that poison was the cause while others attribute his death to heavy drinking. Whatever the case, Attila's heirs fought over who would rule the Huns, which divided them and resulted in the ultimate defeat of the Huns at the hands of a confederation of Germanic tribes.

*cordial: friendly
*dowry: money or other items of value a bride gives to her husband when they are married

Vocabulary

• _____ = to name	• _____ = a very large group
• _____ = a stimulation; a motivation	• _____ = a tie

1   In paragraph 3, the author implies that the Huns

    (A) frequently violated the terms of their agreements with the Romans

    (B) carried out raids against many small towns in the Eastern Roman Empire

    (C) were occasionally defeated in full-scale battles by Roman troops

    (D) possessed no weapons able to breach the walls of Constantinople

Rhetorical Purpose Question

2   In paragraph 5, why does the author mention "the Battle of Chalons"?

    (A) To claim that the Romans considered it a great triumph

    (B) To state how the Huns managed to lose some allies

    (C) To explain the effect that it had on the Huns

    (D) To argue that it helped improve the position of the Huns

Insert Text Question

3   Look at the four squares [■] that indicate where the following sentence could be added to the passage.

How exactly this happened is unknown, but some have suggested that Attila murdered his own brother.

Where would the sentence best fit?

Prose Summary Question

4   An introductory sentence for a brief summary of the passage is provided below. Complete the summary by selecting the THREE answer choices that express the most important ideas of the passage. Some sentences do not belong because they express ideas that are not presented in the passage or are minor ideas in the passage.

Attila the Hun successfully led his men in battle first against the Eastern Roman Empire and then against the Western Roman Empire until his death.

ANSWER CHOICES

1   Attila managed to attract many allies as he marched through Gaul and then went on to fight the Romans both in Gaul and Italy.

2   The Huns had a tradition in which two brothers ruled the tribe together, so Attila began his leadership of the Huns with his brother Bleda.

3   The sister of the Roman emperor wrote to Attila to beg him for assistance since she was being forced to marry a person she did not want to.

4   Attila died on his wedding night for some reason that remains unknown to historians up to the present day.

5   While the Huns could not force their way into Constantinople, they received gold and tribute and were able to ransom Roman prisoners.

6   Attila claimed that Honoria, the emperor's sister, proposed to him, so he began his invasion of the Roman Empire in the hope of gaining more territory.

| # The First Talkies

Motion pictures were invented late in the nineteenth century, yet it was not until the 1920s that they featured sound. Prior to then, movies were silent but were usually accompanied by printed words or **subtitles** on the screen to serve as dialogue or descriptions. Many theaters additionally employed a piano player or music record player to provide live music during the showing of a film. Silent film actors were famed for their ability to show expressive emotions rather than to recite dialogue, such as what was done during staged dramatic performances. When the first sound motion pictures—talkies—came out, however, the landscape of the motion picture industry changed forever.

Since motion pictures were invented, people desired to include sound along with the moving images. Some early devices utilized sound discs, which were similar to record albums, to produce sounds for short films; however, the difficulty was getting the sounds and images to **synchronize**. This was a problematic task because both had to be started at precisely the same moment for the sounds and images to match. Due to this problem, the motion picture industry searched for a way to put sounds and images onto a single medium. By 1920, several European inventors had experienced minor success in putting sound waves on celluloid film strips, but the technology was deemed inadequate for large-scale motion pictures.

Meanwhile, in the United States, inventor Lee de Forrest strived to perfect recording sound on celluloid, and, by the mid-1920s, he had solved the problem. He started producing short sound films for public exhibition. At the same time, other inventors successfully worked on sound on disc technology, which synchronized sounds on a record disc with the images in a film. The first major motion picture to take advantage of this system was *Don Juan*, which premiered in August 1926. It used recorded music and sound effects, yet it had no recorded dialogue, so it is usually not considered the first talkie. That honor went to *The Jazz Singer*, which was released in October 1927. It was the first major motion picture with prerecorded music, effects, and, in some scenes, singing and dialogue. *The Jazz Singer* used sound on disc technology, but the standard soon became sound on celluloid, or film, due to the better synchronization between sounds and images that it provided.

At first, the big Hollywood studios resisted changing from silent movies to talkies. A major issue was that theaters, which were owned by many of the major studios then, were unequipped to project talkies, so converting them would be expensive. There were also difficulties on movie sets as directors and actors struggled with the new sound recording technology. Nevertheless the success of *The Jazz Singer* and other talkies changed their minds. In July 1928, *Lights of New York*, the first film with all its dialogue recorded and played for the audience, became a smash hit. Audiences were amazed by the new technology and clamored for more as they wanted to see their favorite stars singing and talking on the silver screen. For the next few years, studios continued to produce both silent movies and talkies. However, by the mid-1930s, most studios were only producing talkies as silent movies practically disappeared.

*subtitle: words in a film that are printed at the bottom of a screen
*synchronize: to match; to coordinate

Vocabulary

- _____ = to repeat something from memory
- _____ = to consider; to believe
- _____ = to take place for the first time; to open
- _____ = to call for

1 The word "problematic" in the passage is closest in meaning to

   Ⓐ challenging

   Ⓑ dismaying

   Ⓒ impossible

   Ⓓ questionable

2 The author discusses "*Don Juan*" in paragraph 3 in order to

   Ⓐ claim that it should be acknowledged as the first full-length talkie

   Ⓑ compare the dialogue used in it to the dialogue used in *The Jazz Singer*

   Ⓒ mention that it lacked the dialogue that made other talkies successful

   Ⓓ point out the technology that it was the first film ever to make use of

3 In paragraph 4, the author's description of talkies mentions all of the following EXCEPT:

   Ⓐ how profitable they were in comparison to the silent films made in the 1920s

   Ⓑ the title of the film that encouraged audiences to demand more talkies be made

   Ⓒ one of the reasons that there was some initial resistance to producing them

   Ⓓ why some performers had trouble during the filming process of the movies

4 An introductory sentence for a brief summary of the passage is provided below. Complete the summary by selecting the THREE answer choices that express the most important ideas of the passage. Some sentences do not belong because they express ideas that are not presented in the passage or are minor ideas in the passage.

Once the technical requirements for making talkies were perfected, studios began to film them, and they became popular with audiences.

ANSWER CHOICES

1 Lee de Forrest and other inventors learned the process of how to put sound on both celluloid and disc.

2 Many actors in silent films could not make the transition to talkies since filming them required a completely different type of acting.

3 *Lights of New York* was a talkie with all its dialogue recorded, and it was so successful that it convinced studios to create more talkies.

4 *Don Juan* and *The Jazz Singer* were two of the first films that used sound on disc technology, and the latter is considered the first talkie.

5 Many movie theaters hired piano players to play live music for their audiences while they were watching films.

6 Most studios released both talkies and silent movies in the 1930s since they were able to profit from both of them.

CH07_4A

The Unsaturated and Saturated Zones

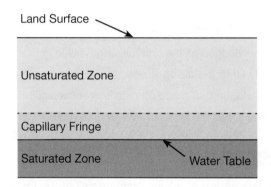

The two primary divisions in the upper layers of the Earth are called the unsaturated and saturated zones. These two terms refer to the amount of water each zone holds in addition to the ability of that water to move. Each zone has special characteristics which make the movement of water possible or not based primarily on the amount of soil and the types of rocks found in the ground. These zones have no defined limits, their depths may vary considerably, and they are both vital for agriculture and for use as sources of fresh water for animals, plants, and people.

The unsaturated zone is found in the upper level of the soil, where water may be confined in small spaces between particles of soil and rocks. Because of the greater amount of soil and rock compared to water, water has a difficult time moving through the unsaturated zone. It is more restrained and compressed than water located in the saturated zone beneath it. More solid rock, such as granite, permits water little movement while more porous rocks and soil, such as sand and clay, allow water greater movement. Nevertheless, despite the solidity of the unsaturated zone, water can still move through it by flowing both upward and downward. Rainwater seeps through it to the saturated zone while plant root systems draw water from this zone, making it a crucial component for plant survivability.

The saturated zone lies beneath the unsaturated zone, and its upper level is commonly called the water table. In the saturated zone, water flows more freely because there is less solid rock to interfere with it. The depth of the saturated zone depends upon a variety of factors, including what types of rock and soil are underneath it, the amount of rainfall the area gets, the presence of nearby rivers and lakes, and the amount of water that is consumed by humans. Layers of solid bedrock beneath the saturated zone limit its depth while the presence of more porous rocks and soil causes it to be deeper. Heavy rainfall means that more water seeps into it and that water exists in greater concentrations. Rivers and lakes, however, tend to drain water from the saturated zone as some geologists estimate that up to thirty percent of the water in some rivers comes from the saturated zone. Finally, when humans dig wells to take water from the ground, the saturated zone gets depleted of water.

The area between the unsaturated and saturated zones is a narrow region termed the capillary fringe zone. In this place, which varies in thickness from a few centimeters to more than half a meter, the water in the saturated zone is drawn up by capillary action into the unsaturated zone. The distance the water moves upward depends upon the types of rocks and soil. If the rocks and soil there have large pores, only a small amount of water will be drawn up a relatively small distance. If the rocks and soil have smaller pores, however, more water will be drawn up, and it will travel a greater distance into the unsaturated zone. The reason is that capillary action works better in objects with smaller pores due to the properties of liquid surface tension, which is required for capillary action.

The human usage of water from the saturated zone can have tremendous effects on the environment as taking too much water for both agriculture and human consumption can have disastrous results. In some places, the loss of water from the saturated zone causes the subsidence of the unsaturated zone, resulting in large depressions in the land's surface. ◼1 In other cases, overconsumption can cause the disruption of agriculture. ◼2 For example, one of the largest saturated zones in the United States, the Ogallala Aquifer in the Midwest, has 170,000 wells pumping twenty trillion cubic meters of water to the surface annually. ◼3 The result of this extraction has been an average drop in the depth of the water table of almost four meters in the past few decades, and there have been extreme drops of up to sixty meters in some regions in Kansas. ◼4 This has led to a decline in agriculture and an increase in the cost of pumping water from the saturated zone.

*Glossary

bedrock: the solid rock located beneath the soil and broken rock near the surface

capillary action: a result of surface tension that causes a liquid to be elevated or depressed depending on its properties

1   According to paragraph 1, which of the following is true about the unsaturated and saturated zones?

    (A) Their positions can sometimes be reversed depending upon how much moisture is in the soil.

    (B) Each of these two regions is capable of holding roughly the same amount of water.

    (C) How deep into the ground they descend is consistent in regions all around the planet.

    (D) Water can be extracted from both of them for usage by various types of organisms.

2   In paragraph 2, the author uses "sand and clay" as examples of

    (A) soil that lets water move freely through it on account of its physical composition

    (B) the two soil types that are found in the greatest amounts in the unsaturated zone

    (C) two kinds of soil that are not as porous as rocks such as granite are

    (D) soil found in the unsaturated zone that hinders water from moving up and down

3   Which of the sentences below best expresses the essential information in the highlighted sentence in the passage? Incorrect answer choices change the meaning in important ways or leave out essential information.

Rivers and lakes, however, tend to drain water from the saturated zone as some geologists estimate that up to thirty percent of the water in some rivers comes from the saturated zone.

    (A) Geologists believe that rivers and lakes have up to thirty percent of their water absorbed by the saturated zone.

    (B) The saturated zone is thought to account for almost thirty percent of the water in all the planet's bodies of water.

    (C) Nearly one third of all the water in rivers and lakes is thought to come from the saturated zone.

    (D) Roughly one third of all rivers and lakes get a large percentage of their water from the saturated zone.

4   The phrase "depleted of" in the passage is closest in meaning to

    (A) filled with

    (B) bypassed by

    (C) weakened by

    (D) exhausted of

5   According to paragraph 4, which of the following is NOT true about the capillary fringe zone?

   (A) Water from the saturated zone moves to the unsaturated zone by passing through it.

   (B) Its size varies because of the types of rocks and soil that are contained in it.

   (C) It is located in the place where the unsaturated zone and the saturated zone meet.

   (D) The amount of water in it is greater than that in the unsaturated and saturated zones.

6   The author discusses "the Ogallala Aquifer" in paragraph 5 in order to

   (A) argue that so much water should not be taken from certain geographical regions

   (B) explain how the saturated zone in the Midwest came to be so full of water

   (C) claim that there should be laws against overconsuming natural resources

   (D) show how pumping large amounts of water from it has affected the region

7   According to paragraph 5, what effect can the usage of water from the saturated zone by humans have on the environment?

   (A) It can cause some parts of the land to sink.

   (B) It can result in the degradation of the soil.

   (C) It can lead to the rapid erosion of the land.

   (D) It can extract valuable nutrients from the soil.

8   Which of the following can be inferred from paragraph 5 about the Midwest part of the United States?

   (A) It has very few mountains and the lowest average elevation in the entire country.

   (B) Fewer crops are being grown in the parts of it that are above the Ogallala Aquifer.

   (C) Water must be piped in from other parts of the country to serve the people living there.

   (D) A drought that occurs there could result in the Ogallala Aquifer completely drying up.

9   Look at the four squares [■] that indicate where the following sentence could be added to the passage.

This is especially true when there is a pronounced lack of rainfall in a region for a substantial amount of time.

Where would the sentence best fit?

Click on a square [■] to add the sentence to the passage.

10 Directions: Select the appropriate statements from the answer choices and match them to the division of the earth to which they relate. TWO of the answer choices will NOT be used. **This question is worth 3 points.**

Drag your answer choices to the spaces where they belong. To remove an answer choice, click on it. To review the passage, click on VIEW TEXT.

STATEMENTS

1 Can be replenished when humans pipe water into the ground
2 Contains the area that is known as the water table
3 May have some of its water taken out by the roots of plants
4 Is the area in the ground where capillary action draws water upward
5 Can negatively affect the environment if much of its water is removed
6 May be hard for water to move through this layer of the ground
7 Can have its water removed through both natural and manmade means

DIVISION OF THE EARTH

Unsaturated Zone (Select 2)

-
-

Saturated Zone (Select 3)

-
-
-

PASSAGE 2

Brown Tree Snakes on Guam

Guam is a lush tropical Pacific island in the Marianas chain that was once a habitat for numerous colorful native species of birds, small rodents, lizards, and other tiny mammals. Then, sometime during or after World War II, a new species arrived on Guam and began devastating the natural fauna on the island. This was the brown tree snake, a native of Papua New Guinea, Indonesia, the Solomon Islands, and the northern coast of Australia. The snake was first discovered on Guam in 1952 but likely arrived years earlier. With no natural predators and an abundance of food, the brown tree snake population grew dramatically, and the snake eventually began causing serious problems both for the native people and the natural wildlife on Guam.

The brown tree snake is a slightly venomous nocturnal animal averaging roughly a meter or two in length as an adult. Breeding twice a year, it produces between four and twelve offspring. It hunts by using its vision and chemical scents to detect prey. The snake stalks its prey and then lunges at and bites the animal in order to hold its victim in place. Then, the snake wraps its body around the animal to constrict it before consuming its prey. During the day, the snake shelters in shady spots such as in trees and caves. The snake's slender body allows it to wriggle into tight places, so it easily slithers through pipes, into pet cages, and even into tiny cracks in walls. This has caused residents of Guam to be highly vigilant in protecting their homes from invasion. While the snake's venom is too weak to seriously harm adult humans, it can still injure small children.

How and when the brown tree snake arrived on Guam remains a mystery. During World War II, the American military constructed enormous bases on islands in the south Pacific Ocean, including on Guam, and all of them were connected by sea and air transport routes. ◼ There is a high probability that the snake arrived on Guam as a stowaway on a cargo ship or airplane coming from its native range of habitation. ◼ This theory is given legitimacy by the fact that ship and airplane crews leaving Guam always search their vessels for the invasive species, a task which frequently results in their finding the brown tree snake hidden amongst the cargo. **3** Despite their valiant efforts, people on other islands in the Marianas, including Tinian and Saipan, have reported sighting the snake in recent years. **4**

The fauna on Guam began declining in the 1960s, which was when the brown tree snake population exploded. In its native lands, wild pigs and lizards prey upon the snake, yet no such predators exist on Guam. Wildlife experts on Guam noticed in the 1960s that the southern third of the island was suffering gigantic losses of native bird species. The area with disappearing birds slowly extended, creeping toward the northern part of Guam year by year. By 1985, virtually the entire island—except for a few small, isolated pockets in the northern part—was devoid of native bird species. To date, wildlife experts on Guam have recorded the total extinction of at least twelve bird species that were once plentiful there. Scientists were puzzled at first, and they believed that pesticides had perhaps caused the decline in bird populations, but after conducting more research, they concluded that the brown tree snake was responsible. They then started noticing the decline in lizard and small rodent populations, and people even began reporting attacks on their pets and snake invasions in their homes.

To counter the growing problem, the people of Guam developed traps that would attract the snake and then kill it. Each trap contained a dead rodent laced with the drug acetaminophen, which is capable of killing the brown tree snake. These traps were dropped from airplanes into the dense jungle foliage all over the island. In recent years, the brown tree snake population has declined, yet experts believe this has more to do with the dwindling food supply than human efforts as the snake has effectively reached a balance point between how many can exist on the island without there being any more food sources.

*Glossary

stowaway: one that hides aboard a ship or plane and uses it to go to another place

acetaminophen: a substance used in medicine that can relieve pain and reduce fevers

11 According to paragraph 1, which of the following is true about the brown tree snake?

  Ⓐ It is now considered by zoologists to be a native species of the island of Guam.

  Ⓑ People believe that it made its first appearance on Guam prior to the year 1952.

  Ⓒ It has become one of the most dangerous animals to humans living on Guam.

  Ⓓ There are few animals living on Guam that actively hunt the snake for food.

12 In stating that the snake "stalks its prey," the author means that the snake

  Ⓐ hides before attacking

  Ⓑ uses venom on its prey

  Ⓒ overpowers its victim

  Ⓓ uses speed to kill animals

13 Which of the following can be inferred from paragraph 2 about the residents of Guam?

  Ⓐ They believe the brown tree snake may be able to kill both children and adults.

  Ⓑ They are encouraging their government to eliminate the brown tree snake.

  Ⓒ They are concerned about the problems the brown tree snake poses.

  Ⓓ They feel that the brown tree snake is nothing to be overly worried about.

14 The author discusses "the American military" in paragraph 3 in order to

  Ⓐ mention that it requires its air and ship crews to search for snakes before leaving Guam

  Ⓑ claim that it is working to come up with some ways to eliminate the brown tree snake

  Ⓒ argue that it should not receive too much blame for bringing the brown tree snake to Guam

  Ⓓ suggest that it is the most likely reason the brown tree snake arrived in Guam

15 In paragraph 3, the author implies that the brown tree snake

  Ⓐ is capable of swimming long distances and can even cross the ocean

  Ⓑ has moved from Guam to other islands located in the Marianas chain

  Ⓒ is believed to be extinct on the islands of Tinian and Saipan

  Ⓓ reacts in a violent manner when air and ship crews find it hiding somewhere

16 The phrase "prey upon" in the passage is closest in meaning to

  Ⓐ poison

  Ⓑ chase

  Ⓒ avoid

  Ⓓ hunt

17 Which of the sentences below best expresses the essential information in the highlighted sentence in the passage? Incorrect answer choices change the meaning in important ways or leave out essential information.

Scientists were puzzled at first, and they believed that pesticides had perhaps caused the decline in bird populations, but after conducting more research, they concluded that the brown tree snake was responsible.

(A) People generally agreed that while pesticides killed some native birds, it was the brown tree snake that should receive the most blame.

(B) Scientists came to believe that the brown tree snake was killing the birds after first being confused and thinking that pesticides had been responsible.

(C) The brown tree snake was discovered to be killing all of the birds that pesticides had not already eliminated from the island.

(D) There were calls to conduct more research into why it was the brown tree snake, and not pesticides, that was killing local bird populations.

18 According to paragraph 5, the brown tree snake population on Guam has decreased because

(A) the snake traps that were used against it in the jungle were highly effective

(B) people began using traps with acetaminophen inside their homes and on their property

(C) the government made a concerted effort to catch and kill large numbers of snakes

(D) there is no longer enough food on the island to support so many snakes

19 Look at the four squares [■] that indicate where the following sentence could be added to the passage.

There was therefore frequent contact between the islands as ships and planes were constantly moving from one place to another.

Where would the sentence best fit?

Click on a square [■] to add the sentence to the passage.

20 **Directions:** An introductory sentence for a brief summary of the passage is provided below. Complete the summary by selecting the THREE answer choices that express the most important ideas of the passage. Some sentences do not belong because they express ideas that are not presented in the passage or are minor ideas in the passage. **This question is worth 2 points.**

> Drag your answer choices to the spaces where they belong. To remove an answer choice, click on it. To review the passage, click on VIEW TEXT.

Ever since the brown tree snake arrived in Guam, it has been killing large numbers of the local animal population.

-

-

-

ANSWER CHOICES

1. The venom of the brown tree snake can harm human children but has little to no effect on human adults.

2. The brown tree snake is an invasive species on some Pacific islands, where it has lived for a few centuries.

3. It is believed that the snake first came to Guam either on a ship or a plane operated by the American military.

4. There are almost no native birds, lizards, and small rodents still alive anywhere on Guam today because of the snake.

5. The snake slowly began eliminating birds across the island until only a few places with native birds alive remained.

6. Despite human efforts to reduce the snake population that were not very successful, it has still declined in number in recent years.

◢ Vocabulary Review

A Complete each sentence with the appropriate word from the box.

> instantaneously   impetus   evoked   aggrieved   lush

1   Building a moon colony was the _____ for increasing funding for the space program.

2   The orchestra's performance _____ strong emotions in the audience members.

3   Mr. Jackson felt _____ by the treatment he was given by his employer.

4   The _____ jungle is full of trees, flowers, and other kinds of tropical plants.

5   The two contestants _____ shouted the correct answer out loud.

B Complete each sentence with the correct answer.

1   Eric **recited** the entire fifteen-minute speech _____.

   a. from memory   b. by using a teleprompter

2   The woman's face went **slack** as she suddenly _____ and fell asleep.

   a. got stressed out   b. relaxed

3   The prisoner is **confined** in his cell and is therefore _____ it.

   a. restricted to   b. avoiding

4   Most people **sympathized** with the grieving family and felt _____ their loss.

   a. compassion for   b. anger about

5   They plan to **counter** the advances of their enemy by finding a way to _____ them.

   a. destroy   b. oppose

6   The patterns on the jewelry are **intricately** designed in a very _____ manner.

   a. complex   b. casual

7   Some **fauna** in the area is endangered as a few _____ appear to be dying off.

   a. plants   b. animals

8   The **extraction** of the tooth caused some pain for the patient during its _____.

   a. removal   b. repair

9   The two sides arrived at a **stalemate** with neither being able to _____ the other.

   a. speak truthfully to   b. gain an advantage over

10 **Deemed** a great person, Julius Caesar is _____ an important man in Roman history.

   a. suggested   b. considered

Chapter 08

Insert Text

Question Type | Insert Text

■ About the Question

Insert Text questions focus on an additional sentence that could be included in the passage. You are asked to read a new sentence and then to determine where in the passage it could be added. These questions require you to consider several factors, including grammar, logic, flow, and connecting words, when you are trying to determine the correct answer. There are 0-1 Insert Text questions for each passage. There is a special emphasis on these questions. Almost every passage now has 1 Insert Text question.

Recognizing Insert Text questions:

- Look at the four squares [■] that indicate where the following sentence could be added to the passage.

  [You will see a sentence in bold.]

  Where would the sentence best fit?

Helpful hints for answering the questions correctly:

- The squares are always placed after four consecutive sentences.

- Try reading the passage to yourself by adding the sentence after each square. That can help you determine where it should be added.

- Many times, the sentence to be added contains a connecting word or phrase. Pay attention to words or phrases such as *in addition, for instance, for example, therefore, consequently, on the other hand, finally,* and *as a result*. These connecting words and phrases can affect the flow of the passage.

Project Mohole

　　　Geologists have long been interested in acquiring samples of the Earth's mantle but have been unable to do so primarily on account of the crust's relative thickness. However, attempts at reaching the mantle have been made, with arguably the best-known venture being Project Mohole, which was initiated in 1961. The geologists involved decided to drill through the seafloor because the crust is the thinnest underneath the oceans. ■ Project Mohole was intended to have three phases. ■ The first phase involved drilling five holes, one of which descended 183 meters, in water 3,600 meters deep off the coast of Guadalupe, Mexico. ■ Phases two and three were never implemented since the project was terminated by Congress because of its cost in 1966. ■ Nevertheless, Project Mohole was not considered a failure because geologists learned a tremendous amount from the samples they extracted. They also managed successfully to utilize the technology that did the digging, which, up until that time, was purely theoretical in nature and had not been implemented in the field.

Look at the four squares [■] that indicate where the following sentence could be added to the passage.

In addition, digging on land would have guaranteed the failure of the project since the drilling equipment would not have been able to handle the extreme pressure and temperature.

Where would the sentence best fit?

| Answer Explanation |

The first square is the correct answer. The sentence before the first square reads, "The geologists involved decided to drill through the seafloor because the crust is the thinnest underneath the oceans." Note that the sentence to be added begins with the connecting phrase "In addition." This indicates that the sentence to be added is going to provide more information to the sentence preceding it. The sentence to be added mentions another reason that the drilling was attempted in water and not on land. Therefore, it should be placed following the first square.

A | The Red-Billed Quelea

🎧 CH08_2A

Native to Africa, the red-billed quelea is arguably the most prolific bird species in the world as ornithologists estimate there may be ten billion individual birds living on the planet. In addition to its great numbers, the quelea is noted for the ability of the male to change its plumage and beak coloring during its breeding season. Normally, both males and females have a dull, grayish-brown plumage, yet when it is time to mate, the male's plumage transforms into a pinkish color while its beak becomes bright red, which enables females to distinguish males in the massive flocks the birds form.

The quelea has a fairly short breeding period of merely a few weeks each year. It occurs at the beginning of the rainy season in various parts of its African homelands. Its habitat is the grasslands of **sub-Saharan Africa**, where the males make nests from flexible green strips of grass in thorn bushes or trees. Once a male begins constructing a nest, females visit to examine it, and if one appreciates the male's efforts, she mates with him. **1** Once breeding is accomplished, both the male and female work together on the nest to complete it by the time the eggs are laid. **2** The female quelea lays anywhere from one to five eggs, which are green or blue in color and require ten to twelve days to hatch. **3** Upon hatching, both parents feed the chicks, but after merely two or three weeks, the chicks become independent so can forage and feed themselves. **4**

Before the newborn chicks leave the nest, the main sustenance they receive is insects that their parents capture. **5** After departing the nest, however, the quelea's primary food source is seeds from crops such as wheat, millet, rice, and sorghum. **6** Obtaining any of these requires that the quelea visit inhabited areas where humans are practicing agriculture. **7** Millions of these small birds frequently unite to form gigantic flocks which move across the African **savannah** in dense, cloudlike formations and cause serious disruptions to agriculture when they swoop down on farmers' fields. **8** Despite intensive efforts to eradicate them by killing millions of birds annually, the quelea's numbers never appear to be significantly reduced.

*sub-Saharan Africa: the part of Africa that is located south of the Sahara Desert
*savannah: a plain that has scattered grass and few trees and that receives seasonal rainfall

1 Look at the four squares [**1** – **4**] that indicate where the following sentence could be added to the passage.

This is an incubation period much swifter than that of most other bird species, which typically require at least twice that amount of time.

Where would the sentence best fit?

2 Look at the four squares [**5** – **8**] that indicate where the following sentence could be added to the passage.

Because of the damage they subsequently cause, African farmers consider them a major pest.

Where would the sentence best fit?

Vocabulary

- _____ = a scientist who studies birds
- _____ = the pointed end of a bird's mouth; a bird's bill
- _____ = to search for food
- _____ = food; nutrition

B | Metamorphic Rocks

The three main types of rocks are igneous, sedimentary, and metamorphic. Of those, metamorphic rocks, which include schist, slate, marble, gneiss, quartzite, and lapis lazuli, are the most complex because they are formed when other rocks are subjected to intense heat and pressure. They all begin as igneous, sedimentary, or other metamorphic rocks, but then their mineral composition is transformed by intense heat and pressure deep underground. On some occasions, they may be changed through tectonic forces when the plates comprising the Earth's crust collide.

There are both foliated and non-foliated metamorphic rocks. The term foliate refers to the visible colored bands present in some metamorphic rocks, so foliated rocks have these bands while non-foliated ones do not. **1** The creation of these two types of metamorphic rocks is the result of the different ways that pressure acts on the original rocks before they are transformed. **2** Foliated metamorphic rocks have pressure applied on a single plane, or direction, while non-foliated metamorphic rocks have pressure from several directions at once or from several directions at differing times. **3** The main result of this pressure is the **recrystallization** of the minerals in the original rocks. **4**

Slate is a common type of foliated metamorphic rock that is produced from the sedimentary rock shale. Heat and pressure transform the clay minerals in shale to become mica, which is found in slate. Schist is another example of a foliated metamorphic rock. **5** It contains high levels of mica, which allows it to be broken up into thinner pieces. **6** Two common non-foliated metamorphic rocks are marble and quartzite. **7** Marble is formed from limestone, a type of sedimentary rock. **8** It is regularly found in places where two of the Earth's plates are colliding and applying great pressure against each other. Under this pressure, the calcite crystals in limestone transform from being small, loose crystals to being larger, more **interlocking** crystals. Quartzite forms in much the same way as it changes from sandstone, another sedimentary rock. The loose sandstone crystals undergo an interlocking, binding transformation to create quartzite, a tougher and more durable rock.

*recrystallization: the act of becoming crystal again
*interlocking: interlaced; connected with one another

1   Look at the four squares [**1** – **4**] that indicate where the following sentence could be added to the passage.

The bands can be easy to see in rocks such as gneiss but are not as apparent in slate and phyllite.

Where would the sentence best fit?

2   Look at the four squares [**5** – **8**] that indicate where the following sentence could be added to the passage.

The absence of bands makes it appealing to look at, so sculptors commonly utilize this material to make statues with.

Where would the sentence best fit?

Vocabulary

- _____ = to change
- _____ = to run into something
- _____ = a long strip
- _____ = strong; long-lasting

C | John B. Watson and Behaviorism

American psychologist John B. Watson was the founder of the school of psychology known as behaviorism. Watson first publicized his theories while lecturing at Columbia University in 1913, and he later refined his notions in articles and books after conducting experiments relating to animal behavior and the raising of children. His ideas on behaviorism established an entirely new branch of psychology that was later explored and enhanced by various **luminaries** in the field, including B.F. Skinner.

The main tenet of behaviorism is that only observable behavior can show a person's true mind. Until Watson's 1913 lecture, there had been tremendous disagreement in the field regarding how exactly to investigate the human mind. **1** Watson proposed discarding the old **methodologies** of being introspective and trying to understand consciousness and instead suggested that people concentrate on behavior that could be observed and predicted. **2** Watson came to his conclusions by way of his experiments with animal behavior, particularly white rats, which was the focus of his PhD dissertation. **3** Watson was also a proponent of the theories of Russian Ivan Pavlov, who did conditioning experiments with dogs that established the basis for theories on classical conditioning. **4**

Watson believed that all people began life with three basic emotions—fear, rage, and love—and that these emotions drove their reactions to external stimulations. **5** To prove his point, he conducted the Little Albert experiment, during which he subjected an eleven-month-old child named Albert to external stimulations. **6** Watson showed a white rat to Albert, who initially showed no fear. **7** Then, he began loudly clanging an iron bar when he showed Albert the rat. **8** This caused Albert to begin showing fear of the rat. Even when Watson presented the rat without clanging the bar, Albert cried at the sight of the animal. In Watson's thinking, he had conditioned the child to fear something he had originally not been scared of, and this was proof that people could be conditioned to behave in certain ways. He even stated that he could take a dozen infants and condition them to become any profession he chose later in their adult lives.

*luminary: a top name; a celebrity
*methodology: a way of doing something; a procedure

1 Look at the four squares [**1** – **4**] that indicate where the following sentence could be added to the passage.

This work of his was published a decade prior to the seminal lecture he gave that brought him so much fame.

Where would the sentence best fit?

2 Look at the four squares [**5** – **8**] that indicate where the following sentence could be added to the passage.

This would prove to be an extremely controversial experiment for which Watson was heavily criticized by others in his profession.

Where would the sentence best fit?

Vocabulary

- _____ = to improve
- _____ = a supporter
- _____ = to expose a person to something
- _____ = to put into a certain state

172

◢ Mapping

The following chart shows the structure of the passage. Fill in the blanks with the appropriate words.

```
                    John B. Watson and Behaviorism

              Founded the ❶ _____ of behaviorism
              - published his theories in ❷ _____
              - refined them through ❸ _____ on
                animals and children


  Thought only ❹ _____ behavior      Believed people started with three basic
  can show person's mind                      emotions: fear, ❻ _____, and
  - focused on observable and                 love
    ❺ _____ human behavior            - conducted Little ❼ _____
  - did experiments on white rats               experiment
                                               - caused baby to fear white rat
                                               - proved people could be
                                                 ❽ _____ to behave in certain
                                                 ways
```

◢ Summary

The following is a summary of the passage. Fill in the blanks with the appropriate words.

John B. Watson founded the psychological school of ❶ _____. He first publicized

his theories in 1913 and later ❷ _____ them over time. He believed that only

observable behavior can show a person's true ❸ _____. He wanted people to

focus on ❹ _____ that could be observed and predicted. He did work on white

rats and believed in the theories of ❺ _____. Watson thought people started

life with the emotions fear, rage, and ❻ _____. He became famous for the Little

Albert ❼ _____ he ran in which he conditioned a baby to be

❽ _____ of a rat.

A | The Roman Conquest of Italy

CH08_3A

The Roman Empire had its origins in a small village alongside the Tiber River. Over time, the village increased in size to become a town and, later, a city, whereupon it was ruled by a series of kings—seven according to tradition—for more than two centuries. In 509 B.C., however, the people of Rome deposed the last king and established a republican system of government. During the next 250 years, the Romans proceeded to dominate Latium, the land around their city, and then conquered the entire Italian peninsula.

In the early years after the foundation of the Roman Republic, the Romans were confined to a narrow strip of land around their city and the Tiber River. During the next couple of centuries, the city expanded slowly because of the numerous warlike tribes and city-states located nearby. Rome's primary enemy, which it ultimately conquered in 396 B.C., was the city-state of Veii; nevertheless, Rome's victory did not ensure peace because, in 390 B.C., the Gauls, another barbarian tribe, invaded Italy and conquered numerous city-states, including Rome, which they **sacked**. Fortunately for the Romans, the Gauls were concerned with looting rather than conquest, so they departed afterward. Sensing Rome's weakness following that defeat, a group of Latium city-states called the Latin League rose in rebellion, but the Romans crushed them.

Next, Rome dealt with the Samnites, a tribe of warriors in southern Italy who threatened the city-state of Campania, which beseeched Rome for help. The Samnites heartily resisted Roman attacks, so the warfare between them and Rome lasted decades and required three long wars before the Romans emerged triumphant in 290 B.C. The Roman army attempted to employ the Greek **phalanx** as its tactical formation, yet it was ill-suited for fighting the Samnites in their hilly homeland. The Romans consequently adopted the looser Samnite formation of smaller tactical units equipped with javelins and short swords, which enabled them to defeat the Samnites, and then those weapons were used by the Roman legions for centuries.

By that time, most of the Italian peninsula, except for the extreme southern part, where Greek city-states had established many colonies, was under Roman control. Fearing Rome, the city-states there banded together and, in 280 B.C., hired an army led by King Pyrrhus of Epirus. **1** Pyrrhus defeated the Romans several times, but his own armies suffered great losses as well. **2** In spite of these setbacks, Rome refused to surrender, and a Roman army finally defeated Pyrrhus's army in 272 B.C. **3** This was the last major enemy Rome faced in Italy, so almost the entire peninsula was possessed by Rome by 265 B.C. **4**

After vanquishing their foes, the Romans needed to retain power over them, and they accomplished this by being benevolent masters rather than cruel conquerors. They gave most defeated people the opportunity to become Roman citizens, thereby entitling them to numerous benefits. Additionally, Roman soldiers were granted land in occupied regions, so they remained in those places as farmers. This policy had two advantages. First, the Romans served as a force of experienced soldiers who could swiftly form military units to quell any rebellions that started. It also infused the conquered people with individuals loyal to Rome who, over the course of time, married local women and had families that themselves became loyal to Rome.

*sack: to pillage or loot after taking control of a place
*phalanx: a group of heavily armed infantry that fight closely together while joining their shields

Vocabulary

- _____ = to control; to rule over
- _____ = a defeat
- _____ = kind
- _____ = to defeat; to put down

1   In paragraph 2, all of the following questions are answered EXCEPT:

      (A) What was the relationship between Rome and the city-state Veii?

      (B) What caused some city-states to unite and to establish the Latin League?

      (C) What part of the Italian peninsula did Rome control by 396 B.C.?

      (D) What happened to Rome after the Italian peninsula was invaded by barbarians?

Vocabulary Question

2   The word "beseeched" in the passage is closest in meaning to

      (A) demanded

      (B) approached

      (C) begged

      (D) considered

Insert Text Question

3   Look at the four squares [■] that indicate where the following sentence could be added to the passage.

His actions gave rise to the term Pyrrhic victory, which refers to a battle that is won but in which the victor suffers heavy losses.

Where would the sentence best fit?

Prose Summary Question

4   An introductory sentence for a brief summary of the passage is provided below. Complete the summary by selecting the THREE answer choices that express the most important ideas of the passage. Some sentences do not belong because they express ideas that are not presented in the passage or are minor ideas in the passage.

Once the Roman Republic was established, the Romans slowly but steadily began to expand their territory until, around 250 years later, they controlled the entire Italian peninsula.

ANSWER CHOICES

1. Many Roman soldiers were stationed in conquered lands so that they could be organized quickly in case there were rebellions.

2. Although they suffered several defeats at the hands of King Pyrrhus, the Romans persisted and defeated him, so they gained control of the rest of the Italian peninsula.

3. When the Roman Republic began expanding at a slow rate in its early years, many Romans demanded a return to the rule of kings.

4. The Romans used the tactics employed by the Samnites to defeat them in battle and to gain control of part of southern Italy.

5. The Latin League posed a serious challenge to the power of Rome, so the Romans sought allies in order to fight it.

6. City-states such as the Veii were warlike in nature and close to Rome, which prevented the city from expanding very quickly.

CH08_3B

Plants reproduce when **pollen** from the anther—the male part—spreads to the stigma—the female part—and fertilizes the plant, enabling it to produce the seeds necessary for reproduction. Because the anther and stigma are far apart in most plants—and not even present in the same plant at times—the pollen must spread from the anther to the stigma by external means. Pollination occurs in most plants by one of two methods: The pollen can be spread by the actions of insects and birds, or it can be carried by the wind. Insects and birds spread pollen in most flowering plants while the wind carries pollen in a few flowering plants and most nonflowering plants, including members of the **conifer** family, grasses, and cereal crops such as wheat.

The majority of plants pollinated by the wind have evolved without colorful, scented flowers that contain the nectar which attracts insects and birds, so they cannot rely on them for pollination. In addition, while many nonflowering plants have both male and female parts, nature has made them unable to inbreed, so a plant cannot use the pollen from its anther to pollinate its own stigma. ■1 Therefore, these plants must spread their pollen to the female parts of other plants, which could be growing nearby or might be hundreds of meters away. ■2 These plants must therefore rely on the wind to carry their pollen to other plants of the same species. ■3 Some nonflowering plants have developed so that they contain only male parts or only female parts, making it impossible for them to inbreed, so they must be pollinated by another plant. ■4

Nonflowering plants have, however, evolved in a manner that has bestowed them with several characteristics making it simpler for them to be pollinated by the wind. For example, pollen is produced in the anther in far greater quantities in nonflowering plants than in flowering plants to increase the success rate of pollination. The majority of this pollen never arrives at its intended destination, but some does, so having more pollen increases the chances of successful interaction with the stigma of another plant. Furthermore, the anther in nonflowering plants is very loosely attached and dangles more outside the plant compared to the anther in flowering plants. This allows the wind to strike it and then carry pollen away. Plants that receive pollen also possess enhanced abilities to catch it. The stigma hangs outside these plants so that it can lie in the path of windblown pollen, and many nonflowering plants have a feathery or netlike stigma, permitting them more easily to capture pollen.

Unlike flowering plants, which have sticky pollen that can cling to insects and birds, nonflowering plants have loose pollen that the wind can pick up and distribute. The pollen is also light, ensuring that it can travel great distances. The pollen is small and not particularly nutritious, so it is unattractive to insects and birds. These characteristics all combine to increase the likelihood that, of the entire mass of pollen released by a plant's anther, at least some will survive the journey to the stigma of another plant and permit reproduction to take place.

*pollen: the fertilizing part of a plant, which often appears in powder form
*conifer: a type of tree that produces pollen in cones and includes evergreen trees

Vocabulary

• _____ = having a strong smell, usually pleasant in nature
• _____ = to give; to grant

• _____ = improved
• _____ = to hold on to; to stick to

1   According to paragraph 2, which of the following is true about nonflowering plants?

(A) They produce nectar in their stems and branches in order to attract birds and insects.

(B) They typically contain both male and female parts located close to one another.

(C) They rely upon both the wind and the actions of animals in order to pollinate other plants.

(D) They can only reproduce by spreading their pollen to other plants of the same species.

Reference Question

2   The word "it" in the passage refers to

(A) the stigma

(B) the plant

(C) the anther

(D) the wind

Insert Text Question

3   Look at the four squares [■] that indicate where the following sentence could be added to the passage.

The gingko tree, which is native to China but is cultivated all around the world, is one of these plants as there are both male trees and female trees of that species.

Where would the sentence best fit?

Fill in a Table Question

4   Select the appropriate statements from the answer choices and match them to the type of plant to which they relate. TWO of the answer choices will NOT be used.

Flowering Plant (Select 2)	Nonflowering Plant (Select 3)
•	•
•	•
	•

STATEMENTS

1   Is only capable of reproducing during certain months of the year

2   May have its pollen consumed by animals because of its particular taste

3   Is mostly pollinated thanks to the actions of various animals

4   May have its anther or stigma dangling outside the plant

5   Has pollen that is sticky so does not need to be transported by the wind

6   Produces large amounts of pollen to increase the chances of fertilization happening

7   May have only male or female parts

CH08_4A

Woodrow Wilson's Economic Policies

Woodrow Wilson

Woodrow Wilson served as the president of the United States from 1913 to 1921. While he is mostly remembered for leading the country into World War I and for his peace efforts following the war, he was also heavily involved in domestic affairs, particularly those regarding the American economy. During his presidency, the Federal Reserve banking system was established, <u>antitrust laws</u> were strengthened, tariff reforms were instituted, and the first broad income tax became law. On top of those measures, the eight-hour workday was established, and financial assistance was provided to farmers during Wilson's two terms in office.

One of Wilson's first moves toward economic reform was the Revenue Act of 1913, which had two objectives: the lowering of tariffs and the implementing of a broad income tax on all income sources. The income tax was intended to maintain government revenues that would be lost through the lowering of tariffs. The income tax had become law once the Sixteenth Amendment was ratified in February 1913, one month prior to Wilson taking office; however, the details of the new law had not been worked out yet. Wilson's government proposed a one-percent tax on all annual incomes exceeding $4,000 for couples and $3,000 for singles. ■ The new law also allowed higher taxes to be levied on those earning greater incomes. ■ And it lowered tariffs on foreign goods, which was done in the hope of increasing international trade. ■ The immediate effectiveness of this act on the American economy is difficult to calculate though because the outbreak of World War I in 1914 tremendously upset global trade. ■

Wilson additionally set his sights on reforming the American banking system. Most American banks were <u>private enterprises</u>, and numerous banks had failed, leaving their depositors impoverished when their life savings were lost. Wilson was determined to create a federal banking system which would have a wide range of responsibilities, among them protecting people's savings and serving as the government's bank. This new bank would additionally be the only legal authority permitted to issue American money. After considerable debate, the Federal Reserve Act was passed in December 1913.

Antitrust reform and consumer protection were Wilson's next targets. During his time, many of the largest American companies dominated certain aspects of the economy, including oil, steel, and shopping. Antitrust laws were designed to halt these practices, which they accomplished with the breakup of Standard Oil into several small companies in 1911. The court system handled antitrust cases, but Wilson believed they should be the responsibility of a regulatory body that would oversee all such business practices. Therefore, the Federal Trade Commission was established in 1914 to regulate competition between companies and to protect consumers from unfair business practices.

Wilson continued to focus on reforming the American economy when he tackled two more major issues, agriculture and labor laws. Farming was the livelihood of a great majority of Americans in the 1910s, but farms were notoriously susceptible to instability, suffering both good and bad years. Most farmers were cash poor and unable to improve their farms or equipment. Banks frequently refused to lend money to farmers, or, if they did, the loans were short term and had interest rates that were ruinous in nature. The Federal Farm Loan Act of 1916 was passed to enable farmers to borrow money by using their land as collateral. Under this act, farmers could borrow up to $10,000 at low interest rates and had up to forty years to repay the funds. The main results were the revitalization of the small American farmer and the protection of these farmers from absorption by big agricultural companies.

Labor reform during Wilson's administration came about due to a threatened major railway strike in 1916 that was averted only when workers were promised an eight-hour workday, which would reduce the work they did on a daily basis. This established a precedent that later led to most workers getting eight-hour workdays. Wilson attempted to reform child labor laws through the Keating-Owen Labor Act of 1916, but the Supreme Court ruled it was unconstitutional and struck it down in 1918. Despite this setback, Wilson's economic reforms as a whole had a significant and long-lasting impact on the American economy.

*Glossary

antitrust law: a law that is aimed at breaking up monopolies or preventing their creation

private enterprise: a business

1   In paragraph 1, the author's description of Woodrow Wilson mentions all of the following EXCEPT:

- (A) the reasons he is primarily recalled by people thinking back on his time as president
- (B) the manner in which the American economy changed on account of his reforms
- (C) some of the economic reforms that he was responsible for during his presidency
- (D) the years during which he served as the president of the United States

2   The author discusses "the Revenue Act of 1913" in paragraph 2 in order to

- (A) explain how the American people felt about the reforms it instituted
- (B) argue that it was actually less influential than the Sixteenth Amendment was
- (C) describe the manner in which it affected the economy after it was passed
- (D) discuss its effects on the global economy prior to the outbreak of World War I

3   Select the TWO answer choices from paragraph 2 that identify the results of the Revenue Act of 1913. *To receive credit, you must select TWO answers.*

- (A) The Sixteenth Amendment was ratified and became law.
- (B) Taxes on foreign imports to the United States were lowered.
- (C) Global trade was affected in a negative manner.
- (D) Some people were taxed on the income that they earned.

4   According to paragraph 3, Woodrow Wilson wanted to institute a federal banking system because

- (A) it would prevent the savings of individuals from being lost in case of bank failures
- (B) the government would be able to offer better interest rates than private banks would
- (C) there was a severe problem with banks printing their own currency and distributing it
- (D) too many people had lost faith in banking since so many financial institutions had gone bankrupt

5   In paragraph 4, the author's description of the Federal Trade Commission mentions which of the following?

- (A) The role that Standard Oil played in getting it established
- (B) How it was intended to assist both companies and private individuals
- (C) The year in which its formation was first proposed by Woodrow Wilson
- (D) The first antitrust case that it became involved in after its founding

6 In stating that the loans had interest rates that were "ruinous in nature," the author means that the interest rates

A required immediate payment

B were against the law

C were excessively high

D took personal situations into account

7 According to paragraph 5, which of the following is NOT true about the Federal Farm Loan Act of 1916?

A It kept farmers from having their land taken from them and from being absorbed by larger entities.

B It permitted farmers to spend several decades paying back any of the loans they took out.

C It was passed with the intention of making cash-poor farmers better able to borrow money.

D It allowed farmers to use their land as collateral when taking out short-term loans.

8 In paragraph 6, the author uses "the Keating-Owen Labor Act of 1916" as an example of

A a time when one of Woodrow Wilson's reforms was rejected

B a law passed during the last year of Woodrow Wilson's time as president

C one of the reforms that Woodrow Wilson considered very important

D a bill that became law due to the threat of a strike by workers

9 Look at the four squares [■] that indicate where the following sentence could be added to the passage.

Thus those individuals who made greater amounts of money than others could be forced to turn over a larger percentage of their income to the government.

Where would the sentence best fit?

Click on a square [■] to add the sentence to the passage.

10 **Directions:** An introductory sentence for a brief summary of the passage is provided below. Complete the summary by selecting the THREE answer choices that express the most important ideas of the passage. Some sentences do not belong because they express ideas that are not presented in the passage or are minor ideas in the passage. **This question is worth 2 points.**

Drag your answer choices to the spaces where they belong. To remove an answer choice, click on it. To review the passage, click on VIEW TEXT.

During his two-term presidency, Woodrow Wilson focused on reforming the American economy by passing a number of new laws.

-
-
-

ANSWER CHOICES

1   The Federal Farm Loan Act of 1916 helped small farmers gain access to bank loans and led to the improvement of the American farming industry.

2   Even though Woodrow Wilson is known more for his role in World War I, many people still remember his intense involvement in the American economy.

3   Woodrow Wilson and his supporters worked hard to get the Sixteenth Amendment ratified so that Americans would have to pay income tax.

4   The Revenue Act of 1913 had a powerful effect on the American economy even after World War I started one year later.

5   After the Federal Trade Commission was passed, it was used to protect businesses and consumers from unfair business practices.

6   Woodrow Wilson got the Federal Reserve Act passed in order to help keep the savings of Americans from being lost to bank failures.

Animal Social Play

   Researchers on animal behavior have long noted that animals engage in activities which can be described as play. While these researchers have developed various theories as to why animals participate in play, they have difficulty actually proving their notions with field observations. In addition, engaging in play appears to counter the belief that animals always do activities which benefit their survival while avoiding those that lessen their chances of living. Darwinian theory states that over time, species with greater survival chances will outcompete other species, yet the fact that animals play is contrary to this notion.

   First, it is vital to consider the definition of animal play. Researchers state that animal play consists of activities that are voluntary and associated with enjoyment yet have no bearing on an animal's survival. In addition, play is a creative activity during which animals try to test their limits in a controlled environment. Examples include elephants sliding down muddy slopes, meerkats engaging in mass-colony melees, and cats and dogs mock fighting with their siblings while never actually clawing or biting. ■ While play is more common among younger animals, it should be noted that it continues into adulthood for many species. ■ Researchers believe the majority of animals that engage in social play are mammals due to their more complex brains and nervous systems in comparison to other types of animals. ■ Some examples of play have been seen exhibited by birds and a few reptiles, but it is mostly limited to animals in captivity and is also a very simplified form. ■

   The theories that exist on what motivates animals to play are various. One notion is that play starts as an aspect of parental bonding and that parents begin playing with their offspring to prepare them to engage with other young animals. Primate researchers have noted that chimpanzee mothers caress, tickle, and make vocalizations to their offspring as soon as they are born. Then, they permit their offspring six months of age or older to engage in play with other young chimpanzees. Touching their offspring and making vocalizations may also be part of an effort by the parents to help their young develop cognitive skills. Play may be a way for young animals to test the limits of their bodies and strength and to see how high they can jump or how fast they can run as well. Some young chimps play with objects such as branches and rocks in what may be an effort to prepare to use them as tools to find food in the future, too.

Interacting with other animals is the most common form of animal play. Researchers long believed that such play in groups allowed animals to learn the ways of adulthood by engaging in certain activities in a safe environment. Play with other animals allows young ones to learn how to fit into their social group and may teach them skills and abilities they require to survive in adulthood. Play may additionally teach predators how to hunt for food. Chasing other animals helps increase speed and endurance, play fighting prepares animals for combat with others, and play biting prepares animals to make kills. Play may teach prey animals to survive by learning to run fast and to hide, too.

Despite all these theories, research proving them valid is lacking. This is partially due to the fact that it is difficult to measure play. Comparing the amount of time an animal plays and measuring the vigor the animal does it with is not a simple task. One researcher noted that she had to spend an inordinate amount of time in the hot African scrublands while observing meerkats just to catch them when they spontaneously began playing. Other researchers tried following groups of animals over long periods of time to discover if those that had engaged in extensive play were better at socializing and surviving. They concluded that playing more made no difference. In the end, it may be possible that animals engage in play for the same reason humans do so: because it is fun. While realizing that it could cause injury or even death, both people and animals engage in some activities purely for enjoyment.

*Glossary

melee: a fight that takes place between several individuals

scrubland: land where most of the vegetation is small trees and shrubs

11 According to paragraph 1, animal play appears to go against Darwinian theory because

- (A) it claims that animals need to play in order to learn various skills
- (B) it proposes the notion that animals should rest more than they should play
- (C) it states that animals should only do activities that help them survive
- (D) it argues that few animals are intelligent enough to play with others

12 The word "mock" in the passage is closest in meaning to

- (A) serious
- (B) pretend
- (C) dangerous
- (D) extended

13 According to paragraph 2, mammals are the most common animals to engage in play because

- (A) they are normally raised to adulthood by their parents
- (B) their brains and nervous systems are highly developed
- (C) they spend many years as youths before they reach maturity
- (D) their parents encourage them to play with their siblings

14 Paragraph 3 supports which of the following ideas about animal play?

- (A) Play is primarily a way to teach young animals how to find the food they need to survive.
- (B) Primates tend to play very roughly, so primate youths sometimes get hurt while playing.
- (C) Once young animals are old enough to move on their own, their parents encourage them to play.
- (D) Parents may start playing with their offspring to get them ready to interact with other animals.

15 In paragraph 3, the author's description of young chimpanzees mentions all of the following EXCEPT:

- (A) what kinds of games they play with other young chimpanzees
- (B) why their parents sometimes help them play
- (C) how playing helps prepare them for life in the future
- (D) which skills some of them may learn when they play

16 Which of the sentences below best expresses the essential information in the highlighted sentence in the passage? Incorrect answer choices change the meaning in important ways or leave out essential information.

Researchers long believed that such play in groups allowed animals to learn the ways of adulthood by engaging in certain activities in a safe environment.

- (A) It is normally safe for animals to play with one another unless there are some adults playing with young animals.
- (B) When animals play together with one another, they are trying to act like they would when they are adults.
- (C) Scientists used to believe some animals played in groups to learn how to be adults in a safe manner.
- (D) Most researchers have noticed that both young and old animals tend to form groups in which they play with others.

17 The word "inordinate" in the passage is closest in meaning to

- (A) unimpressive
- (B) arrogant
- (C) irresponsible
- (D) excessive

18 Which of the following can be inferred from paragraph 5 about theories on animal play?

- (A) Researchers do not have enough information to prove that their ideas are correct.
- (B) Most scientists believe that they can verify their theories by communicating with animals.
- (C) The majority of them conclude that animals play because they think it is fun.
- (D) Some of them can be proved correct by conducting more experiments in laboratories.

19 Look at the four squares [■] that indicate where the following sentence could be added to the passage.

It is also not uncommon for pet owners to see their young animals playing with stuffed animals or other types of toys.

Where would the sentence best fit?

Click on a square [■] to add the sentence to the passage.

20 **Directions:** An introductory sentence for a brief summary of the passage is provided below. Complete the summary by selecting the THREE answer choices that express the most important ideas of the passage. Some sentences do not belong because they express ideas that are not presented in the passage or are minor ideas in the passage. **This question is worth 2 points.**

Drag your answer choices to the spaces where they belong. To remove an answer choice, click on it. To review the passage, click on VIEW TEXT.

Researchers have observed that playing provides some benefits to animals.

-
-
-

ANSWER CHOICES

1 Scientists do not have enough information about why animals play yet.

2 Researchers know that most animals interact with others when they play.

3 Not only young animals but also adults have been observed engaging in play.

4 Some people believe animals learn important skills when they play in their youth.

5 The complex brains and nervous systems of mammals and birds let them play well.

6 Many animals appear to play to test their physical abilities in controlled environments.

Vocabulary Review

A Complete each sentence with the appropriate word from the box.

ornithologist	vigor	setback	outcompete	band

1 Kevin's lack of _____ was explained by him having worked too much the previous day.

2 Many invasive species manage to _____ native species in their own habitats.

3 As a(n) _____, Katherine enjoys spending a lot of time outdoors.

4 We suffered a _____ when our application for a grant was rejected.

5 A thin _____ of land on the island was completely unaffected by the typhoon.

B Complete each sentence with the correct answer.

1 Some mussels _____ the bottoms of ships by **clinging** to their hulls.

   a. hold on to   b. eat through

2 People _____ extremely cold weather often do not appreciate being **subjected** to it.

   a. immune to   b. exposed to

3 The **impoverished** man hoped that his children would not be _____ like him.

   a. poor   b. unhappy

4 By **refining** the ore, the miners can _____ the quality and the purity of it.

   a. register   b. improve

5 Susan **bestowed** a gift upon her friend by _____ him an antique vase.

   a. selling   b. giving

6 There was a lack of _____ in the city, so people suffered by not getting enough **sustenance**.

   a. food   b. money

7 The general **quelled** the revolt by _____ the soldiers who had started it.

   a. speaking with   b. defeating

8 Children love to **engage** in fun activities such as sports, so they _____ them willingly.

   a. participate in   b. try to win

9 Jasmine **tackled** the problem by _____ an effort to solve it at once.

   a. promoting   b. undertaking

10 These _____ of Mr. Bond were the biggest **proponents** of him running for governor.

   a. supporters   b. family members

Chapter 09

Prose Summary

◢ About the Question

Prose Summary questions focus on the main theme or idea of the passage. You must read a thesis sentence that covers the main points in the passage. Then, you must read six sentences that cover parts of the passage and choose the three sentences that describe the main theme or idea of the passage the closest. These questions always appear last, but they do not always appear. When there is a Fill in a Table question, there is not a Prose Summary question. However, Prose Summary questions are much more common than Fill in a Table questions. Almost every passage now has 1 Prose Summary question.

Recognizing Prose Summary questions:

- **Directions:** An introductory sentence for a brief summary of the passage is provided below. Complete the summary by selecting the THREE answer choices that express the most important ideas of the passage. Some sentences do not belong because they express ideas that are not presented in the passage or are minor ideas in the passage. **This question is worth 2 points.**

  [You will see an introductory sentence and six answer choices.]

Helpful hints for answering the questions correctly:

- Try to understand the main theme or idea of the passage as you are reading it.

- Only select answer choices that focus on the main theme. Ignore answer choices that focus on minor themes.

- Do not select answer choices that contain incorrect information. In addition, ignore answer choices that contain information which is correct but which is not mentioned in the passage.

The Impact of the Light Bulb on Society

In the late 1870s, Thomas Edison perfected the incandescent light bulb and therefore changed the world in a number of ways. It was actually not private homes that first got light bulbs but large buildings and workplaces instead. Thanks to the availability of artificial light, workers were able to see better, which resulted in a couple of improvements. First, people could suddenly work longer hours, so companies—especially manufacturers—became much more productive because they could add night shifts. In addition, workplaces became less dangerous environments since their lighting was improved and since the possibility of fires breaking out from candles or lamps that used oil no longer existed once they were replaced by light bulbs. As private residences became equipped with electricity later in the nineteenth and twentieth centuries, they dramatically changed people's lives as well. Light bulbs not only made people's homes safer for the same reasons that workplaces had become safer but also gave people more time in the day. Previously, people had lived their lives according to the sun. When the sun rose, so did they, and then they went to bed when the sun went down. However, with the advent of electric lighting in homes, people's days were extended, which enabled them to engage in various leisure activities at night.

Directions: An introductory sentence for a brief summary of the passage is provided below. Complete the summary by selecting the THREE answer choices that express the most important ideas of the passage. Some sentences do not belong because they express ideas that are not presented in the passage or are minor ideas in the passage. **This question is worth 2 points.**

The invention of the electric light bulb had a positive effect in both workplaces and people's homes.

ANSWER CHOICES

1 The first light bulbs were very expensive, so only businesses could purchase them in large amounts.

2 Days were extended for people once their homes were equipped with incandescent light bulbs.

3 It took a relatively long time for electricity to be connected to the majority of people's homes.

4 The incandescent light bulb was improved by Thomas Edison during the 1870s.

5 Companies were able to produce more since they could have employees work at night.

6 The dangers to people's homes and businesses decreased once they could stop using candles and gas lamps for illumination.

| **Answer Explanation** |

Choices 2, 5, and 6 are the correct answers. The passage reads, "However, with the advent of electric lighting in homes, people's days were extended, which enabled them to engage in various leisure activities at night," and, "People could suddenly work longer hours, so companies—especially manufacturers—became much more productive since they could add night shifts." It also notes, "In addition, workplaces became less dangerous environments since their lighting was improved and since the possibility of fires breaking out from candles or lamps that used oil no longer existed once they were replaced by light bulbs," and, "Light bulbs not only made people's homes safer for the same reasons that workplaces had become safer." Choices 1 and 3 are not mentioned in the passage, so they are incorrect. And choice 4 is a minor point, so it is wrong as well.

A | The Formation of Civilization

🎧 CH09_2A

The criteria for a body of people to be considered a civilization includes the construction of permanent settlements, the use of agriculture for food, the emergence of a leadership class, the worship of one or more deities, and the development of art and writing. For most of human history, these features were beyond the reach of the roving bands of <u>hunter-gatherers</u> whose primary concern was obtaining food. Some tribes may have settled in areas to hunt, fish, or gather fruits or nuts for short periods, but their shelters were not permanent, and they inevitably moved on when their food supplies became exhausted.

This changed once humans discovered how to farm. Agriculture developed at different times around the world, but sometime around 8000 B.C., people in the Middle East learned how to sow wild grains to produce crops. Since raising crops takes time, these individuals built permanent shelters and stood guard over their plants to protect them from other people and wild animals. This required a degree of organization and specialization, so people began doing various tasks. Some worked the land, others protected the settlements, and others raised animals or made crafts such as pottery and woven baskets. Hunter-gatherer groups had always had leaders; therefore, it was natural for them to emerge in these permanent settlements. Because agriculture depended upon good weather and timely rain or floodwaters, people started worshipping deities and praying for sunshine and rain.

Over time, the practice of agriculture led to population explosions and the founding of civilizations in Egypt, Mesopotamia, China, and the Indus Valley. The leaders became kings, the protectors became soldiers, the <u>shamans</u> who prayed to deities became priests in organized religions, and the majority of people became peasants who farmed the land and worked on massive construction projects in honor of their kings and gods. Craftsmen also began creating beautiful works of art, and, in some places, writing was developed to record history and to communicate with others. In these places, civilization was born.

*hunter-gatherer: a human that has no permanent home but wanders the land while hunting, fishing, and gathering wild fruits, grains, and vegetables
*shaman: a person that acts as an intermediary between the real world and the spirit world

---

An introductory sentence for a brief summary of the passage is provided below. Complete the summary by selecting the THREE answer choices that express the most important ideas of the passage. Some sentences do not belong because they express ideas that are not presented in the passage or are minor ideas in the passage.

Thousands of years ago, hunter-gatherers learned to farm the land and then developed civilizations based around the permanent settlements they established.

ANSWER CHOICES

1. There are still some groups of people in the world who can be said not to have established civilizations yet.

2. Once people started settling down in one place, individuals began taking on roles such as those of king, soldier, shaman, and peasant.

3. Some of the first civilizations were established in China, Egypt, Mesopotamia, and the Indus Valley.

4. Having organized religions, creating art, and developing writing systems are three of the characteristics of human civilizations.

5. It was necessary for people to learn how to raise crops by farming the land for them to start establishing civilizations.

6. Most of the people in the earliest civilizations were peasants who had to farm the land and serve their masters.

The Expanding Universe Theory

The Big Bang Theory, which posits that the universe began from a single point of incredibly dense matter, is the most widely accepted theory regarding the creation of the universe. According to it, roughly fourteen billion years ago, this matter exploded and expanded to form the present-day universe. This theory is based upon observations of the universe suggesting that it is not **static** but is instead continually expanding outward.

For centuries, astronomers believed that the universe was fixed and that Earth was located at its center. By the early twentieth century, the notion that Earth was at the center of the universe had been dispelled, but the static universe theory was still the prevailing model. Even Albert Einstein was a great believer in it. Then, in 1917, he had a revelation. His general theory of relativity did not precisely agree with the static universe model, yet he could not reconcile his strong belief in a static universe with his theories, so he concluded that some unknown force was preventing the universe from expanding. Simultaneously, other astronomers were discovering that Earth and the sun belonged to a large collection of stars they called a galaxy. In 1925, American astronomer Edwin Hubble proved other galaxies existed in addition to Earth's galaxy, which had been dubbed the Milky Way.

Hubble made further observations that had a profound effect on the static universe theory. In 1929, he realized that the light coming from the galaxies he was observing had a distinctive red shift on the light spectrum. This was due to the **Doppler Effect**, which makes an object moving away from an observer appear red in color. This meant that the galaxies were moving away from one another and that the universe was expanding outward. There was resistance to Hubble's theory, but Einstein accepted it, and others soon agreed with the expanding universe theory as well. From it, astronomers concluded that if the universe was expanding, then it must have been much smaller at some point. That led to the Big Bang Theory becoming the accepted model for the creation of the universe.

*static: stationary; unmoving
*Doppler Effect: a shift in the frequency of the radiation emitted by a source that is moving relative to an observer

An introductory sentence for a brief summary of the passage is provided below. Complete the summary by selecting the THREE answer choices that express the most important ideas of the passage. Some sentences do not belong because they express ideas that are not presented in the passage or are minor ideas in the passage.

Thanks to discoveries made by astronomers in the twentieth century, the expanding universe model replaced the static universe model as accepted science.

ANSWER CHOICES

1. Edwin Hubble made a discovery that showed that the galaxies in the universe were spreading apart from one another.

2. The theory of relativity showed Albert Einstein that his notion that the universe was static was incorrect.

3. Most people throughout history have believed that the universe is static and that Earth can be found at its center.

4. The belief in the expanding universe model indicated to astronomers that the universe was probably started due to the Big Bang.

5. Albert Einstein and Edwin Hubble worked together to come up with the expanding universe model.

6. The Doppler Effect is what makes an object appear red when it is moving away from another object.

C Prions and Illness

CH09_2C

Prions are proteins responsible for several infectious diseases that can affect both humans and animals. In humans, prions cause a number of neurological diseases which result in a decrease in cognitive functions and that almost always end in death. Creutzfeldt-Jacob Disease—often called mad cow disease because of its debilitating effect on **bovines**—is one such prion disease that strikes the human brain. Some others are fatal familial insomnia, kuru, and Gerstmann-Straussler-Scheinker Disease (GSS).

These diseases, while different, share some similarities, particularly their cause. Prion proteins are attached to cell surfaces and are usually not harmful; however, in each of the aforementioned diseases, a prion protein in the brain assumes a wrong shape, disrupting the cell it is attached to. This signals nearby prion proteins to form improper shapes, too. The process slowly spreads across the brain as it destroys **neurons**, builds up plaque-like matter, and makes holes in brain tissue. It is slow moving, so it may take several years before the first symptoms are recognized.

There are three main forms of prion diseases: acquired, genetic, and sporadic. People get acquired prion diseases through infections by bad prions, typically through food. Kuru, a prion disease that was once common in New Guinea, was caused by cannibals eating the brains of people with bad prions, and Creutzfeldt-Jacob Disease, which humans get from ingesting infected beef, is another example. Genetic prion diseases are passed from parents to children through genes as an error causes the genes that code prion proteins to make mutant prion proteins that, as the children age, attach to cells in the wrong shapes. Fatal familial insomnia, which is found in a few families worldwide, causes people to be unable to sleep, and eventually leads to death, is one such example. As for sporadic prion diseases, they have no definitive causes. Experts believe they manifest because of mutant genes but are not certain why people acquire the diseases. Roughly 85% of prion diseases are sporadic as their victims are not exposed to infected food and have no family history of prion diseases.

*bovine: an animal such as a cow or buffalo
*neuron: a specialized cell that is a part of the nervous system

An introductory sentence for a brief summary of the passage is provided below. Complete the summary by selecting the THREE answer choices that express the most important ideas of the passage. Some sentences do not belong because they express ideas that are not presented in the passage or are minor ideas in the passage.

Prions are proteins that can cause various types of diseases to infect the brains of their victims.

ANSWER CHOICES

1. Sporadic prion diseases are not caused by infected food or genetics, so their causes are a complete mystery.

2. Medical researchers believe that they can cure some of the best-known prion diseases, including Creutzfeldt-Jacob Disease.

3. Sporadic prion diseases are the most common, but there are also acquired and genetic prion diseases.

4. When prions take the wrong shape, they cause other prions to do the same thing, and this can spread through the brain.

5. When a person is infected by a prion disease, that individual's thinking processes are weakened, and the disease is nearly always fatal.

6. Only a few families around the world are affected by the genetic prion disease that is called fatal familial insomnia.

▮ Mapping

The following chart shows the structure of the passage. Fill in the blanks with the appropriate words.

> **Prions and Illness**

> Responsible for several ❶ _____ diseases
> - can affect humans and animals
> - decrease ❷ _____ functions and usually kill victims

> Causes: prion protein in brain assumes wrong shape
> - makes ❸ _____ prion proteins do same thing
> - spread across the brain
> - destroy ❹ _____, build up plaque-like matter, and make holes in brain tissue

> Forms of prion diseases: acquired, genetic, and sporadic
> - acquired ones often come from ❺ _____
> - genetic ones are ❻ _____ from parents to children
> - sporadic ones have no known ❼ _____

▮ Summary

The following is a summary of the passage. Fill in the blanks with the appropriate words.

Prions are ❶ _____ that can cause various diseases in both humans and animals. The diseases they cause in humans, such as Creutzfeldt-Jacobs Disease, fatal familial insomnia, kuru, and Gerstmann-Straussler-Scheinker Disease, almost always ❷ _____ the infected people. What happens is that a prion protein in the brain assumes the wrong ❸ _____, and then it causes nearby prion proteins to do the same thing. This spreads across the brain, destroys neurons, builds up plaque-like matter, and creates ❹ _____ in brain tissue. Prion diseases can be acquired, genetic, or sporadic. ❺ _____ prion diseases are typically gotten from food. ❻ _____ prion diseases are passed from parents to children, and ❼ _____ prion diseases have no known causes.

A | Humanism and Renaissance Art

CH09_3A

Humanism is the idea that human life and its natural surroundings are more important than a religious-centered view of the world. Its origins lie in ancient Greece and can be seen in Greek art, which depicts humans with **anatomically correct** proportions. The notion of humanism spread to other parts of the ancient world but then declined when the Roman Empire fell. Gradually, humanism was replaced by religion as the primary focus of life as well as art. Artwork produced in the Middle Ages, which began roughly after the fall of Rome, is almost entirely focused on religion while human aspects are secondary concerns. For instance, saints and other religious figures are depicted in medieval paintings as having **halos**, and the holy people themselves are much larger than normal humans. In addition, the mathematical precision with which the ancients showed both scale and depth in their works became a lost art.

It was not until the late fourteenth century in Florence, Italy, that a revival of humanistic thinking began. At first, it was mostly scholarly and literary in form, but over time, this rediscovered philosophy spread and had a profound influence on establishing the era known today as the Renaissance. Humanism had a particularly powerful effect on artists then. Slowly, artists moved away from religion being the focal point of their work as they began showing humans in a more realistic manner. In artwork in which religious figures were depicted, they were no longer wearing halos or looming over other humans. They were instead drawn or painted on the same scale. In Leonardo da Vinci's *The Last Supper*, for instance, Jesus and his disciples are represented naturally as real people rather than as iconic figures of Christianity.

Nature became prominent in Renaissance art, too, as humans were placed in natural scenes, and nature was represented more realistically. The rediscovering of the ancient mathematical method of drawing humans and the using of depth in artwork led the way to paintings showing people more realistically. Painters learned the art of foreshortening, which gave paintings an illusion of depth not found in prior periods. The depth and lifelike aspect of Renaissance art was further enhanced by the invention of oil paints, which enabled artists to work in more detail and to include more naturalism in their works. **1** Furthermore, artists of that time embraced the human body as a work of art. **2** They accomplished this by showing the body nude more often than clothed and by putting the beauty of the human body on full display. **3** Michelangelo's sculpture *David* is the prime example of this as it shows a nude human body in perfectly chiseled proportions. **4**

Art patrons, such as the Medici family of Florence, also encouraged the influence of humanism on art. Not satisfied only with artwork with religious themes, individuals of wealth and social standing sought artists who could provide more secular views in their art and commissioned works with humanist aspects. A final way in which humanism affected Renaissance art concerned how people perceived artists. At one time, artists were regarded as craftsmen rather than specialists, which is why hardly any artists from the Middle Ages are known today. However, people recognized the true genius of men such as Michelangelo, Leonardo, and Raphael, so they—and many others—are remembered today for the brilliance of their work.

*anatomically correct: properly representing the human body
*halo: a disc or circle of light around the head of a divine or holy individual

Vocabulary

• _____ = exactness	• _____ = carved
• _____ = to improve; to make better	• _____ = to think of; to consider

1   The word "art" in the passage is closest in meaning to

    (A) skill

    (B) replica

    (C) painting

    (D) work

Negative Factual Information Question

2   In paragraph 2, all of the following questions are answered EXCEPT:

    (A) What changes in the representation of religious figures in art did humanism cause?

    (B) How influential was *The Last Supper* on other art produced in the Renaissance?

    (C) How important was the idea of humanism to the Renaissance?

    (D) When and where did humanism start to become prominent again?

Insert Text Question

3   Look at the four squares [■] that indicate where the following sentence could be added to the passage.

The paints that had been used previously had dried more quickly and been less vivid, which made them produce works of inferior quality.

Where would the sentence best fit?

Prose Summary Question

4   An introductory sentence for a brief summary of the passage is provided below. Complete the summary by selecting the THREE answer choices that express the most important ideas of the passage. Some sentences do not belong because they express ideas that are not presented in the passage or are minor ideas in the passage.

The notion of humanism had a great impact on the artwork that was produced during the Renaissance.

ANSWER CHOICES

1   Leonardo da Vinci's *The Last Supper* is considered one of the greatest works of humanism in the Renaissance.

2   Michelangelo, Leonardo, and Raphael could not have created the artwork they made without the influence of humanistic ideas.

3   The relearning of artistic techniques from ancient times enabled Renaissance artists to portray their figures more realistically.

4   Renaissance artists influenced by humanism began portraying religious figures as normal-sized humans lacking halos.

5   The desire of rich individuals to possess artwork of a secular nature induced many artists to abandon painting pictures with religious themes.

6   The ancient Greeks were among the first people to develop various notions of humanism and to implement those ideas in their artwork.

The Wilderness Road

For the first century and a half following their founding, the American colonies—as well as the American people—were mainly confined to the **Eastern Seaboard** along the coast of the Atlantic Ocean. West of the Appalachian Mountains, the land was too rugged for easy travel, and it was also the territory of numerous Native American tribes that contested attempts at westward settlement with violence. It was not until 1775 that a route to the west was established when frontiersman Daniel Boone cut a trail from Tennessee northwest through the tail end of Virginia and then through the Cumberland Gap into Kentucky. Called the Wilderness Road, this trail, which eventually stretched more than 300 kilometers, became the principal route westward for the next fifty years.

The Wilderness Road was not entirely hacked out of the forests as it followed long-used animal and native trails. Previous expeditions into Kentucky had followed these paths, but the explorers had been harassed by bands of Cherokee and Shawnee Indians. Daniel Boone tried to lead a group of settlers into the region in 1773 but was turned back by an attack during which his oldest son was captured and later killed. Two years later, a group of wealthy investors from North Carolina who were led by Richard Henderson, a prominent judge, formed the Transylvania Company for the purpose of making a trail into Kentucky to settle in the region and to create a new colony, which they intended to name Transylvania. To lead the expedition, the investors hired Daniel Boone, who was reputed to be the man who knew the most about Kentucky and the way west. Before Boone set out, he and Henderson negotiated peace with the local tribes, but not all of their members were willing to abide by the terms of the settlement.

On March 10, 1775, Boone led a large party of men wielding axes to begin cutting a trail from Tennessee. Their starting point was the Holston River near Kingsport. The men made good progress by following existing trails when they could and by crossing rivers at shallow **fords**. They passed through a notch in the Appalachians that was known as the Cumberland Gap and went down into Kentucky. Boone and his men suffered some losses when they were attacked by hostile natives in violation of the peace settlement, but the attacks failed to deter them, and they reached the Kentucky River in April. There, Boone founded a settlement that was named Boonesborough after him. Arriving later were Henderson and a larger body of men and wagons as they had followed Boone, widened the trail, and brought along plenty of provisions for the new settlement.

The way west was now open, but the Wilderness Road was not much more than a muddy path barely wide enough for wagons to traverse in its first few years. It was also dangerous since warfare with the natives that would last for twenty years erupted. Travelers went well armed, and attacks were frequent. Nevertheless, the lure of land attracted many westward, and it is estimated that 300,000 settlers had moved into Kentucky by 1810. Henderson's attempts to form the colony of Transylvania were opposed by Virginia, which laid claim to the region. When the American Revolution broke out in 1775, Henderson appealed to the Continental Congress for statehood, but the representatives refused to recognize Transylvania as a state. Eventually, in 1792, the American government admitted Kentucky as the fifteenth state in the United States.

*Eastern Seaboard: the land in the American colonies, and later the United States, alongside the Atlantic Ocean
*ford: a place where a river, stream, or other body of water is shallow enough to be crossed by walking

Vocabulary

- _____ = rough; rocky
- _____ = to challenge; to attempt to stop
- _____ = to follow; to obey
- _____ = to hold and use a tool or weapon

1 In paragraph 1, why does the author mention "Daniel Boone"?

   Ⓐ To point out that he discovered the existence of the Cumberland Gap

   Ⓑ To blame him for the hostilities settlers faced from Native Americans

   Ⓒ To argue that he was responsible for the colonizing of the land west of the Appalachians

   Ⓓ To give him credit as the person who created the Wilderness Road

Factual Information Question

2 In paragraph 2, the author's description of Transylvania mentions which of the following?

   Ⓐ Why the founders of it decided to give the colony that particular name

   Ⓑ The general area that the colony was intended to be established in

   Ⓒ The individuals who were supposed to have executive positions in it

   Ⓓ The number of people who were hoping that they could settle in it

Reference Question

3 The word "them" in the passage refers to

   Ⓐ Boone and his men

   Ⓑ some losses

   Ⓒ hostile natives

   Ⓓ the attacks

Prose Summary Question

4 An introductory sentence for a brief summary of the passage is provided below. Complete the summary by selecting the THREE answer choices that express the most important ideas of the passage. Some sentences do not belong because they express ideas that are not presented in the passage or are minor ideas in the passage.

Daniel Boone was the person mostly responsible for the making of the Wilderness Road, which opened the interior of America to colonists.

ANSWER CHOICES

1 The application of the colony of Transylvania for American statehood was rejected by the Continental Congress.

2 In 1775, a group of men under the leadership of Daniel Boone cut a path through the Appalachian Mountains from Tennessee to Kentucky.

3 The creating of the Wilderness Road was difficult because Native Americans often attacked and even destroyed some parts of the trail.

4 The Wilderness Road was utilized by hundreds of thousands of settlers heading west in the half century after it was created.

5 Richard Henderson was the man who hired Daniel Boone to make the Wilderness Road since he wanted to found a new American state.

6 Once Daniel Boone's men made it to Kentucky, they founded Boonesborough for the larger group that was following them.

CH09_4A

Pacific Island Plant and Animal Migration

The Pacific Ocean is covered by a vast archipelago of islands spread out in long chains covering thousands of kilometers with some close to large landmasses and others much farther away. When European explorers chanced upon these islands, almost all of them were inhabited, and most had significant amounts of vegetation as well as large populations of various species of animals. Because nearly all of these islands were created by volcanic activity, such life—both plant and animal—would have been absent when they rose above the ocean's surface. The plants and animals living on them migrated from elsewhere by both air and sea. In many cases, they accomplished this on their own, but some got helping hands from humans.

Plant life on the desolate volcanic Pacific islands most likely initially arrived due to the wind. Small seeds such as thistle seeds and the spores of ferns are lightweight enough to have been carried aloft great distances whereas heavy seeds would have had more difficulty being transported that way, especially to remote, isolated islands such as Easter Island and the Galapagos Islands. The latter group has many lichens, ferns, and mosses, which all grow from light spores, yet it has few vascular plants, which have heavier seeds. As for vascular plant life, it could have arrived on other islands through two ways: by water or birds. The coconut tree is widespread throughout the Pacific islands in spite of its enormous seeds being too heavy to be carried by the wind, yet it is light enough to float, so it has moved across the ocean in that way. Birds may have also consumed various heavy seeds, flown to islands, and then defecated the seeds onto these new lands, whereupon plants began to grow. There may not have been suitable soil for seeds to grow in on volcanic islands at first, but, over time, as new plant life arrived, the soil was sufficiently broken up and filled with nutrients, thereby allowing many plant species to take root.

Similarly, animals arrived by air and sea. The birds that first arrived on the Pacific islands indisputably flew from nearby larger landmasses. Over many generations, they could have island-hopped from one place to another. Small insects—and possibly tiny invertebrates—may have been light enough to be windblown to various islands. Certainly, sea creatures such as turtles and penguins arrived by swimming to the islands. Small mammals and reptiles may have arrived by water, most likely after floating on rafts of dense vegetation which were blown out to sea during strong storms. Some species of mice have been known to do this, and lizards have also been found on rafts far from their native homelands.

Today, many Pacific islands are home to numerous plants and animals that reside throughout the rest of the world. The reason is that they were brought to the islands as a result of human migration. Over thousands of years, people spread from mainland Asia into the Pacific islands as they reached as far south as New Zealand, as far east as Easter Island, and as far north as Hawaii. During these great migrations, people took plants and animals with them. One example is the chicken, which is found virtually everywhere in the Pacific today because it was transported in large canoes from island to island. The pig was also widespread throughout the Pacific and became an important source of protein for Pacific islanders. Some animals, such as mice, were most likely stowaways on islanders' canoes. Furthermore, people took their staple plants, such as taro and yams, which they planted on the islands as they slowly made their way across the Pacific Ocean.

The Pacific natives were not the only ones who contributed to animal and plant migration as Europeans also played a role of their own. Unfortunately, European explorers brought many animals that caused disruptions on the islands. **1** Dogs, rats, snakes, and cats, for instance, hunted many species of small mammals and birds to extinction. **2** Plant eaters such as goats and sheep had negative effects on small islands' vegetation as well. **3** Nevertheless, these new animals provided some benefits. **4** Goats and sheep, for instance, became important to the settlements of Europeans on New Zealand.

*Glossary

vascular plant: a plant with vascular tissues that move nutrients through various parts of its body

invertebrate: an organism that lacks a spine

1. In paragraph 1, the author implies that many of the Pacific islands

   (A) contained plants and animals despite having active volcanoes

   (B) had civilized tribes of humans living on them

   (C) were discovered accidentally by European explorers

   (D) were larger than the islands in other oceans on the planet

2. The word "desolate" in the passage is closest in meaning to

   (A) promising

   (B) destroyed

   (C) barren

   (D) fertile

3. Which of the sentences below best expresses the essential information in the highlighted sentence in the passage? Incorrect answer choices change the meaning in important ways or leave out essential information.

   The coconut tree is widespread throughout the Pacific islands in spite of its enormous seeds being too heavy to be carried by the wind, yet it is light enough to float, so it has moved all across the ocean in that way.

   (A) Despite the fact that the seeds of the coconut tree are too heavy for the wind to move them, there are still coconut trees on islands all across the Pacific Ocean.

   (B) Explorers have found coconut trees growing on most of the islands in the Pacific Ocean because coconuts seeds have been transported by the water since they float.

   (C) While the wind cannot carry coconut seeds, the coconut is still found on most Pacific islands because its seeds are capable of floating on the ocean water.

   (D) There are coconut trees on islands throughout the Pacific Ocean because both the wind and the water have moved coconut seeds from island to island.

4. According to paragraph 2, the Galapagos Islands lack vascular plants because

   (A) the soil in the rocky islands is not conducive for them to grow in

   (B) the islands are so remote that the wind cannot transport the plants' seeds that far

   (C) the plants are not capable of living in the harsh climate of the islands

   (D) lichens, ferns, and mosses have made the ecosystem there unhospitable for vascular plants

5 The word "indisputably" in the passage is closest in meaning to

   (A) perhaps

   (B) apparently

   (C) certainly

   (D) arguably

6 According to paragraph 3, which of the following is NOT true about the animals that arrived on islands in the Pacific?

   (A) Many of the tiniest animals arrived on them due to the action of the wind.

   (B) The birds that went to the islands flew to various ones over the course of years.

   (C) Some of them arrived by staying on plant matter that floated to certain islands.

   (D) Both reptiles and mammals most likely swam across the ocean to the islands.

7 Which of the following can be inferred from paragraph 4 about the animals on Pacific islands?

   (A) Almost all of them were capable of flight or of being blown by the wind.

   (B) A few of them were unintentionally brought to some islands by humans.

   (C) A large number of them helped improve the ecosystems of the islands.

   (D) Not all of them were capable of adapting to their new environments.

8 According to paragraph 5, European explorers caused problems on some Pacific islands by

   (A) spreading diseases to natives who had no natural immunity to them

   (B) importing animals that killed large numbers of native species

   (C) engaging in violence and warfare that resulted in large numbers of dead

   (D) negatively affecting the vegetation that lived on most islands

9 Look at the four squares [■] that indicate where the following sentence could be added to the passage.

And in just four decades, the brown tree snake caused ten of Guam's twelve native bird species to go extinct.

Where would the sentence best fit?

Click on a square [■] to add the sentence to the passage.

10 Directions: An introductory sentence for a brief summary of the passage is provided below. Complete the summary by selecting the THREE answer choices that express the most important ideas of the passage. Some sentences do not belong because they express ideas that are not presented in the passage or are minor ideas in the passage. **This question is worth 2 points.**

Drag your answer choices to the spaces where they belong. To remove an answer choice, click on it. To review the passage, click on VIEW TEXT.

Both the plants and animals that live on islands in the Pacific Ocean arrived on these islands through a variety of ways.

-

-

-

ANSWER CHOICES

1. The Galapagos Islands and Easter Island were too far away from the mainland for most animals and vascular plants to find their way to them.

2. Birds and insects often went to islands by traveling in the air while larger animals traversed the ocean to get to some islands.

3. Humans are responsible for importing animals as well as plants to many of the islands that they sailed to in the past.

4. A large number of imported plants and animals have resulted in the extinction of plants and animals native to the islands.

5. Since the Pacific islands are all volcanic in nature, they had a great deal of life on them in the years immediately following their creation.

6. Plants that had lightweight seeds were the first to arrive on many islands since they were carried great distances by the wind.

Trees outside the Forest

While most of the world's trees grow in large groups called forests, many do not. These non-forest trees are classified by botanists as trees outside the forest. They exist in a variety of locations and contain a wide spectrum of species. Trees outside the forest are key assets which provide both economic and environmental benefits to the world. Some include providing food, being sources of firewood for cooking and heating, providing shade and shelter to people and animals, enhancing the aesthetic qualities of urban landscapes, and playing a role in the reduction of carbon emissions in the atmosphere.

Trees outside the forest are those which exist on what experts call other lands, meaning places not defined as forests or woodlands. Among these other lands are parks, farmland, land inside urban regions, fruit orchards, cropland such as coffee plantations that have large tree coverings, home gardens, and land with rows of trees alongside rivers, canals, and roads. Therefore, a tree outside the forest may stand as an individual one in a family's backyard, as one of many thousands in an apple orchard, or as one in a small woodlot where people in a nearby village acquire timber for cooking and heating. The volume of trees outside the forest compared to woodlands is uncertain, and an exact accounting of the difference between the two is practically impossible to determine due to the scattered nature of trees in so many various places.

One key role of trees outside the forest is in environmental protection. Trees have substantial root systems, which help prevent soil erosion by keeping the earth in place. Trees outside the forest additionally act as windbreaks and protect the land by preventing the wind from blowing topsoil away. This is especially important on farmland and flatland, where there are typically no nearby forests to serve as windbreaks. ◼1 Alongside rivers and streams, trees outside the forest halt riverbank soil erosion and provide shade and food sources that attract fish and land animals, too. ◼2 This enhances the biodiversity of such regions and stabilizes them. ◼3 Trees outside the forest play a crucial role in absorbing carbon emissions from the atmosphere as well, so they improve the quality of the air. ◼4

These trees also provide food and wood for people around the world. Fruit and nut trees are major sources of food for billions of people and amount to a small percentage of all trees outside the forest. In Morocco, for instance, fruit and nut trees, which include almond, palm, walnut, and fig trees, comprise twelve percent of such trees. As for wood, a large percentage of the world's population still depends on wood as a primary source of fuel for cooking and heating. In the state of Kerala in India, for instance, residents acquire almost ninety percent of their fuel from trees outside the forest, and about seventy percent of that amount comes from coconut trees alone. In Kenya, careful management and the establishment of tree-planting programs on farmland in the 1970s and 1980s means that Kenyan farmers currently produce around eighteen million cubic meters of wood for their own use and for sale as a means of supplementing their incomes.

The aesthetic qualities of towns and cities are additionally improved by trees outside the forest. People with homes on lots frequently plant trees to improve the beauty of their property. Such trees provide shade, a necessity in warm and hot climates that receive many hours of sunlight. Parks with trees also contribute to the quality of life in cities as they act as havens for people to find pleasure walking amongst the trees and enjoying other recreational activities. Trees in urban regions help regulate temperatures since they can reduce some of the effects of the urban heat island effect as well.

With many regions suffering from deforestation, it is vital that people be encouraged by their governments to promote the growth of trees outside the forest. The major challenges today are to find practical ways to measure such growth and to implement national policies encouraging the planting of trees. These trees will become essential as sources of food and wood in the future and will also have a positive environmental effect on the world.

*Glossary

topsoil: fertile soil near the land's surface

urban heat island effect: a phenomenon which makes cities hotter than nearby rural areas because of the actions of humans, particularly the construction of buildings and roads

11 The word "spectrum" in the passage is closest in meaning to

(A) range

(B) color

(C) appointment

(D) habitat

12 In paragraph 1, the author's description of trees outside the forest mentions all of the following EXCEPT:

(A) the most popular species of trees found in some of these places

(B) some of the benefits that they are able to provide for people

(C) the reason why they have been given their name by scientists

(D) some of the effects that they can have on local environments

13 Which of the sentences below best expresses the essential information in the highlighted sentence in the passage? Incorrect answer choices change the meaning in important ways or leave out essential information.

The volume of trees outside the forest compared to woodlands is uncertain, and an exact accounting of the difference between the two is practically impossible to determine due to the scattered nature of trees in so many various places.

(A) Once scientists calculate the number of trees outside the forest, they will be able to make better comparisons with those trees that are actually growing in forests.

(B) It is possible that the volume of trees outside the forest is equivalent to trees in woodlands, but scientists are not sure if they will ever be able to figure that out or not.

(C) Because trees outside the forest grow in so many different places, scientists often compare them to the trees that are growing in woodland areas.

(D) Nobody is sure how many trees outside the forest there are in comparison to trees in forests, and finding the answer probably cannot be done.

14 The author discusses "windbreaks" in paragraph 3 in order to

(A) describe the need to have waterways and small areas of trees near farmland

(B) discuss one of the major benefits that trees outside the forest provide land

(C) point out why many farmers like to plant tall trees in areas around their fields

(D) explain the most common way that valuable topsoil often gets eroded

15 In paragraph 4, the author implies that people in Morocco

(A) utilize many trees outside the forest for both food and other purposes

(B) have vegetarian diets thanks to the large number of fruit trees in the country

(C) acquire lots of food from some of the trees outside the forest growing there

(D) have extensive farms where they grow all kinds of fruits and nuts on trees

16 According to paragraph 4, which of the following is true about Kenyan farmers?

(A) They are taking advantage of trees planted decades ago to make money in the present day.

(B) They cut down the country's forests in the 1970s and 1980s but then replanted many trees.

(C) They make the majority of their money not from selling crops but from selling wood they cut.

(D) They use wood they acquire from trees outside the forest only for personal consumption.

17 The word "regulate" in the passage is closest in meaning to

(A) monitor

(B) report

(C) normalize

(D) rescind

18 Select the TWO answer choices from paragraph 6 that identify issues facing trees outside the forest in the present day. *To receive credit, you must select TWO answers.*

(A) Governments ought to try various ways to get people to plant more of these trees.

(B) People must think of better ways to monetize trees growing outside the forest.

(C) Experts need to be able to determine how much these types of trees are growing.

(D) Scientists should figure out how to make trees outside the forest become woodland areas.

19 Look at the four squares [■] that indicate where the following sentence could be added to the passage.

For instance, trees that bear fruits and nuts can provide plenty of sustenance for animals primarily during the summer and fall months.

Where would the sentence best fit?

Click on a square [■] to add the sentence to the passage.

20 **Directions:** An introductory sentence for a brief summary of the passage is provided below. Complete the summary by selecting the THREE answer choices that express the most important ideas of the passage. Some sentences do not belong because they express ideas that are not presented in the passage or are minor ideas in the passage. **This question is worth 2 points.**

> Drag your answer choices to the spaces where they belong. To remove an answer choice, click on it. To review the passage, click on VIEW TEXT.

Trees outside the forest grow in many places around the world and provide all kinds of advantages for people.

-
-
-

ANSWER CHOICES

1. There are not only many different species of trees growing outside the forest, but they also reach varying heights.

2. The beauty that trees outside the forest provide as well as the way they can affect the temperature benefit urban areas.

3. Trees outside the forest are able to prevent land from being eroded while providing food for animals.

4. People around the world are bestowed with food, fuel, and extra income thanks to trees outside the forest.

5. Scientists believe that the number of trees outside the forest globally may be the same as those inside forests.

6. Deforestation is becoming a big problem, so people are being encouraged to plant more trees anywhere they can.

◼ Vocabulary Review

A Complete each sentence with the appropriate word from the box.

posits	implement	abide	aesthetic	dispel

1 All citizens should _____ by the laws in order to create a peaceful society.

2 You should _____ your doubts and be confident in your abilities.

3 We must find a way to _____ the new technology being developed.

4 The engineer _____ that faster-than-light travel will be possible someday.

5 The _____ beauty of the artist's paintings impressed visitors to the gallery.

B Complete each sentence with the correct answer.

1 Susan suddenly **perceived** the correct answer when she took a moment to _____ about it.

   a. think   b. write

2 Nobody currently **inhabits** that island in the Pacific Ocean as people no longer _____ there.

   a. travel   b. live

3 This **staple** food is one of the _____ forms of sustenance for the locals.

   a. popular   b. primary

4 Zebulon Pike **dubbed** the mountain Highest Peak, hence its _____.

   a. name   b. height

5 It often seems that clouds **manifest** from nothingness when they suddenly _____ at times.

   a. move   b. form

6 The **deity** in that ancient religion is a very powerful _____.

   a. god   b. warrior

7 The **rugged** road was too _____ for any vehicles to drive on it.

   a. rocky   b. slippery

8 **Infectious** diseases are highly _____, and some can be fatal to their victims.

   a. studied   b. contagious

9 **Precision** measuring is important because if _____ is not achieved, the cut will be wrong.

   a. speed   b. exactness

10 Birds look for **havens** during storms, so they try to find _____.

   a. safe places   b. high places

Chapter **10**

Fill in a Table

◢ About the Question

Fill in a Table questions focus on the entire passage. You are asked to answer a question that breaks down the passage into two or three major theme or topics. There will be a number of sentences about these themes. You have to determine which theme each of the sentences you read refers to. These questions may ask about cause and effect, problem and solution, and compare and contrast, or they may focus on other themes. These questions always appear last, but they do not always appear. When there is a Prose Summary question, there is not a Fill in a Table question. Fill in a Table questions rarely appear anymore. Prose Summary questions are much more common than Fill in a Table questions.

Recognizing Fill in a Table questions:

- **Directions:** Select the appropriate statements from the answer choices and match them to X to which they relate. TWO of the answer choices will NOT be used. **This question is worth 3 points.**

  [You will see seven statements.]

- **Directions:** Select the appropriate statements from the answer choices and match them to X to which they relate. TWO of the answer choices will NOT be used. **This question is worth 4 points.**

  [You will see nine statements.]

Helpful hints for answering the questions correctly:

- These questions only ask about the major themes or topics in the passage.

- Passages that have two or three major themes or topics frequently have this type of question.

- Ignore any minor themes or topics in the passage. These are not covered on this type of question.

- There are always two answer choices that are incorrect. They may have irrelevant information, incorrect information, or information that is correct but which does not appear in the passage.

Glaciers

Glaciers are enormous sheets of ice that can take decades or even centuries to form and, depending on the weather, may expand or recede at various rates. Currently, they cover approximately ten percent of the Earth's surface and contain roughly four-fifths of the planet's fresh water. There are several types of glaciers, but they can all be categorized as either alpine or continental glaciers. Alpine glaciers, which include cirque, valley, piedmont, and tidewater glaciers, are those which form in mountains. Cirque glaciers are found at the heads of valleys, valley glaciers are typically quite long, and piedmont glaciers are combinations of several valley glaciers that unite to form a single extensive glacier. As for tidewater glaciers, they descend from mountains and stretch to the sea, where they frequently calve and create icebergs. Continental glaciers, meanwhile, are much larger than alpine glaciers and mostly consist of ice sheets, ice caps, and ice fields. Ice sheets cover more than 50,000 square kilometers of land and are located only in Antarctica and Greenland. Their enormous sizes and weights enable them to bend the continental crust lying beneath them. Ice caps are smaller than ice sheets and form circular structures with domes while ice fields fail to cover all the land they are above but are still quite large.

Directions: Select the appropriate statements from the answer choices and match them to the type of glacier to which they relate. TWO of the answer choices will NOT be used. **This question is worth 3 points.**

STATEMENTS

1. May go to the sea and then create icebergs
2. Is able to alter the shape of the crust due to its mass
3. Can sometimes combine with other glaciers to make one large glacier
4. Usually takes centuries until it reaches its greatest size
5. Includes the largest of the Earth's glaciers
6. Can recede quickly when the weather becomes warmer
7. Forms in areas that have mountains

TYPE OF GLACIER

Alpine (Select 3)

-
-
-

Continental (Select 2)

-
-

| Answer Explanation |

Alpine glaciers are choices 1, 3, and 7. About them, the author writes, "They descend from mountains and stretch to the sea, where they frequently calve and create icebergs," (1) "Piedmont glaciers are combinations of several valley glaciers that unite to form a single extensive glacier," (3) and, "Alpine glaciers, which include cirque, valley, piedmont, and tidewater glaciers, are those which form in mountains." (7) Continental glaciers are choices 2 and 5. Regarding them, the author points out, "Their enormous sizes and weights enable them to bend the continental crust lying beneath them," (2) and, "Continental glaciers, meanwhile, are much larger than alpine glaciers."(5)

A | The Outer and Inner Cores

🎧 CH10_2A

The Earth's center is an enormous ball of superheated nickel and iron that is called the core and has two main parts: the outer core and the inner core. While not identical, both play important roles in heating the inner Earth and in maintaining the planet's **magnetic field**. Younger than the Earth itself, the core was created 500 million years after the planet's formation. Due to radioactive decay inside the Earth and the heat left over from the space rock collisions which formed the planet, the interior became extremely hot. This created movement in the planet's interior as heavy elements such as iron and nickel melted, gravitated to the planet's center, and formed the core.

The outer core is mostly comprised of liquid iron and nickel and lies between the mantle and the inner core. It starts roughly 2,900 kilometers beneath the Earth's surface, is approximately 2,200 kilometers thick, and has temperatures anywhere between 4,500 and 5,500 degrees Celsius. As a result, the metals there are in a viscous state so are highly malleable and in constant flux. This creates waves of **convection** forces, which play a major role in creating the Earth's magnetic field. Without it, life on the planet would not be possible since it protects the Earth's ozone layer from dangerous solar winds and ionized particles by deflecting them. If these particles managed to strike the ozone layer, they would rapidly destroy it and thereby allow harmful ultraviolet radiation to reach the planet's surface.

The inner core is also mostly iron and nickel yet is solid. It is roughly 1,220 kilometers in diameter, and its temperature reaches around 5,200 degrees Celsius. Despite this high temperature, the incredible pressure placed on the inner core by the weight of the planet prevents the atoms in the metals there from transforming from solids into liquids. Like the outer core, the inner core also moves, but it rotates rather than move in convection waves. The inner core revolves eastward—the same direction as the surface—but moves at a slightly faster rate than the planet does.

*magnetic field: an electrically charged field which stretches from the interior of the Earth to an area into outer space and which protects the planet from various forces
*convection: the transfer of heat through the movement of heated liquids or gases

Select the appropriate statements from the answer choices and match them to the part of the Earth's core to which they relate. TWO of the answer choices will NOT be used.

Outer Core (Select 3)	Inner Core (Select 2)
•	•
•	•
•	

STATEMENTS

1. Has metals that mostly exist in their liquid forms
2. Is the largest of all of the layers that comprise the Earth
3. Rotates in the same direction that the entire planet is moving
4. Contains solid metals due to the extreme pressure in it
5. Is primarily responsible for the formation of the planet's magnetic field
6. Is getting larger as it expands into parts of the Earth's mantle
7. Is very hot and is around 2,200 kilometers thick

B | Carnivorous Plant Traps

 CH10_2B

Most plants obtain nourishment through photosynthesis, but some species actually consume other living things for sustenance. The majority of these plants grow in regions with rocky terrain or bogs, where the soil lacks nutrients, so they utilize a couple of methods to catch their prey, which are primarily insects and small **vertebrates**. The two hunting methods these carnivorous plants use are active traps and passive traps.

An active carnivorous plant trap involves some type of movement by the plant when capturing prey. The best-known plant with this kind of trap is the Venus flytrap, which has clamshell-like leaves that snap closed on animals landing on them. The plant has tiny glands that produce nectar on the open faces of its leaves and therefore attract animals. The leaves have small surface hairs that act as trigger mechanisms, so when an animal sucking the nectar touches them more than once in a short period of time, the trap swiftly shuts, capturing the animal. The leaf next releases enzymes that slowly digest the creature over a period of three to five days. The waterwheel plant is another carnivorous plant that catches animals in a similar manner. Its trap, however, is smaller than that of the Venus flytrap and exclusively captures underwater invertebrates.

Most carnivorous plants use passive traps, so no movement is required to capture their prey. The flypaper trap, utilized by sundews and butterworts, is one such passive trap. A leaf or tentacle-like protrusion has a sticky substance—called **mucilage**—on it, and it acts like sweet nectar to attract prey that subsequently gets stuck in the mucilage of the flypaper trap. Other passive carnivorous plants include the various species of pitcher plants, each of which has a deep hollow resembling a water pitcher. Toxic nectar attracts prey to the plant's rim, where the creatures, after consuming the nectar, become disoriented and fall into the hollow of the plant. Downward-pointing, stiff bristle-like hairs prevent them from crawling back up, and they are consequently slowly digested inside the plant.

*vertebrate: an animal that has a backbone
*mucilage: a liquid gummy secretion of a plant

Select the appropriate statements from the answer choices and match them to the carnivorous plant trap to which they relate. TWO of the answer choices will NOT be used.

Active Trap (Select 3)	Passive Trap (Select 2)
•	
•	•
•	•

STATEMENTS

1. Requires part of the trap to move to capture its prey
2. Includes the traps used by the butterwort and pitcher plant
3. May require a long period of time to catch its prey
4. Is the type of trap that is used by the waterwheel plant
5. Can involve the use of tiny hairs that trigger a trap when they move
6. Is used by the sundew and the cobra plant to catch animals
7. May involve the utilization of nectar that is poisonous to prey

How Animals Regulate Their Body Temperatures

Both land and water animals possess a variety of ways to regulate their body temperatures to avoid overheating or freezing. Nearly all mammals and birds are endotherms that can control their internal body temperatures without external means. In contrast, most reptiles, amphibians, and fish are ectotherms that require external sources to adjust their body temperatures.

Mammals and birds maintain their body temperatures mainly through the **metabolizing** of food, which generates internal heat. In extreme environments, however, they rely on other methods. The fur of most mammals acts like a warm coat, and mammals living in polar climates, such as polar bears, walruses, and seals, additionally have thick layers of blubber providing them with extra protection. Birds' feathers act in a similar manner and also keep water away from their skin, thereby preventing them from getting too cold. Numerous mammals and birds build lairs or nests that can keep them warm in frigid conditions, too. In tropical zones, many endotherms sweat to make their skin cooler and to draw heat from their bodies. Most fur-bearing mammals cannot sweat well and therefore pant through the mouth, which increases the **evaporation** that removes heat and cools their bodies. As for birds, they may flap their wings close to their throats to cool down.

Ectotherms typically regulate their body temperatures by using the environment. Lizards and snakes lie on hot rocks to absorb heat from the sun or find shaded spots when it is overly hot. In some cases, they climb to higher, cooler spots when the temperature becomes too hot. Crocodiles and other reptiles bury themselves in cool mud to escape from the heat while fish seek warm currents to maintain their body temperatures or spend time near the surface, where sunlight heats the water. Some species of fish have internal methods to control their temperatures though. For example, tuna swimming in cold water can transfer warm blood from the heart to the outer regions of their bodies. Additionally, some Arctic fish have special enzymes that act like antifreeze and prevent their cells from freezing in extremely cold temperatures.

*metabolize: to undergo the basic functions of one's body
*evaporation: the act of changing from a liquid or solid state to a gaseous one

Select the appropriate statements from the answer choices and match them to the type of animal to which they relate. TWO of the answer choices will NOT be used.

Endotherm (Select 3)	Ectotherm (Select 2)
•	•
•	•
•	

STATEMENTS

1. Can easily freeze in winter temperatures if it does not find shelter
2. Primarily consists of most birds and mammals
3. May cool its body by sweating or panting
4. Uses the sun's heat to avoid getting too cold
5. Can use both blubber and fur to keep itself warm in cold places
6. Mostly consists of amphibians, reptiles, and some mammals
7. May dig in the mud to cool off or find warm currents to get warm

■ Mapping

The following chart shows the structure of the passage. Fill in the blanks with the appropriate words.

How Animals Regulate Their Body Temperatures

Have various ways to regulate body temperatures
- endotherms = most ❶ _____ and birds
- ectotherms = most ❷ _____, amphibians, and fish

Endotherms: can control ❸ _____ body temperatures
- mostly metabolize food
- use fur, ❹ _____, and feathers to keep warm
- can sweat, pant, or flap wings to cool off

Ectotherms: need ❺ _____ sources to control internal body temperatures
- lie in sun to get warm or shade to cool off
- bury selves in mud to cool off
- fish stay warm near water's ❻ _____
- tuna and some Arctic fish can regulate internal ❼ _____

■ Summary

The following is a summary of the passage. Fill in the blanks with the appropriate words.

Land and water animals use various ways to keep ❶ _____. Mammals and birds are mostly ❷ _____ whereas reptiles, amphibians, and fish are primarily ❸ _____. Endotherms can control their internal body temperatures by ❹ _____ food. They also use fur, blubber, and feathers. They may build ❺ _____ to keep warm and sweat to become cooler. Ectotherms need external ❻ _____ such as the sun to adjust their body temperatures. They may lie in the sun or cool off in shady spots. Some ❼ _____ themselves in mud to stay cool. Certain fish, such as tuna and Arctic fish, are capable of controlling their temperatures ❽ _____ though.

A | The Western and Eastern Roman Empires

🎧 CH10_3A

At the height of its power, the Roman Empire was so immense that Emperor Diocletian divided the empire into western and eastern halves in 285. The Western Roman Empire was based in Rome while the Eastern Roman Empire later had its capital in Constantinople. Over time, the two empires exhibited distinct methods of rule reflecting their regions. Eventually, the Western Roman Empire fell to barbarian invaders in the late fifth century whereas the Eastern Roman Empire evolved into the Byzantine Empire, which survived for more than 1,000 years before being conquered by the Ottoman Turks in 1453.

Diocletian opted to divide the empire primarily due to the unwieldiness of ruling a huge amount of territory. By 285, the Roman Empire covered all of Southern Europe and parts of Western Europe, Northern Africa, and the Middle East. Despite having an extensive network of roads and secure **shipping lanes**, communications were terribly slow. Messages from Rome could take weeks to reach their destinations. Thus provincial governors had a level of autonomy that practically made them minor emperors. A series of conflicts in the decades prior to the split also showed the weakness of far-flung military commands as invasions by border people in the east and west were barely beaten back. In such conditions, local military commanders had to wield absolute power to respond promptly to threats. Such power went to the heads of some of them to the point that generals contemplating usurping the throne were constant threats to the imperial throne. The forming of two empires, each led by a different ruler, was meant to end these problems and to bring stability by giving each emperor more control than a single ruler could wield.

The reforms accomplished Diocletian's objectives to some degree, but the split also led to great differences between the two halves of the once-united empire. Diocletian had intended for the Eastern ruler to be subordinate to the Western one, but, over time, every emperor ruled as if his empire were separate. This was **exacerbated** by the differences between the two lands. For instance, despite being a part of the Roman Empire, Greece had dominated the eastern Mediterranean world for centuries. Hence it was natural that the Greek language and Greek customs replaced the Latin language and Roman customs in the Eastern Roman Empire.

Further problems centered on economic differences between the two halves. The eastern empire was urban based and derived its wealth from trade and work done by artisans. The western empire was more rural and agricultural, and its wealth depended on large populations of people working the land. In time, this weakness led to the decline of the western empire as waves of barbarian invaders devastated the population and land. Diocletian also initiated economic reforms by raising taxes to fund the defense of the empire. In the west, tax collectors had problems getting money from the rural populace, who were spread out, had little currency, and preferred paying taxes in farm produce. In the east, most people lived in cities and had hard currency, so tax collectors had an easier time, making money pour into Constantinople. The end result was a rich, stable Eastern Roman Empire that withstood multiple invasions for a millennium and a poor, unstable Western Roman Empire that succumbed to invasion fewer than two centuries after the split.

*shipping lane: a region of water, especially in an ocean or sea, in which numerous ships sail
*exacerbate: to make worse

Vocabulary

- _____ = awkwardness
- _____ = distant
- _____ = to take over as a ruler, often by force
- _____ = lower in status or power

1 The word "autonomy" in the passage is closest in meaning to

(A) difficulty

(B) independence

(C) respect

(D) power

2 The word "them" in the passage refers to

(A) far-flung military commands

(B) border people in the east and west

(C) local military commanders

(D) threats

3 According to paragraph 4, the Eastern Roman Empire became wealthy because

(A) it did not have to spend large amounts of money fighting invading barbarians

(B) the people who lived there tended to pay their taxes in money rather than with items

(C) the eastern emperors levied higher taxes than the emperors in the western lands

(D) the people who lived there tended to pay all of the taxes that were demanded of them

4 Select the appropriate statements from the answer choices and match them to the cause and effect of the splitting of the Roman Empire to which they relate. TWO of the answer choices will NOT be used.

Cause (Select 3)	Effect (Select 2)
•	•
•	•
•	

STATEMENTS

1 Greek culture dominated the region in the eastern Mediterranean.

2 The empire was so large that ruling it became too difficult.

3 The number of generals attempting to usurp the throne declined greatly.

4 Barbarian tribes constantly attacked the empire at certain places.

5 The Byzantines were able to preserve much of the legacy of the Roman Empire.

6 Communications to various parts of the empire took a long period of time.

7 Places in the west were overrun by invaders in a relatively short amount of time.

B | Different Types of Stars

When viewed from the ground, the thousands of stars in the night sky have relatively similar appearances, yet in reality, there are a wide variety of stars, each with its own distinct characteristics. There are three main types of stars: main sequence stars, giant stars, and white dwarf stars. They are actually stages in the lives of stars since, as they age, they change in size, **luminosity**, and temperature until the only things that eventually remain are their inner cores.

All stars begin as main sequence stars. They are called that because they fall on the mid-range of the Hertzsprung-Russell diagram of star classification, which categorizes stars based upon their size, luminosity, and temperature. Main sequence stars, of which the Earth's sun is one, constitute the vast majority of stars in the universe. When stars form from stellar gas and dust, the process of fusion eventually begins, whereby the stars convert hydrogen into helium, which creates light and heat and also provides stability as the stars' internal energy pushes out and gravity pushes in to form their spherical shapes. Main sequence stars are roughly the same size of the sun but can have up to six times its luminosity, and their surface temperatures average around 3,500 to 7,500 degrees **Kelvin**. Most main sequence stars are neither very large nor hot though. Instead, they are red dwarf stars, which are smaller and much cooler than the sun and are not even visible to the naked eye from the Earth.

Giant stars are the first stage dying main sequence stars experience. Main sequence stars lack an infinite amount of hydrogen, so they eventually exhaust their supply and begin dying. The largest of these stars burn through their hydrogen supply faster than smaller ones because of their greater internal pressure and temperature. As gravity contracts these stars, their last remaining inner shell of hydrogen ignites and causes their rapid expansion, pushing them to giant size. Most dying main sequence stars become red giant stars, like the star Betelgeuse, although some become blue giant stars. Giant stars can be gargantuan in scale, with some being more than 1,000 times the size of the sun, but most never attain sizes that big. Their temperatures vary from around 7,500 degrees Kelvin to approximately 30,000 degrees Kelvin.

After some time, the last remnants of energy in giant stars are nearly depleted, so there is nothing holding their remaining matter together. At that point, some stars explode into supernovas, yet many fail to do so as their outer layers simply dissipate into space and form planetary nebulae while gravity collapses their inner layers and leaves a dense core of material that astronomers call a white dwarf. While white dwarves are not stars but are merely their remains, they are still bright and observable as they cool. Most white dwarves are the size of the Earth but possess much higher densities and masses. Their temperatures fluctuate as they cool, but they begin at a high of roughly 100,000 degrees Kelvin when they form, making them among the hottest stars in the universe. As their remaining heat scatters into space, they slowly cool.

*luminosity: brightness
*Kelvin: a unit of temperature

Vocabulary

- _____ = to make up; to comprise
- _____ = without ending; countless
- _____ = to catch on fire
- _____ = something remaining from a larger object

1   Which of the sentences below best expresses the essential information in the highlighted sentence in the passage? Incorrect answer choices change the meaning in important ways or leave out essential information.

When viewed from the ground, the thousands of stars in the night sky have relatively similar appearances, yet in reality, there are a wide variety of stars, each with its own distinct characteristics.

Ⓐ Even though there are various kinds of stars with their own characteristics, only a few of the thousands of stars in the sky can be identified from the ground.

Ⓑ While stars look similar, in reality, there are many kinds of stars that are different from one another.

Ⓒ There are many different types of stars with unique characteristics, and it is possible to identify them when viewing them from the ground.

Ⓓ A person who is on the ground is able to look at the night sky and see thousands of different kinds of stars.

Inference Question

2   In paragraph 2, the author implies that the sun

Ⓐ is going to become a red dwarf star in the next few million years

Ⓑ is different from the majority of other stars in the universe

Ⓒ has an average temperature at the upper level of most main sequence stars

Ⓓ is much less bright than some other main sequence stars are

Rhetorical Purpose Question

3   In paragraph 3, the author uses "the star Betelgeuse" as an example of

Ⓐ one of the most visible stars in the Earth's night sky

Ⓑ one of the few blue giant stars that exist in the galaxy

Ⓒ a star that is likely to become a supernova when it dies

Ⓓ a red giant star that used to be a main sequence star

Fill in a Table Question

4   Select the appropriate statements from the answer choices and match them to the type of star to which they relate. TWO of the answer choices will NOT be used.

Main Sequence Star (Select 3)	Giant Star (Select 2)	White Dwarf Star (Select 2)
•		•
•	•	•
•	•	

STATEMENTS

1 Is the most common type of star found in the galaxy

2 May become a thousand times larger than the Earth's sun

3 Can be among the hottest stars in the galaxy

4 Includes stars that are much dimmer and smaller than the Earth's sun

5 Is believed to be the rarest of all the types of stars in the universe

6 Can often be invisible to people observing the sky from the Earth

7 Forms when a star suddenly expands to a great size

8 Is the last stage in a star's life before it becomes a black hole

9 Is comprised of what remains of a star's inner core

🎧 CH10_4A

Tropical Rainforest Animal Adaptations

A toco toucan

Lying between the Tropic of Cancer in the north and the Tropic of Capricorn in the south, the tropics, which straddle the equator, are noted for the high amount of rainfall and humidity that help create the dense tropical rainforests in the area. There are large rainforests in the tropics in Central and South America as well as in parts of Central Africa, Southeast Asia, and Northern Australia. Both predators and prey animals dwelling in these rainforests have adapted in various ways to enable them to survive in their harsh environments.

A tropical rainforest has four distinct layers of vegetation, and different species of animals, all of which compete for food resources, reside in them. The top is the emergent layer, which consists of the tallest trees rising above everything else. Within the emergent layer live many species of birds and insects. Directly below the emergent layer is the canopy, a thick layer of tall, leafy trees that prevents most sunlight from reaching the ground below. The canopy is home to numerous species of insects, birds, reptiles, and small animals, including monkeys. Under the canopy and closer to the ground is the understory, where the vegetation is not as tall or as thick as the canopy since little sunlight reaches it. The understory is also home to various insects, reptiles, and larger mammals, such as jaguars, which can climb trees. Finally, there is the rainforest floor, where hardly any plant life grows due to the absence of sunlight. This is where the largest mammals and reptiles, including tigers and crocodiles, live, and it is also home to countless species of insects.

Food in tropical rainforests is abundant but hard to acquire with so many animals competing for it. Consequently, large numbers of them have adapted to help them obtain food or to protect them in order to avoid becoming food for predators. Some animals have developed ways to reach food which other animals cannot get. For example, the brightly colored toucan is a bird with a long, strong beak it uses to reach into tight places to grab fruit. The toucan's feet have four toes—two face toward the front while two face backward—that it utilizes to latch onto branches very tightly and securely as it bends its body to reach fruit that is hard to get. Another example of an animal whose body has adapted so that it can acquire food is the jaguar. This big cat is not a fussy eater but will instead devour virtually anything. It has developed powerful jaws that can kill prey with a single bite and has strong legs and sharp claws that let it climb trees to reach prey attempting to stay high above the ground. Two additional adaptations are its padded paws, which permit the jaguar to walk silently to sneak up on its prey, and its fur pattern, which provides it with camouflage while hunting.

Many prey animals also utilize camouflage to hide from predators. The sloth, for example, hides in trees and hardly moves, preventing predators from sighting it, and has blue-green algae growing on its fur, which lets it blend in with its leafy surroundings. ■ Many other reptiles and amphibians have greenish skin enabling them to hide in the rainforest. ■ Others, however, have brightly colored skin that warns predators to avoid them. ■ The poison dart frog comes in several bright colors, indicating to predators that it is poisonous so should neither be hunted nor consumed. ■ Some other species of frogs trick predators by mimicking the bright colors of the poisonous dart frog yet are not toxic if eaten.

Predators have adapted to the camouflage employed by prey animals by hunting at night. Many mammalian and reptilian predators have developed the senses necessary to become nocturnal hunters. Big cats such as the jaguar possess enhanced vision, making it easier to see at night. Most species of snakes can also sense body heat, so they can slither up to prey and attack it without warning, and they can easily climb trees to seek food at most layers in the rainforest, too. These are just a few of the adaptations rainforest animals have developed in the constant battles between predators and prey animals.

*Glossary

equator: the imaginary line that runs around the center of the Earth

slither: to move on the ground in a sliding motion

1 Which of the sentences below best expresses the essential information in the highlighted sentence in the passage? Incorrect answer choices change the meaning in important ways or leave out essential information.

Under the canopy and closer to the ground is the understory, where the vegetation is not as tall or as thick as the canopy since little sunlight reaches it.

- (A) The canopy has trees that are taller and thicker than those in the understory even though it gets less sunlight.
- (B) Due to a lack of sunlight, the vegetation in the understory is not as high or thick as it is in the canopy above it.
- (C) The amount of sunlight they receive is the primary difference between the understory and the canopy.
- (D) There are some tall, thick trees in the understory, but there are many more of them located in the canopy.

2 According to paragraph 2, which of the following is NOT true about the four layers of vegetation in tropical rainforests?

- (A) The layer that is covered with the greatest amount of vegetation is the rainforest floor.
- (B) Birds and insects are the primary animals that may be found in the emergent layer.
- (C) A wide variety of types of animals live in the trees that grow in the understory.
- (D) The trees in the canopy are primarily responsible for little sunlight reaching the ground.

3 Which of the following can be inferred from paragraph 2 about the creatures living in tropical rainforests?

- (A) The emergent layer is the safest region due to the high amount of sunlight it gets.
- (B) There are many more predators in tropical rainforests than there are prey animals.
- (C) Those in the emergent layer and the canopy are safe from the largest predators.
- (D) Mammals can only be found living in the bottom two layers of tropical rainforests.

4 The author discusses "the brightly colored toucan" in paragraph 3 in order to

- (A) explain the manner in which its physical adaptations permit it to obtain food more easily
- (B) describe how it manages to avoid most of the rainforest predators that hunt it
- (C) discuss the reason that it is so colorful in spite of its need to avoid certain predators
- (D) point out how it evolved to become one of the more skilled rainforest hunters

5 The phrase "latch onto" in the passage is closest in meaning to

Ⓐ grasp

Ⓑ land on

Ⓒ remain on

Ⓓ bite

6 Select the TWO answer choices from paragraph 3 that identify how the jaguar has adapted to hunt better. *To receive credit, you must select TWO answers.*

Ⓐ Animals can often not see it because of how its fur looks.

Ⓑ Its padded paws enable it to climb trees more skillfully.

Ⓒ It only needs to bite animals once due to the strength of its jaws.

Ⓓ It has strong legs that let it run faster than most prey animals.

7 In stating that big cats such as the jaguar possess "enhanced vision," the author means that the jaguar

Ⓐ possesses powerful senses

Ⓑ has excellent sight

Ⓒ can focus on distant objects

Ⓓ is sensitive to light

8 According to paragraph 5, snakes in tropical rainforests have adapted by

Ⓐ having camouflage patterns on their skin that make them hard to see

Ⓑ developing eyesight enabling them to see prey animals better

Ⓒ utilizing highly toxic venom that can effectively kill large animals

Ⓓ being able to detect the heat given off by the animals they are hunting

9 Look at the four squares [■] that indicate where the following sentence could be added to the passage.

Predators can easily see these animals on account of their vivid colors, which inform them that these animals are unique in some regard.

Where would the sentence best fit?

Click on a square [■] to add the sentence to the passage.

10 Directions: Select the appropriate statements from the answer choices and match them to the type of animal to which they relate. TWO of the answer choices will NOT be used. **This question is worth 3 points.**

Drag your answer choices to the spaces where they belong. To remove an answer choice, click on it. To review the passage, click on VIEW TEXT.

STATEMENTS

1 Relies on bright colors to warn other animals away from it

2 Tends to be more active at night than during the day

3 Digs into the ground to build dens that other animals cannot see

4 Prefers to live in the emergent layer to avoid most other animals

5 May rely upon its lack of movement to remain hidden from others

6 Uses the ability to move silently to surprise other animals

7 Has learned to climb trees to get to places with other animals

TYPE OF ANIMAL

Predator (Select 3)

-
-
-

Prey (Select 2)

-
-

Ocean Marine Life

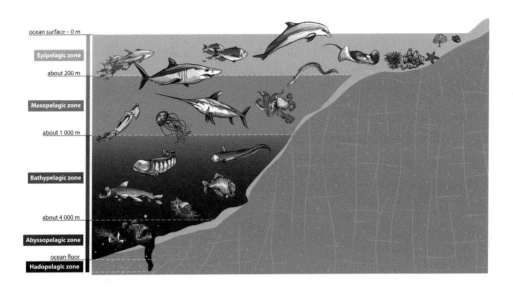

The world's oceans contain an enormous number of diverse organisms, many of which have unique characteristics permitting them to adapt to life in deep water. Oceanographers have divided the ocean depths into five distinct levels, each distinguished by differences in depth, pressure, light, temperature, oxygen level, and mineral nutrients, that these creatures dwell in. From the surface to the ocean floor, these levels are the epipelagic, mesopelagic, bathypelagic, abyssopelagic, and hadalpelagic zones.

The epipelagic zone occupies the top layer of the ocean and extends from the surface to approximately 200 meters beneath it. The vast majority of marine organisms, including most commercial fish species and many marine mammals, reside here. One reason for the teeming diversity of life is the abundance of phytoplankton, which serves as a nutrition source for countless marine organisms. As smaller species consume phytoplankton, they, in turn, are food sources for larger species. In addition, the world's coral reefs, which serve as special ecological regions where myriad marine life dwells, are found in the epipelagic zone.

The next layer is the mesopelagic zone, which extends from roughly 200 to 1,000 meters underneath the surface. Marine biologists also call it the twilight zone due to the lack of sunlight. It is a murky world, so phytoplankton cannot survive there because they depend on sunlight to produce food through photosynthesis. This lack of a nutrient food base does not hamper the existence of life though. Some of the more common species there are giant squid, jellyfish, the lanternfish, and the bristlemouth fish. Many creatures also migrate to the upper epipelagic zone to consume food at night and then descend deeper during daylight hours. ■1 Others survive on marine snow, the particles of decaying dead organisms that sink from the upper layers. ■2 Scientists have trouble studying many of these creatures in detail. ■3

What they currently know is that most have internal bladders filled with gases to help them maintain buoyancy. ◢ If a species is quickly brought to the surface, the pressure change causes the gases to expand rapidly, bursting the bladder and killing the animal.

Under the mesopelagic zone is the bathypelagic zone, which extends 4,000 meters beneath the surface. It is sometimes referred to as the midnight zone due to its extreme darkness and is a region of extreme pressure, freezing temperatures, and low oxygen and nutrient levels. However, some creatures, such as the bristlemouth fish and the humpbacked angler fish, dwell there. Most of the marine lifeforms in this zone have adapted to the extreme pressure by having elongated bodies with weak muscles and cartilage skeletons that bend but do not break under the pressure. Many creatures in this region feed on marine snow or are predators that use bioluminescence to attract prey. These animals have serrated teeth and hinged jaws that expand wide to allow them rapidly to draw in any unwary fish swimming by.

The fourth layer is the abyssopelagic zone, which extends down to 6,000 meters or wherever the water meets the ocean floor. Oceanographers estimate that more than eighty percent of the world's ocean waters comprise this zone. Extreme pressure, freezing cold temperatures, and no sunlight are hallmarks of this region, so there is a lack of diversity in the lifeforms dwelling there. Many creatures there depend on marine snow for food or simply prey on other animals. They have also adapted to the deep water and the pressure by having weak, flexible bodies, gas bladders to let them maintain buoyancy, and wide mouths and expansive stomachs that enable them to consume as much food as possible whenever they find it. Many also have very large eyes or utilize bioluminescence to find their way around in the dark. Most species in this zone, including various types of shellfish, eels, and octopuses, live near the ocean floor.

The final area is the hadalpelagic zone, which extends into the deepest trenches found on the ocean floor all the way down to 11,000 meters beneath the surface. Despite the extreme cold and pressure, some lifeforms survive there. Among them are the amphipod, a form of tiny crustacean, the snailfish, a gelatinous species, and the cusk-eel, which is known for being the creature that lives at the greatest depth beneath the surface.

*Glossary

cartilage: firm, elastic tissue found in some animals

bioluminescence: the production of light by a living creature

11 Which of the sentences below best expresses the essential information in the highlighted sentence in the passage? Incorrect answer choices change the meaning in important ways or leave out essential information.

Oceanographers have divided the ocean depths into five distinct levels, each distinguished by differences in depth, pressure, light, temperature, oxygen level, and mineral nutrients, that these creatures dwell in.

(A) Animals live in five different layers in the ocean, and each level has different characteristics based upon certain factors identified by oceanographers.

(B) Oceanographers have learned that some animals are not capable of living in all five of the different levels of the ocean.

(C) The levels of the ocean are different due to their depth, water pressure, the amount of light they get, the temperature, the amount of oxygen, and the nutrients found in them.

(D) Five ocean levels have been discovered by oceanographers so far, and these levels are all believed to be different from one another.

12 In paragraph 2, the author uses "the world's coral reefs" as an example of

(A) zones that oceanographers know have the most diverse life in the world

(B) places that are teeming with life and are found in the epipelagic zone

(C) areas in the epipelagic zone that are known to be rich in phytoplankton

(D) regions that are not able to survive 200 meters beneath the ocean's surface

13 Which of the following can be inferred from paragraph 2 about phytoplankton?

(A) Its existence is of great importance to the animals living in the epipelagic zone.

(B) It is sometimes responsible for species dying off when it exists in small numbers.

(C) It serves as a major source of food for large fish and mammals in the ocean.

(D) Its presence has been detected in small amounts in coral reefs around the world.

14 According to paragraph 3, some animals in the mesopelagic zone move to the epipelagic zone because

(A) they are heading toward illuminated places in order to see better

(B) they are trying to get away from predators in the mesopelagic zone

(C) they are looking for sources of food that they can consume

(D) they are attempting to find the phytoplankton they need to survive

15 The word "serrated" in the passage is closest in meaning to

(A) jagged

(B) dangerous

(C) diagonal

(D) retractable

16 According to paragraphs 3 and 4, which of the following is true about some creatures living in the mesopelagic and bathypelagic zones?

(A) They tend to travel in large groups in order to defend themselves from predators better.

(B) They acquire sustenance from the bodies of dead animals falling from higher levels of the ocean.

(C) They rely upon bioluminescence in order to see as well as to hunt prey animals at times.

(D) They have special bladders in their bodies which enable them to remain deep beneath the ocean's surface.

17 The word "hallmarks" in the passage is closest in meaning to

(A) requirements

(B) additions

(C) dangers

(D) features

18 In paragraph 6, the author's description of the hadalpelagic zone mentions all of the following EXCEPT:

(A) what the names of some of the creatures that live there are

(B) how certain animals have adapted in order to survive in that zone

(C) how far beneath the surface of the ocean it is believed to extend

(D) which parts of the ocean this zone is considered to be located in

19 Look at the four squares [■] that indicate where the following sentence could be added to the passage.

Fortunately, new technology, particularly cameras and submersibles, is letting them get more glimpses of life in this zone and helping them increase their minimal knowledge.

Where would the sentence best fit?

Click on a square [■] to add the sentence to the passage.

20 **Directions:** Select the appropriate statements from the answer choices and match them to the ocean zone to which they relate. TWO of the answer choices will NOT be used. **This question is worth 4 points.**

Drag your answer choices to the spaces where they belong. To remove an answer choice, click on it. To review the passage, click on VIEW TEXT.

STATEMENTS

1. Has many creatures that live on the floor of the ocean
2. Is home to both the bristlemouth fish and the humpbacked angler fish
3. Is a dim area that is sometimes referred to as the twilight zone
4. Is populated by animals such as the amphipod and the cusk-eel
5. Makes up the vast majority of the world's oceans
6. Features creatures that often move from one zone to another
7. Is located directly beneath the epipelagic zone
8. Contains large amounts of phytoplankton that animals feed on
9. Has some creatures which have skeletons made of cartilage

OCEAN ZONE

Mesopelagic Zone (Select 3)

-
-
-

Bathypelagic Zone (Select 2)

-
-

Abyssopelagic Zone (Select 2)

-
-

Vocabulary Review

A Complete each sentence with the appropriate word from the box.

| extreme | flux | subordinate | infinite | straddles |

1 Lisa is _____ to Carol, who is the manager of the entire department.

2 The ancient city _____ the border between the two countries.

3 _____ weather can cause problems for the people and the animals caught in it.

4 The company is in a state of _____ with so many employees leaving these days.

5 On clear nights, there appear to be an _____ number of stars in the sky.

B Complete each sentence with the correct answer.

1 The **manner** he uses to do research is unique, but it is an effective _____ for him.

   a. result   b. way

2 The animals are **hampered** by a lack of food, and the unsafe environment also _____ them.

   a. hurts   b. annoys

3 Ten people **constitute** the club's membership with it being _____ solely of professionals.

   a. founded   b. comprised

4 Jonah no longer _____ in the city but instead **dwells** in the suburbs.

   a. lives   b. works

5 King Harold **usurped** the throne when he took it from his brother _____.

   a. peacefully   b. by force

6 Some birds **mimic** the sounds made by other animals by _____ them.

   a. hearing   b. replicating

7 The lake is **teeming** with fish as _____ of them live in the water.

   a. huge numbers   b. a few species

8 There is a **protrusion** on the animal that _____ the rest of its body.

   a. somewhat resembles   b. sticks out very far from

9 The scientists hope to **deflect** the asteroid by _____ before it hits the Earth.

   a. turning it aside   b. destroying it

10 The storm is moving **swiftly** and will _____ arrive at the coast in a few hours.

   a. slowly   b. quickly

Actual Test

Reading Section Directions

This section measures your ability to understand academic passages in English. You will have **54 minutes** to read and answer questions about **3 passages**. A clock at the top of the screen will show you how much time is remaining.

Most questions are worth 1 point but the last question for each passage is worth more than 1 point. The directions for the last question indicate how many points you may receive.

Some passages include a word or phrase that is underlined. Click on the word or phrase to see a definition or an explanation.

When you want to move to the next question, click on **NEXT**. You may skip questions and go back to them later. If you want to return to previous questions, click on **BACK**. You can click on **REVIEW** at any time, and the review screen will show you which questions you have answered and which you have not answered. From this review screen, you may go directly to any question you have already seen in the Reading section.

Click on **CONTINUE** to go on.

British Taxation and the American Colonies

When the French and Indian War concluded in 1763, the result was an overwhelming British victory over the French that resulted in the losers being driven from most of their North American colonies. The British government, for its part, was left deeply in debt. After the hostilities ended, the British Parliament enacted several new tax laws intended to raise revenue from Britain's American colonies to pay for the war. The American colonists had no voice in Parliament to speak for or against these laws, so the end result was that they developed strong, negative reactions to what they termed "taxation without representation." The colonists accordingly opposed the taxes, and their protests escalated to violence and were ultimately a leading cause of the American Revolution.

Four main taxes created tension in the colonies: the Sugar Act of 1764, the Stamp Act of 1765, the Townsend Acts of 1767, and the Tea Act of 1773. The first, the Sugar Act, was enacted to prevent the smuggling of molasses. Under the Molasses Act of 1733, colonists had to pay a duty of six pence per gallon of molasses. Yet customs officials routinely accepted bribes of around one and a half pence per gallon and permitted the molasses to be shipped untaxed. The Sugar Act actually reduced the duty to three pence, but the colonists still refused to pay it. Only when it was lowered to one pence in 1766 did it become cheaper to pay the duty than the bribes. The British government subsequently received around 30,000 pounds of revenue annually—a relatively small amount of money—from the molasses trade.

The main effect of the Sugar Act was to make the colonists wonder if the British had the right to interfere in their affairs, particularly in matters of trade. Nevertheless, the Sugar Act was not widely protested because it primarily affected those involved in trade and shipping. The same cannot be said of the Stamp Act, which had wide-ranging effects on every colony. It mandated that many documents the colonists used, especially those related to legal affairs and publishing, could only be written on paper with a crown revenue stamp on it. Essentially, the colonists had to buy special paper from the British government at a higher price than normal paper. Regarding this as a direct form of taxation, the colonists protested the act so vigorously that it was repealed in 1766.

Despite this setback, the British government was determined to extract revenue from the colonies. The Townsend Acts were designed to tax various imported items to raise money to pay the salaries of government officials in the colonies. Once again, however, the colonists objected as they believed that British control of American colonial government officials' salaries would result in more widespread

British influence in the colonies. After extensive American boycotts of British goods, in 1770, the acts were repealed except for a tax on tea. This, in turn, led to the Tea Act, which was an attempt by the British government to bestow a monopoly on the sale of tea in the colonies to the East India Company. Among the most famous reactions to this law happened on the night of December 16, 1773. American colonists dressed as Indians stormed on board British ships in Boston Harbor and cast their cargoes of tea into the water in what came to be known as the Boston Tea Party.

The opposite perceptions each side had of the role of the colonists in the British Empire were the root cause of the difficulties between them. To the British, it appeared reasonable to tax the colonists to pay for the war that drove the encroaching French out of North America. The colonists were also part of the global British Empire and had always been regarded as a support system for the motherland. But by the 1760s, the American colonies had existed for nearly 150 years and attained a high level of autonomy. Though the colonies still belonged to the British Empire, many colonists considered themselves Americans rather than British. This was a recipe for trouble when the British began making demands the colonists thought unreasonable, so this eventually led to the American Revolution and the founding of a new nation.

*Glossary

molasses: a thick syrup made by refining sugar

crown: referring to the sovereign power of a monarchy

1 In paragraph 1, the author's description of the tax laws enacted by the British Parliament mentions all of the following EXCEPT:

    (A) how the American colonists felt about being taxed by the British

    (B) the effect the taxes had on the relationship between the British and Americans

    (C) the negotiations regarding the taxes that the British held with the Americans

    (D) the reason that the British government was attempting to raise money

Paragraph 1 is marked with an arrow (➡).

British Taxation and the American Colonies

➡ When the French and Indian War concluded in 1763, the result was an overwhelming British victory over the French that resulted in the losers being driven from most of their North American colonies. The British government, for its part, was left deeply in debt. After the hostilities ended, the British Parliament enacted several new tax laws intended to raise revenue from Britain's American colonies to pay for the war. The American colonists had no voice in Parliament to speak for or against these laws, so the end result was that they developed strong, negative reactions to what they termed "taxation without representation." The colonists accordingly opposed the taxes, and their protests escalated to violence and were ultimately a leading cause of the American Revolution.

2 The author discusses "the Molasses Act of 1733" in paragraph 2 in order to

Ⓐ point out the manner in which the American colonists evaded following that law

Ⓑ argue that the tax was fair and did not cost the American colonists much money

Ⓒ show the corruption that existed in both the British and American governments

Ⓓ claim it was the first time the British had ever taxed the American colonists

Paragraph 2 is marked with an arrow (➡).

3 According to paragraph 2, which of the following is true about the Sugar Act?

Ⓐ It resulted in an increase in the number of bribes officials received.

Ⓑ It was amended several times over the course of a ten-year period.

Ⓒ It led to the first acts of violence perpetrated by the Americans against the British.

Ⓓ It reduced the duty the colonists had to pay on molasses by fifty percent.

Paragraph 2 is marked with an arrow (➡).

➡ Four main taxes created tension in the colonies: the Sugar Act of 1764, the Stamp Act of 1765, the Townsend Acts of 1767, and the Tea Act of 1773. The first, the Sugar Act, was enacted to prevent the smuggling of molasses. Under the Molasses Act of 1733, colonists had to pay a duty of six pence per gallon of molasses. Yet customs officials routinely accepted bribes of around one and a half pence per gallon and permitted the molasses to be shipped untaxed. The Sugar Act actually reduced the duty to three pence, but the colonists still refused to pay it. Only when it was lowered to one pence in 1766 did it become cheaper to pay the duty than the bribes. The British government subsequently received around 30,000 pounds of revenue per annually—a relatively small amount of money—from the molasses trade.

*Glossary

molasses: a thick syrup made by refining sugar

238

4 The word "mandated" in the passage is closest in meaning to

(A) assumed

(B) required

(C) recommended

(D) appropriated

5 According to paragraph 3, the Stamp Act was repealed because

(A) the British feared that their authority in the American colonies was being undermined

(B) there were a large number of protests made by the American colonists

(C) the British government raised much less money than had been anticipated

(D) the American colonists refused to purchase any paper with revenue stamps on it

Paragraph 3 is marked with an arrow (➡).

➡ The main effect of the Sugar Act was to make the colonists wonder if the British had the right to interfere in their affairs, particularly in matters of trade. Nevertheless, the Sugar Act was not widely protested because it primarily affected those involved in trade and shipping. The same cannot be said of the Stamp Act, which had wide-ranging effects on every colony. It mandated that many documents the colonists used, especially those related to legal affairs and publishing, could only be written on paper with a crown revenue stamp on it. Essentially, the colonists had to buy special paper from the British government at a higher price than normal paper. Regarding this as a direct form of taxation, the colonists protested the act so vigorously that it was repealed in 1766.

*Glossary

crown: referring to the sovereign power of a monarchy

6 In paragraph 4, the author uses "the Boston Tea Party" as an example of

Ⓐ an illegal act by the American colonists that prompted a vigorous British reaction

Ⓑ one of the first acts of violence in the American Revolution

Ⓒ a noted response of the American colonists to British taxation attempts

Ⓓ a way that the American colonists protested the Townsend Acts

Paragraph 4 is marked with an arrow (➡).

➡ Despite this setback, the British government was determined to extract revenue from the colonies. The Townsend Acts were designed to tax various imported items to raise money to pay the salaries of government officials in the colonies. Once again, however, the colonists objected as they believed that British control of American colonial government officials' salaries would result in more widespread British influence in the colonies. After extensive American boycotts of British goods, in 1770, the acts were repealed except for a tax on tea. This, in turn, led to the Tea Act, which was an attempt by the British government to bestow a monopoly on the sale of tea in the colonies to the East India Company. Among the most famous reactions to this law happened on the night of December 16, 1773. American colonists dressed as Indians stormed on board British ships in Boston Harbor and cast their cargoes of tea into the water in what came to be known as the Boston Tea Party.

7 According to paragraph 5, why did the British and Americans have problems with each other?

   Ⓐ Few Americans ever visited Britain while not many British traveled to the colonies.

   Ⓑ The British were regarded by the American colonists as treating them too harshly.

   Ⓒ People from other countries living in the American colonies had no loyalty to Britain.

   Ⓓ They differed in how they thought the American colonists should act toward the British.

Paragraph 5 is marked with an arrow (➡).

8 In paragraph 5, the author implies that the American colonists

   Ⓐ would have been granted independence from England if they had been more patient

   Ⓑ were used to the British government letting them run most of their own affairs

   Ⓒ were wrong to have started the American Revolution over the matter of taxation

   Ⓓ should have been permitted representation in the British Parliament to placate them

Paragraph 5 is marked with an arrow (➡).

➡ The opposite perceptions each side had of the role of the colonists in the British Empire were the root cause of the difficulties between them. To the British, it appeared reasonable to tax the colonists to pay for the war that drove the encroaching French out of North America. The colonists were also part of the global British Empire and had always been regarded as a support system for the motherland. But by the 1760s, the American colonies existed for nearly 150 years and attained a high level of autonomy. Though the colonies still belonged to the British Empire, many colonists considered themselves Americans rather than British. This was a recipe for trouble when the British began making demands the colonists thought unreasonable, so this eventually led to the American Revolution and the founding of a new nation.

More Available ▲

9   Look at the four squares [■] that indicate where the following sentence could be added to the passage.

The actions by the colonists would result in one of the most important events in American history and one that remains influential in modern times.

Where would the sentence best fit?

Click on a square [■] to add the sentence to the passage.

Despite this setback, the British government was determined to extract revenue from the colonies. The Townsend Acts were designed to tax various imported items to raise money to pay the salaries of government officials in the colonies. Once again, however, the colonists objected as they believed that British control of American colonial government officials' salaries would result in more widespread British influence in the colonies. After extensive American boycotts of British goods, in 1770, the acts were repealed except for a tax on tea. **■1** This, in turn, led to the Tea Act, which was an attempt by the British government to bestow a monopoly on the sale of tea in the colonies to the East India Company. **■2** Among the most famous reactions to this law happened on the night of December 16, 1773. **■3** American colonists dressed as Indians stormed on board British ships in Boston Harbor and cast their cargoes of tea into the water in what came to be known as the Boston Tea Party. **■4**

10 **Directions:** Select the appropriate statements from the answer choices and match them to the cause and effect of the tax laws passed by the British to which they relate. TWO of the answer choices will NOT be used. **This question is worth 3 points.**

Drag your answer choices to the spaces where they belong. To remove an answer choice, click on it. To review the passage, click on **VIEW TEXT**.

STATEMENTS

1. The Boston Tea Party was held in 1773.

2. France and Britain fought a costly war against each other.

3. The American colonists refused to buy certain products.

4. Britain had a large amount of debt to pay off.

5. Protests were held by some of the American colonists.

6. The American colonists were given representation in Parliament.

7. The British wanted to cut down on bribes taken by officials.

TAX LAWS PASSED BY THE BRITISH

Cause (Select 2)

-
-

Effect (Select 3)

-
-
-

Darwin's Voyage on the *HMS Beagle*

The *HMS Beagle*

Charles Darwin is famed for the theory of evolution, which was published in *On the Origin of Species* in 1859. A large portion of the theory was developed during an exploratory ocean voyage Darwin made aboard the British Royal Navy vessel *HMS Beagle* from 1831 to 1836. During that long trip, Darwin had the opportunity to observe plant and animal life in a wide variety of ecosystems, and that led him to conclude that many species slowly evolved into their present forms due to the necessity of surviving in their environments. After returning home, Darwin spent the next couple of decades analyzing and refining his ideas before making them public in 1859.

The *Beagle* was a ten-gun naval <u>sloop</u>—a small ship by the standards of the day—and was equipped for long exploratory expeditions with its goal being to survey the coastal waters of foreign lands. The ship made its first such voyage from 1826 to 1830, where it mostly conducted a <u>hydrographic</u> survey of the coastal waters of South America. For its second voyage, the *Beagle* was to continue its survey work. However, Captain Robert Fitzroy wanted a geologist onboard to examine the land since none had been present on the first voyage, so Darwin was contacted to carry out those duties.

Setting sail from England in December 1831, the *Beagle* made an extensive voyage taking it to the Atlantic and Pacific coasts of Central America, South America, the Galapagos Islands, Tahiti, Australia, New Zealand, and Mauritius before returning to England in October 1836. During the trip, Darwin frequently went ashore to examine the local geology, flora, and fauna, and he collected numerous samples and made extensive notes about everything he discovered. Gradually, as the voyage continued,

his observations led him to his pioneering notion about how plants and animals arrived at their present states. After returning home, Darwin published his diary of the expedition in 1839. Known today as *The Voyage of the Beagle*, the book was well received in its time and went through several printings.

Large portions of the diary served as the basis for Darwin's later writings, including his work on evolution. Included in the diary were many of Darwin's observations that contributed to scientific studies. For example, Darwin noted that in many places, beds of fossilized seashells had been found at high elevations, which indicated that the land had undergone a tremendous transformation at some time in the past. Darwin also observed that coral atolls formed when volcanic islands sank, leaving behind coral reefs. But his greatest find was the discrepancy in plant and animal life in places short distances apart from one another. For instance, the flora and the fauna of the Atlantic and Pacific coasts of Panama differed a large amount despite being relatively close to each other. He further noted that the various islands of the Galapagos had similar plants and animals but that they had evolved with slight differences that helped them survive on the particular island on which they dwelled. The most famous example of this observation is the finches Darwin noticed as having different-shaped beaks, each of which was suited for the main food source on its particular island.

In the years following the voyage of the *Beagle*, Darwin contemplated his findings and gradually articulated his famous theory. Nevertheless, he felt unready to publish his work because he wanted to work on other projects to gather more evidence. Then, in the 1850s, he learned that his ideas were similar to those of another naturalist, Alfred Wallace, who had been working in Southeast Asia for years and had come to nearly identical conclusions with Darwin. Once they made contact, in 1858, the two men collaborated on a paper discussing evolution, making it the first published mentioning of the theory. Then, fearful that Wallace would publish a book on the subject first, Darwin's friends urged him to put his work into print. The result was *On the Origin of Species* in 1859. To his credit, Wallace never felt slighted and publicly supported Darwin and his work when both came under attack. As for the *Beagle*, it made a third trip similar to the first two and then spent time serving as a guard ship in England's coastal waters.

*Glossary

sloop: a sailing ship that has a single mast

hydrographic: relating to the science of measuring and mapping the surface of the Earth's waters, mostly for the purpose of navigation

Beginning ▲

11 Which of the sentences below best expresses the essential information in the highlighted sentence in the passage? Incorrect answer choices change the meaning in important ways or leave out essential information.

During that long trip, Darwin had the opportunity to observe plant and animal life in a wide variety of ecosystems, and that led him to conclude that many species slowly evolved into their present forms due to the necessity of surviving in their environments.

Ⓐ Darwin was able to observe the processes through which both plants and animals evolved to survive in their environments while he was on his long trip.

Ⓑ The observations of plants and animals that Darwin made on that journey helped him conclude that those lifeforms slowly evolved to be better fit for survival.

Ⓒ While he was traveling, Darwin made many discoveries which led him to believe that both plants and animals were capable of evolving over a period of time.

Ⓓ Darwin used the opportunity to observe a wide variety of plants and animals evolving in their natural environments when he went on his journey.

Darwin's Voyage on the *HMS Beagle*

Charles Darwin is famed for the theory of evolution, which was published in *On the Origin of Species* in 1859. A large portion of the theory was developed during an exploratory ocean voyage Darwin made aboard the British Royal Navy vessel *HMS Beagle* from 1831 to 1836. During that long trip, Darwin had the opportunity to observe plant and animal life in a wide variety of ecosystems, and that led him to conclude that many species slowly evolved into their present forms due to the necessity of surviving in their environments. After returning home, Darwin spent the next couple of decades analyzing and refining his ideas before making them public in 1859.

Q
REVIEW

?
HELP

<
BACK

>
NEXT

HIDE TIME 00:54:00

More Available ▲

12 In paragraph 2, the author's description of the *Beagle* mentions which of the following?

Ⓐ The names of some of the highest-ranking crew members on board the ship

Ⓑ The purpose that the ship had been both built and prepared for

Ⓒ The number of men that the ship had as members of its crew

Ⓓ Some of the discoveries that the ship made when it went on its first voyage

Paragraph 2 is marked with an arrow (➡).

13 According to paragraph 2, Charles Darwin became a member of the crew of the *Beagle* because

Ⓐ the quality of his scientific work was well known to the ship's captain

Ⓑ the first voyage was considered a failure due to the lack of a geologist onboard

Ⓒ a scientist with his specific knowledge was needed for the ship's next voyage

Ⓓ Captain Fitzroy agreed to hire him when he requested to be made a crew member

Paragraph 2 is marked with an arrow (➡).

14 According to paragraph 3, which of the following is NOT true about the voyage about the *Beagle*?

Ⓐ None of the samples Charles Darwin collected was brought to England.

Ⓑ Charles Darwin wrote a diary about what he learned on the trip.

Ⓒ The ship sailed to several places that were in two separate oceans.

Ⓓ There were explorations that took place both on water and on land.

Paragraph 3 is marked with an arrow (⇨).

➡ The *Beagle* was a ten-gun naval sloop— a small ship by the standards of the day—and was equipped for long exploratory expeditions with its goal being to survey the coastal waters of foreign lands. The ship made its first such voyage from 1826 to 1830, where it mostly conducted a hydrographic survey of the coastal waters of South America. For its second voyage, the *Beagle* was to continue its survey work. However, Captain Robert Fitzroy wanted a geologist onboard to examine the land since none had been present on the first voyage, so Darwin was contacted to carry out those duties.

⇨ Setting sail from England in December 1831, the *Beagle* made an extensive voyage taking it to the Atlantic and Pacific coasts of Central America, South America, the Galapagos Islands, Tahiti, Australia, New Zealand, and Mauritius before returning to England in October 1836. During the trip, Darwin frequently went ashore to examine the local geology, flora, and fauna, and he collected numerous samples and made extensive notes about everything he discovered. Gradually, as the voyage continued, his observations led him to his pioneering notion about how plants and animals arrived at their present states. After returning home, Darwin published his diary of the expedition in 1839. Known today as *The Voyage of the Beagle*, the book was well received in its time and went through several printings.

*Glossary

sloop: a sailing ship that has a single mast
hydrographic: relating to the science of measuring and mapping the surface of the Earth's waters, mostly for the purpose of navigation

15 Which of the following can be inferred from paragraph 4 about Charles Darwin?

(A) He thought it was strange that animals living so closely together could be so different.

(B) He had little knowledge of the flora and fauna of the Pacific region prior to the journey.

(C) He believed that the fossils which he found were only a few thousand years old.

(D) He made arrangements to publish his journal before the *Beagle*'s voyage began.

Paragraph 4 is marked with an arrow (➡).

➡ Large portions of the diary served as the basis for Darwin's later writings, including his work on evolution. Included in the diary were many of Darwin's observations that contributed to scientific studies. For example, Darwin noted that in many places, beds of fossilized seashells had been found at high elevations, which indicated that the land had undergone a tremendous transformation at some time in the past. Darwin also observed that coral atolls formed when volcanic islands sank, leaving behind coral reefs. But his greatest find was the discrepancy in plant and animal life in places short distances apart from one another. For instance, the flora and the fauna of the Atlantic and Pacific coasts of Panama differed a large amount despite being relatively close to each other. He further noted that the various islands of the Galapagos had similar plants and animals but that they had evolved with slight differences that helped them survive on the particular island on which they dwelled. The most famous example of this observation is the finches Darwin noticed as having different-shaped beaks, each of which was suited for the main food source on its particular island.

16 The word "articulated" in the passage is closest in meaning to

Ⓐ expressed

Ⓑ pondered

Ⓒ proved

Ⓓ determined

17 The author discusses "Alfred Wallace" in paragraph 5 in order to

Ⓐ credit him with coming up with the theory of evolution

Ⓑ discuss the great rivalry between him and Charles Darwin

Ⓒ mention some of the discoveries he made in Southeast Asia

Ⓓ describe the relationship he had with Charles Darwin

Paragraph 5 is marked with an arrow (➡).

18 According to paragraph 5, what did Charles Darwin's friends urge him to do?

Ⓐ Spend some time in Southeast Asia together with Alfred Wallace

Ⓑ Publish his work on evolution before another individual could do so

Ⓒ Go on the third journey of the *Beagle* in order to acquire more samples

Ⓓ Reconsider the arguments that he was making before printing them

Paragraph 5 is marked with an arrow (➡).

➡ In the years following the voyage of the *Beagle*, Darwin contemplated his findings and gradually articulated his famous theory. Nevertheless, he felt unready to publish his work because he wanted to work on other projects to gather more evidence. Then, in the 1850s, he learned that his ideas were similar to those of another naturalist, Alfred Wallace, who had been working in Southeast Asia for years and had come to nearly identical conclusions with Darwin. Once they made contact, in 1858, the two men collaborated on a paper discussing evolution, making it the first published mentioning of the theory. Then, fearful that Wallace would publish a book on the subject first, Darwin's friends urged him to put his work into print. The result was *On the Origin of Species* in 1859. To his credit, Wallace never felt slighted and publicly supported Darwin and his work when both came under attack. As for the *Beagle*, it made a third trip similar to the first two and then spent time serving as a guard ship in England's coastal waters.

19 Look at the four squares [■] that indicate where the following sentence could be added to the passage.

It would not gain fame for this trip but for the following one it made.

Where would the sentence best fit?

Click on a square [■] to add the sentence to the passage.

The *Beagle* was a ten-gun naval <u>sloop</u>— a small ship by the standards of the day—and was equipped for long exploratory expeditions with its goal being to survey the coastal waters of foreign lands. **■** The ship made its first such voyage from 1826 to 1830, where it mostly conducted a <u>hydrographic</u> survey of the coastal waters of South America. **■** For its second voyage, the *Beagle* was to continue its survey work. **■** However, Captain Robert Fitzroy wanted a geologist onboard to examine the land since none had been present on the first voyage, so Darwin was contacted to carry out those duties. **■**

*Glossary

sloop: a sailing ship that has a single mast

hydrographic: relating to the science of measuring and mapping the surface of the Earth's waters, mostly for the purpose of navigation

20 Directions: An introductory sentence for a brief summary of the passage is provided below. Complete the summary by selecting the THREE answer choices that express the most important ideas of the passage. Some sentences do not belong because they express ideas that are not presented in the passage or are minor ideas in the passage. **This question is worth 2 points.**

Drag your answer choices to the spaces where they belong. To remove an answer choice, click on it. To review the passage, click on **VIEW TEXT**.

The lengthy voyage of the *Beagle* was when Charles Darwin did much of the research that led him to come up with the theory of evolution.

-
-
-

ANSWER CHOICES

1. Many of the observations that Charles Darwin made were recorded by him in his journal, which was later published.

2. Charles Darwin often went ashore during the trip and conducted research on the flora and fauna of the places he visited.

3. Alfred Wallace came up with many ideas similar to those Darwin had, but he did his research in Southeast Asia rather than in the Atlantic and Pacific regions.

4. After Charles Darwin returned to England, he spent many years considering the data that he had compiled on his trip.

5. Captain Robert Fitzroy invited Charles Darwin on the voyage because he needed a naturalist and his first choice had rejected Fitzroy's offer.

6. A great deal of the arguments made in *On the Origin of Species* were devised thanks to the research Charles Darwin did while on the *Beagle*.

Neutron Stars

While the largest star known to man is roughly 2,000 times the diameter of the Earth's sun, there are also stars so tiny that they are no larger than a small metropolitan area. These are neutron stars. A neutron star is extremely dense and is essentially the corpse of a giant star which collapsed after going supernova. Despite its small size, a neutron star has a mass greater than one and a half times that of the sun, is among the hottest stars in the galaxy, and has one of the strongest magnetic fields of any object in existence. Whenever a neutron star forms, it begins spinning rapidly, which causes the electromagnetic energy it emits to appear to blink, or pulse, to observers on the Earth. Astronomers call these spinning, blinking neutron stars pulsars.

A star must reach a certain size—roughly four to eight times the size of the sun—to be able to form a neutron star. Stars smaller than that typically become white dwarfs when they collapse while those larger than that normally transform into black holes upon collapsing. The formation of a neutron star occurs when a supernova destroys a star's outer layer yet leaves the dense core intact. The star's center is usually comprised of iron, but other elements may be present in smaller amounts. With the star's outer layers gone, nuclear fusion is no longer possible, which results in gravity having no counterbalancing outward force. Therefore, gravity acts strongly on the core and makes it extremely dense. As this density grows in strength, the electrons and the protons in the core's atoms are forced together to form a core of neutrons and neutrinos. The neutron star forms a structure with different layers, much like other bodies in the universe. If the neutron star is relatively young, it is still very hot, so its surface may be more liquid than solid while its inner core is much denser and more solidified.

A neutron star's temperature is at its height soon after its birth, but the star gradually begins cooling

off as it becomes older on account of the loss of neutrinos, which start flying off the star as soon as it is created. Over time, these neutrinos carry away a great amount of the star's energy, so its temperature falls to a level approximately half of what it was at its genesis. Nevertheless, even after this temperature loss, a neutron star ranks among the hottest stars in the universe. In addition, when it forms, a neutron star spins at an extremely high rate—somewhere between sixty and 600 times per second. This high rotation is explained by the law of conservation of angular momentum, which points out that an object rotates at a faster rate the more it is drawn in on itself. This is similar to the way that a figure skater begins spinning faster the moment that she pulls her arms toward her body.

The extreme density of a neutron star creates a very strong electromagnetic field, which is most often observed in the X-ray band. This magnetic field is aligned along a different axis than the spinning motion of the star, so it is like a lighthouse beam rotating in space. If the star is aligned in the right way with the Earth, astronomers using radio telescope arrays can observe this spinning magnetic field. Astronomer Jocelyn Bell first observed this phenomenon in 1967, and such stars were soon called pulsars. Most pulsars emit electromagnetic energy in the X-ray band, but some emit it in the visible light band as well as in the gamma ray band.

These observations led to the discovery of more neutron stars—almost all pulsars—in the following decades. Some are called millisecond pulsars because of the fact that they rotate as many as 700 times per second. At present, astronomers have discovered nearly 2,000 neutron stars; however, it is believed that the number of neutron stars is far greater since all of them cannot be observed from the Earth because their rotating magnetic fields are misaligned with the planet. In addition, as neutron stars age, the speed of their rotation decelerates, preventing them from being discovered as easily as more swiftly rotating neutron stars.

*Glossary

nuclear fusion: a reaction in which the nuclei of light atoms unite to form the nuclei of heavier atoms

neutrino: a massless or nearly massless lepton, an elementary type of particle

21 In paragraph 1, all of the following questions are answered EXCEPT:

   Ⓐ What causes a pulsar to behave in its particular manner?

   Ⓑ What are some of the unique features possessed by a neutron star?

   Ⓒ For what reason do some giant stars suddenly become supernovas?

   Ⓓ How much bigger than the Earth's sun is the biggest known star in the galaxy?

Paragraph 1 is marked with an arrow (➡).

Neutron Stars

➡ While the largest star known to man is roughly 2,000 times the diameter of the Earth's sun, there are also stars so tiny that they are no larger than a small metropolitan area. These are neutron stars. A neutron star is extremely dense and is essentially the corpse of a giant star which collapsed after going supernova. Despite its small size, a neutron star has a mass greater than one and a half times that of the sun, is among the hottest stars in the galaxy, and has one of the strongest magnetic fields of any object in existence. Whenever a neutron star forms, it begins spinning rapidly, which causes the electromagnetic energy it emits to appear to blink, or pulse, to observers on the Earth. Astronomers call these spinning, blinking neutron stars pulsars.

22 The word "counterbalancing" in the passage is closest in meaning to

(A) accelerating

(B) offsetting

(C) viable

(D) positional

23 In paragraph 2, the author implies that the Earth's sun

(A) is probably going to become a pulsar billions of years in the future

(B) has a core that is comprised of iron and other similar heavy elements

(C) lacks the size that is necessary for it to become a supernova

(D) will stop undergoing nuclear fusion at some time in the future

Paragraph 2 is marked with an arrow (➡).

24 According to paragraph 2, a neutron star is very compact because of

(A) the manner in which gravity affects it

(B) the various layers that are found in it

(C) the actions of the protons and neutrons in its atoms

(D) the lack of nuclear fusion in its core

Paragraph 2 is marked with an arrow (➡).

➡ A star must reach a certain size—roughly four to eight times the size of the sun—to be able to form a neutron star. Stars smaller than that typically become white dwarfs when they collapse while those larger than that normally transform into black holes upon collapsing. The formation of a neutron star occurs when a supernova destroys a star's outer layer yet leaves the dense core intact. The star's center is usually comprised of iron, but other elements may be present in smaller amounts. With the star's outer layers gone, nuclear fusion is no longer possible, which results in gravity having no counterbalancing outward force. Therefore, gravity acts strongly on the core and makes it extremely dense. As this density grows in strength, the electrons and the protons in the core's atoms are forced together to form a core of neutrons and neutrinos. The neutron star forms a structure with different layers, much like other bodies in the universe. If the neutron star is relatively young, it is still very hot, so its surface may be more liquid than solid while its inner core is much denser and more solidified.

*Glossary

nuclear fusion: a reaction in which the nuclei of light atoms unite to form the nuclei of heavier atoms

neutrino: a massless or nearly massless lepton, an elementary type of particle

25 In paragraph 3, why does the author mention "a figure skater"?

Ⓐ To argue that astronomers do not fully understand the actions of neutron stars

Ⓑ To make a comparison between the actions of that individual and a neutron star

Ⓒ To provide a mathematical proof of the law of conservation of angular momentum

Ⓓ To explain why neutron stars do not always rotate at such great speeds

Paragraph 3 is marked with an arrow (➡).

26 In paragraph 4, the author's description of pulsars mentions which of the following?

Ⓐ The individual credited with identifying their unique behavior

Ⓑ The strength that their electromagnetic fields can attain

Ⓒ The reason that they emit energy on up to three different bands

Ⓓ The manner in which people on the Earth can identify them by using telescopes

Paragraph 4 is marked with an arrow (⇨).

➡ A neutron star's temperature is at its height soon after its birth, but the star gradually begins cooling off as it becomes older on account of the loss of neutrinos, which start flying off the star as soon as it is created. Over time, these neutrinos carry away a great amount of the star's energy, so its temperature falls to a level approximately half of what it was at its genesis. Nevertheless, even after this temperature loss, a neutron star ranks among the hottest stars in the universe. In addition, when it forms, a neutron star spins at an extremely high rate—somewhere between sixty and 600 times per second. This high rotation is explained by the law of conservation of angular momentum, which points out that an object rotates at a faster rate the more it is drawn in on itself. This is similar to the way that a figure skater begins spinning faster the moment that she pulls her arms toward her body.

⇨ The extreme density of a neutron star creates a very strong electromagnetic field, which is most often observed in the X-ray band. This magnetic field is aligned along a different axis than the spinning motion of the star, so it is like a lighthouse beam rotating in space. If the star is aligned in the right way with the Earth, astronomers using radio telescope arrays can observe this spinning magnetic field. Astronomer Jocelyn Bell first observed this phenomenon in 1967, and such stars were soon called pulsars. Most pulsars emit electromagnetic energy in the X-ray band, but some emit it in the visible light band as well as in the gamma ray band.

27 Which of the following can be inferred from paragraph 5 about millisecond pulsars?

   (A) Most of the pulsars that have been discovered are millisecond pulsars.

   (B) Astronomers believe there are at least 2,000 of them in the Earth's galaxy.

   (C) They rotate at such quick speeds because their magnetic fields are misaligned.

   (D) They are a rare kind of neutron star that rotate faster than normal.

   Paragraph 5 is marked with an arrow (➡).

28 Select the TWO answer choices from paragraph 5 that identify why astronomers have difficulty finding pulsars. *To receive credit, you must select TWO answers.*

   (A) They are hidden behind larger stars so cannot be seen from the Earth.

   (B) The slowness of their rotation makes them hard to identify.

   (C) Their magnetic fields do not line up properly with the Earth.

   (D) They pulse on the X-ray band, which makes them difficult to see.

   Paragraph 5 is marked with an arrow (➡).

➡ These observations led to the discovery of more neutron stars—almost all pulsars—in the following decades. Some are called millisecond pulsars because of the fact that they rotate as many as 700 times per second. At present, astronomers have discovered nearly 2,000 neutron stars; however, it is believed that the number of neutron stars is far greater since all of them cannot be observed from the Earth because their rotating magnetic fields are misaligned with the planet. In addition, as neutron stars age, the speed of their rotation decelerates, preventing them from being discovered as easily as more swiftly rotating neutron stars.

29 Look at the four squares [■] that indicate where the following sentence could be added to the passage.

This is the reason that the star has gotten its particular name.

Where would the sentence best fit?

Click on a square [■] to add the sentence to the passage.

A star must reach a certain size—roughly four to eight times the size of the sun—to be able to form a neutron star. Stars smaller than that typically become white dwarfs when they collapse while those larger than that normally transform into black holes upon collapsing. The formation of a neutron star occurs when a supernova destroys a star's outer layer yet leaves the dense core intact. The center of the star is usually comprised of iron, but other elements may be present in smaller amounts. **1** With the star's outer layers gone, nuclear fusion is no longer possible, which results in gravity having no counterbalancing outward force. **2** Therefore, gravity acts strongly on the core and makes it extremely dense. **3** As this density grows in strength, the electrons and protons in the core's atoms are forced together to form a core of neutrons and neutrinos. **4** The neutron star forms a structure with different layers, much like other bodies in the universe. If the neutron star is relatively young, it is still very hot, so its surface may be more liquid than solid while its inner core is much denser and more solidified.

*Glossary

nuclear fusion: a reaction in which the nuclei of light atoms unite to form the nuclei of heavier atoms

neutrino: a massless or nearly massless lepton, an elementary type of particle

30 **Directions:** An introductory sentence for a brief summary of the passage is provided below. Complete the summary by selecting the THREE answer choices that express the most important ideas of the passage. Some sentences do not belong because they express ideas that are not presented in the passage or are minor ideas in the passage. **This question is worth 2 points.**

Drag your answer choices to the spaces where they belong. To remove an answer choice, click on it. To review the passage, click on **VIEW TEXT**.

While neutron stars are small, they are both very dense and hot, and they blink on account of their rapid spinning.

-
-
-

ANSWER CHOICES

1. Only stars of a particular size will ever become neutron stars when their lives come to an end.

2. Astronomers have only identified around 2,000 neutron stars because of the difficulty involved in finding them.

3. A neutron star forms when a star larger than the Earth's sun becomes a supernova but keeps its core intact.

4. Some neutron stars spin very quickly, and the resultant blinking can be seen from the Earth at times.

5. Neutron stars have only been known about since 1967, when an astronomer first noticed one of them.

6. The force of gravity makes neutron stars quite dense, and their temperature remains very high over the course of their lives.

Authors

Michael A. Putlack
- MA in History, Tufts University, Medford, MA, USA
- Expert test developer of TOEFL, TOEIC, and TEPS
- Main author of the Darakwon *How to Master Skills for the TOEFL® iBT* series and *TOEFL® MAP* series

Stephen Poirier
- Candidate for PhD in History, University of Western Ontario, Canada
- Certificate of Professional Technical Writing, Carleton University, Canada
- Co-author of the Darakwon *How to Master Skills for the TOEFL® iBT* series and *TOEFL® MAP* series

Allen C. Jacobs
- BS in Physics, Presbyterian College, Clinton, SC, USA
- BCE in Civil Engineering, Auburn University, Auburn, AL, USA
- MS in Civil Engineering, University of Alabama, Tuscaloosa, AL, USA

Decoding the TOEFL® iBT
READING Advanced NEW TOEFL® EDITION

Publisher Chung Kyudo
Editor Kim Minju
Authors Michael A. Putlack, Stephen Poirier, Allen C. Jacobs
Proofreader Michael A. Putlack
Designers Koo Soojung, Park Sunyoung

First published in November 2020
By Darakwon, Inc.
Darakwon Bldg., 211, Munbal-ro, Paju-si, Gyeonggi-do 10881
Republic of Korea
Tel: 82-2-736-2031 (Ext. 250)
Fax: 82-2-732-2037

ISBN 978-89-277-0884-1 14740
         978-89-277-0875-9 14740 (set)

www.darakwon.co.kr

Photo Credits
p. 51 Benoit Daoust / Shutterstock.com
p. 117 David Shankbone / Wikimedia Commons
https://commons.wikimedia.org/wiki/File:Suburbia_by_David_
Shankbone.jpg

Components Student Book / Answer Book
12 11 10 9 8 7 6   24 25 26 27 28